# THE CONCORD, (NH) DIRECTORY FOR 1867 - 8

CONTAINING A
GENERAL DIRECTORY OF
THE INHABITANTS,

AND A
BUSINESS DIRECTORY
INCLUDING FISHERVILLE
CITY AND COUNTY REGISTERS, &C., &C.

COMPILED ON A NEW AND COMPREHENSIVE PLAN,
BY

DUDLEY & GREENOUGH,
DIRECTORY PUBLISHERS

HERITAGE BOOKS
2025

**HERITAGE BOOKS**
***AN IMPRINT OF HERITAGE BOOKS, INC.***

**Books, CDs, and more—Worldwide**

For our listing of thousands of titles see our website
at
www.HeritageBooks.com

A Facsimile Reprint
Published 2025 by
HERITAGE BOOKS, INC.
Publishing Division
5810 Ruatan Street
Berwyn Heights, MD 20740



— Publisher's Notice —
In reprints such as this, it is often not possible to remove
blemishes from the original. We feel the contents of this
book warrant its reissue despite these blemishes and
hope you will agree and read it with pleasure.

International Standard Book Number
Paperbound: 978-0-7884-2851-7

THE

# CONCORD DIRECTORY,

FOR

## 1867-8,

CONTAINING A

## GENERAL DIRECTORY OF THE INHABITANTS,

AND A

## BUSINESS DIRECTORY,

INCLUDING FISHERVILLE,

**CITY AND COUNTY REGISTERS, &c., &c.**

---

COMPILED ON A NEW AND COMPREHENSIVE PLAN, BY

## DUDLEY & GREENOUGH,

DIRECTORY PUBLISHERS,

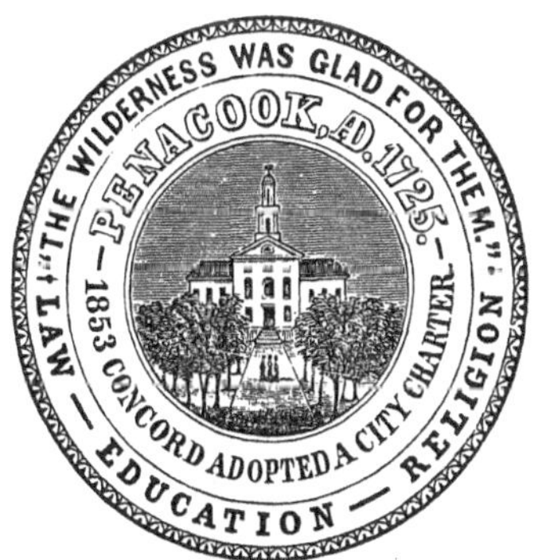


NO. 10 ELM STREET, BOSTON.
1867.

---

CONCORD:

FOR SALE BY D. L. GUERNSEY & CO.

# FARNAM & OSGOOD,

DEALERS IN

## WEST INDIA GOODS,

## GROCERIES,

**FLOUR, CORN MEAL, PORK, LARD, HAMS, FISH, SALT, &c.**

Also, FOREIGN AND DOMESTIC

## DRY GOODS,

A large and well-selected stock at lowest prices.

*Farmers' Produce taken in exchange at the highest market rates.*

**Stickney's North Block,**

CORNER MAIN STREET AND FREE BRIDGE ROAD,

**CONCORD, N. H.**

---

# NORMAN G. CARR,

## WATCHMAKER

AND

## JEWELLER,

And Dealer in

Watches, Clocks, Jewelry, and Fancy Goods.

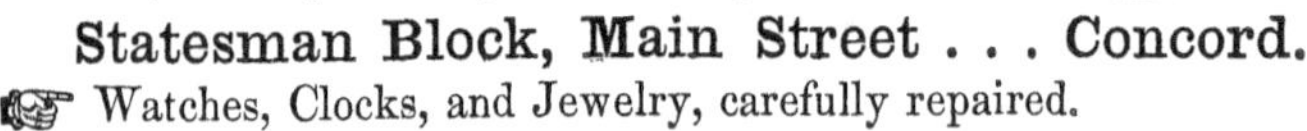

**Statesman Block, Main Street . . . Concord.**

☞ Watches, Clocks, and Jewelry, carefully repaired.

---

# JEWETT'S PATENT ARTIFICIAL LEGS

Manufactured at CENTRAL BLOCK, CONCORD, N. H.

*A Leg superior for its Strength, Lightness, Durability, Simplicity of Mechanical Arrangement, and Noiseless Movement.*

**CIVILIANS, SOLDIERS, AND SAILORS,**

WANTING LIMBS ARE INVITED TO EXAMINE THEM.

Artificial Legs and Arms of all kinds Repaired at Short Notice.

*Address Capt. WM. CARR, or JEWETT LEG CO., Concord, N.H.*

# PREFACE.

We take pleasure in presenting to the public our first volume of the Concord Directory. Great pains have been taken to produce a complete and reliable work; and everything has been done that experience could suggest, and our large facilities aid, to present the work in such a manner as would be a credit to the Capital of the Granite State.

The size of the book has been increased, and it is printed with new type, on extra paper, and bound in a handsome and substantial manner.

A complete Business Directory has been added, comprising every description of business, alphabetically arranged under appropriate headings.

The General Directory is compiled on a new and comprehensive plan, and the large number of names it contains over any previous Directory of Concord, is an assurance of its superiority.

Special care has been taken to give a full list of Public Officers, Societies, Churches, &c.

We would respectfully call the attention of the public to the Advertising Department of our work, as it embraces many of the first class business men of Concord.

It is our intention to make the Concord Directory a standard work, and we shall issue it as often as the public interest demands, and the business men will sustain it.

| | |
|---|---|
| Number of names in Directory of 1860, . . . | 1,990 |
| " " " " " " 1864, . . . | 2,338 |
| " " " " " " 1867–8, . . | 3,300 |

We herewith present our thanks to all who have aided us in any way.

Respectfully,

DUDLEY & GREENOUGH.

# CONTENTS.



## ADDITIONS AND REMOVALS RECEIVED TOO LATE FOR INSERTION IN THEIR PROPER PLACE.

ÆTNA FIRE INS. CO., Hartford, Conn. C. W. Moore, agt. Hill's block, Main

Ætna Life Ins. Co. of Hartford, Webster & Smith, agts., State [block, Main

BACHELDER G. H. boot manuf. moved to 160 Main, over E. C. Eastman's book store

Blanchard George S. lawyer, office moved to Exchange Bldg.

Blood Samuel, crockery and picture frame dealer, 132 Main, house 174 State

Brown George W. farmer, house W. Concord

Chandler George Henry, bds. 9 Centre

Chandler John K. bds 9 Centre

Columbian Hotel, G. C. Fuller, prop. 163 Main

Commerce Fire Ins. Co. Albany, office Stickney's new block

CONCORD DAILY MONITOR, Durgin's block, School

Concord Gas Light Co., John M. Hill, agt. 4 White's blk. Capitol

Concord Granite Co., E. C. Sargent, agt. nr. Union Steam Mill

Gale Perkins Mrs. widow, house State, cor. School

Gates A. M. Miss, teacher of painting, Central block

George Geo. W. A. farmer, house State, near new Cemetery

INDEPENDENT DEMOCRAT, Durgin's block, School

INDEPENDENT PRESS ASSOCIATION, Durgin's blk. School

Rollins John F. apothecary, residence removed to 95 State

Savary Thomas W. boot maker, Main, Fisherville

# J. H. MORRILL,

Wholesale and Retail Dealer in

## CONFECTIONERY, WEDDING CAKE,

**Cake, Pastry, Ice Cream, &c.**

**Ladies' and Gents' Ice Cream Saloon.**

***Opp. State House, Main St.***

Parties, Picnics, and Families supplied at short notice. Wedding Cake of a superior quality, frosted and ornamented in the latest styles.

---

# STAINED & CUT GLASS

## By J. M. COOK,

***Nos. 131, 139, and 141 Congress Street, Boston.***

J. M. C. having perfected arrangements for doing a more extensive business in the manufacturing of Stained and Cut Glass in all its branches, and especially in getting up MEMORIAL CHURCH WINDOWS in all the best styles, hopes to give the best of satisfaction.

We also get up the best style of Panel Lights, Skylights, Flock, Enamelled, Embossed, Plain and Stained Glass of all colors.

---

# DANIEL J. CARRUTH & CO.

IMPORTERS AND WHOLESALE DEALERS IN

## Wines, Liquors,

## TOBACCO,

## Snuff and Cigars,

## ALE, PORTER, AND CIDER,

Meerschaum, French, Briar, German, Dutch, Wood, Shaker, and Common Pipes.

AGENTS FOR THE SALE OF

**Virginia Manufactured Tobacco,**

ALSO,

**FINE OLD KENTUCKY BOURBON, AND MONONGAHELA WHISKIES.**

***61 and 63 Blackstone Street . . . Boston.***

DANIEL J. CARRUTH. STILLMAN P. MARSH.

# EAGLE CLOTHING HOUSE,

## EAGLE BLOCK, CONCORD, N. H.

I take pleasure in calling your attention to my choice selection of

## Gentlemen's Dress Goods,

Both Foreign and Domestic, from the most celebrated manufacturers in the world, which I am prepared to manufacture into Garments of all kinds, to suit the most careful connoisseurs in the art of dress, every garment being drafted to suit each individual customer, — not cut by a piece of paper, misnamed pattern, selected from the packages put up in great style, like some patent drugs, whose only merit is their artistic labels.

I am asssisted in the cutting department by Mr. CHARLES L. STONE, the well known pantaloons and vest cutter, whose many years of constant experience renders comment unnecessary to ensure all who may favor him with a trial, that satisfaction not to be had elsewhere.

I give my personal attention to Coat Cutting. I am also prepared to execute all orders for

## MILITARY GARMENTS,

In a manner second to none in the country. Also on hand, and constantly receiving, all the choice styles of

## READY-MADE CLOTHING,

AND

## GENTLEMEN'S FURNISHING GOODS,

Consisting in part as follows:

**Coats, Vests, Pantaloons, all kinds of Under Vests, and Pants, from the Heaviest Woolen to the Thinnest Gauze.**

Paper Collars, Gloves, Ties, Scarfs,

**HANDKERCHIEFS, STOCKS, HOSIERY, UMBRELLAS,**

In fact every thing to be found in a First Class Furnishing House. I would call particular attention to my new invoice of LINEN CLOTHING, consisting of entire suits, and the finest WRAPPERS ever offered to the public, which for style and workmanship challenge the world, as all will admit upon a personal examination.

My prices are reasonable. Terms, cash.

## A. J. EDMUNDS.

# INDEX TO CONCORD ADVERTISEMENTS.

## INDEX TO BOSTON ADVERTISEMENTS.

# KIMBALL BROTHERS,

# PHOTOGRAPHERS,

## STATE BLOCK, CONCORD, N. H.

PHOTOGRAPHS of every style, from "Gem" to Life Size, Plain, Colored, and finished in Ink. Also, PORCELAIN PORTRAITS, AMBROTYPES, FERREOTYPES, TINTYPES, &c., &c. Copying of all kinds done with unsurpassed excellence.

## PHOTOGRAPHS OF THE BATTLE FLAGS

Of all the New Hampshire Regiments, and other Military Organizations (copy-righted), for sale, either grouped by regiments, 8 by 10 size, or singly as cards.

All work entrusted to them will be executed faithfully and with despatch.

THEY ARE ALSO AGENTS FOR THE

## FLORENCE SEWING MACHINE,

Which was awarded a SILVER MEDAL, at the Paris Exposition; the highest award for any Family Machine — Mr. Howe being awarded a gold medal, not for his machine, *but as a designer and inventor generally.*

*Concord, September*, 1867.

---

# STEVENS & DUNCKLEE,

Wholesale and Retail Dealers in

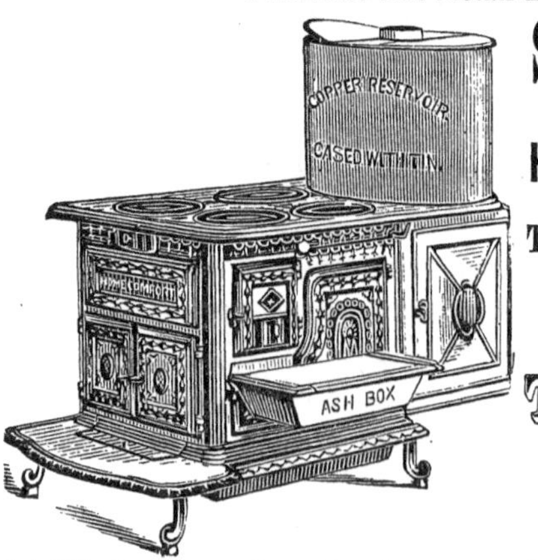


# STOVES

AND

## KITCHEN FURNISHING GOODS,

**TIN, WOODEN, JAPAN, GLASS, BRASS, AND BRITANNIA WARE.**

ALSO,

## TIN PLATE

AND

## Sheet Iron WORKERS.

Job Work executed at the shortest notice in a thorough and workmanlike manner.

**Main Street, opposite Phenix Hotel,**

**CONCORD, N. H.**

P. F. STEVENS. C. H. DUNCKLEE.

# STREETS, COURTS, AND AVENUES.

---

Academy Street, westerly of Spring street, extends from Cambridge to Washington street.

Allison Street is south of West street, and extends westerly from Turnpike street.

Auburn Street, from High to Long Pond.

Badger Street is west of State street, and extends from West to Allison street.

Beacon Street, from Union to Walnut street.

Beaver Street extends from Cross to Monroe street.

Blake Street is between Pleasant and Warren streets, and extends from State to Green street.

Bowery Avenue, from 19 Green street, westerly.

Bradley Street is west of State street, and extends from Franklin to Penacook street.

Cambridge Street is between Centre and Washington street, and extends from Spring to Rumford street.

Capitol Street, from Main to State street, north of School.

Cedar Street runs westerly from State street to Union, and is opposite Montgomery street.

Centre Street extends westerly from Main street, over Sand hill, where it intersects with Washington street.

Chandler Street, from Main to R. R. sq. south of Depot.

Chapel is on the north side of the Methodist church, and runs easterly from State street to railroad.

Chestnut Street, from Fountain to High.

Church Lane extends northerly from Park street to Centre street.

Church Street is on the south side of the Methodist Institute, extending westerly from Main to Walnut street.

Clinton Street, westerly from South, opposite Downing.

Common Street, from Fountain to High street.

Court Street extends westerly from Main street, by the north side of the City Hall, to State street.

Cross Street extends westerly from Main to Spring street.

Depot street, runs easterly from Main street to the Passenger Depot.

Downing Street extends westerly from Main street, by J. S. & E. A. Abbot's carriage manufactory to South street.

Elm Street extends southerly from Pleasant to Thompson street.

Essex Street extends northerly from Centre to Washington street.

Fayette Street is north of Thompson street, and extends westerly from Main to South street.

Ferry Street, from Main, above Washington, east to Merrimack River.

Forest Street runs westerly from High street to Fountain.

Fosterville extends easterly from the north end of State street, to Merrimack and Conn. River Railroad.

Fountain Street, from Franklin to Common, west of Saline.

Franklin Street extends westerly from Main street to High street.

Free Bridge Road, east from Main, above Park.

Fremont Street extends from Pleasant street northerly to Warren by the house of R. H. Sherburne.

Freight Street runs easterly from Main street to the Freight Depot.

Fruit Street, south from junction Pleasant and Washington to Clinton.

Fulton Street extends easterly from South, opp. Thompson to Spring street.

Garden Street, from Huntington to Rumford.

Gay Street, from Allison to West, changed to Depot street.

Granite Street, from High street to Fountain, south of Franklin.

Green Street is west of State street, and extends northerly from Pleasant to Centre street.

Hall Street, from Water below R. R. Bridge

Hanover Street is west of Spring street, and extends northerly from School to Centre street.

Henry Street is next westerly of Jackson street, and runs from Franklin street to Church street.

High Street extends from Washington to Franklin street.

Hill's Avenue runs easterly from Main street, by the house of James R. Hill, to Railroad Square.

Huntingdon Street is west of Rumford, and extends northerly from Warren to Centre street.

Hutchins Street, changed to Depot street

Jackson Street is west of Bradley street, and extends from Franklin to Church street.

Jefferson Street extends southerly from Thompson to Cross street.

Liberty Street is west of Pine street, and extends northerly from Pleasant to Washington street.

Lincoln Court is northerly of Fulton street, and extends easterly from Spring street.

Main Street runs from Water northerly to Horseshoe Pond.

Maple Street extends westerly from Union to Spring street.

Mechanic's Row, east from Main street, opp. State House.

Merrimack Street is west of Rumford street, and extends northerly from Pleasant to Centre street

Monroe Street extends westerly from State to South street.

Montgomery Street extends westerly from Main to State street.

Myrtle Street runs from Thompson street to Cross.

Orchard Street is north of Pleasant street, and runs westerly from Merrimack to Pine street.

Park Street is on the north side of the State House, and extends westerly from Main to State street.

Pearl Street extends westerly from Main to State street opposite the State Prison.

Penacook Street extends from Main to Walnut street, at Horse-shoe Pond, westerly, by the residence of R. Bradley, to the foot of the hill on Little Pond road.

Perley Street is north of Downing street, and runs parallel with it.

Pine Street is west of Merrimack street and extends northerly from Pleasant to Centre street.

Pleasant Avenue is south of Pleasant street, and runs westerly from Spring street.

Pleasant Street extends westerly from Main street, by the South church, to its junction with Washington street.

Prince Street extends westerly from Green street, by Horace Call's house, to Spring street.

Railroad Square is between Main street and the Depot.

Rumford Street is west of Spring street, and extends northerly from Pleasant to Washington street.

Saline Street, from Franklin street to Common, west of Auburn.

School Street extends westerly from Main to Washington street, north of Warren.

Short Street, from Spring to Huntingdon, north of Warren

South Street extends southerly from Pleasant street to Mrs. Benjamin Wheeler's residence.

Spring Street is west of Green street, and extends northerly from Clinton to Washington street.

State Street is west of Main street, and extends from the Turnpike road northerly, to Wood brook, on the Boscawen road.

St. John Street from High to Fountain.

Summer Street runs north from Winter to Court street.

Tahanto Street is west of Merrimack street, and extends northerly from Warren to Centre street.

Thompson Street extends westerly from Main to South street.

Thorndike Street is south of Monroe street, and extends westerly from Main to South street.

Tremont Street is on the north side of the State Prison wall, and extends westerly from State street to Walnut.

Turnpike Street extends south-westerly from Main street, by the head of State street.

Union Street extends northerly from Centre to Washington street.

Valley Street, from Chestnut to High street.

Vernon Street from High to St. John street.

Wall Street is south of Pleasant, and extends westerly from State to South street.

Walker Street extends westerly from State to Union, north of Church.

Walnut Street extends northerly from Washington to Franklin street.

Warren Street is north of Pleasant, and extends westerly from Main to Washington street.

Washington Street runs westerly from Main street by the North church, over the hill, where it intersects with Pleasant street.

Water Street, southeasterly from junction of Main and Turnpike.

West Street is north of Turnpike road, and extends from Main, junction Water, to South street.

Winter Street is north of Montgomery, and extends easterly from State street.

The North and South Lanes, running westerly from State to Green street, and under the arches of Call's block, are private ways.

---

## WARD BOUNDARIES.

The city of Concord hereby is, and shall continue to be, divided into seven wards, which shall be constituted as follows, viz :—

Ward No. 1 shall embrace all the territory, with its inhabitants, comprised within the limits of school districts numbered two and twenty, in said Concord.

Ward No. 2 shall embrace all the territory, with its inhabitants, situate on the east side of Merrimack River, northerly of the centre of the highway leading from Free Bridge to North Pembroke.

Ward No. 3 shall embrace all the territory, with its inhabitants, comprised within the limits of school districts numbered three, four, and five, together with the John Alexander farm, in said Concord.

Ward No. 4 shall embrace all the territory, with its inhabitants, comprised within the limits of school districts, numbered six and eleven, together with all that portion of school district number ten situate northerly of a line passing through the centre of Free Bridge Road, thence across Main and through the centre of Centre Street to Washington Street, thence through the centre of Washington Street to the old road leading from Washington Street to Franklin Street, thence up said road to Franklin Street.

Ward No. 5 shall embrace all the territory, with its inhabitants, comprised between the south line of Ward 4 and a line drawn through the centre of Washington Street, from a point opposite the old road aforesaid to its intersection with Pleasant Street, thence through the centre of Pleasant Street and across Main Street, and thence in a line at right angles to said Main Street at that point to Merrimack River, thence up said river to the centre of Free Bridge Road.

Ward No. 6 shall embrace all the territory, with its inhabitants, comprised between the south line of Ward 5 and a line drawn from the centre of Washington Street, at its intersection with Pleasant Street, through the centre of the road leading from Washington Street to the Bog Road, to its intersection with the Bog Road, thence through the centre of Bog Road and across South Street, through the centre of Downing Street, across Main Street, thence in a line due east to Merrimack River, thence up said river to the south line of Ward 5.

Ward No. 7 shall embrace all the remaining territory of said city, with its inhabitants, not included in either of the other wards, also about forty acres taken from the town of Bow, and annexed to Concord.—*Act of General Court*, 1849. *Section* 3.

## PUBLIC BUILDINGS, HALLS, &c.

Call's Block, 15 State
Central Block, Main, corner Warren
Central Buildings, Main, opp. Columbian Hotel
Central Hall, Central Block
City Block, Main, corner Warren
City Hall, Main, between Court and Montgomery
City Marshal's Office, Police Station
Columbian Hotel, Main, between School and Capital
Court House, Main, between Court and Montgomery
Depot, Railroad Square
Durgin's Block, School, between Main and State
Eagle Hall, Stickney's Block, Main
Eagle Hotel, Main, opp. the State House
Elm House, Main, opp. Pleasant
Exchange Block, Main, opp. Capital
Hill's Block, Main, next to Phenix Hotel
Jail, Washington, junction Pleasant
Lee's Block, Chandler
Low's Block, Main, opp. School
Main's Block, rear 40 Main
Masonic Temple, Main, corner Pleasant
Merrimack County Bank, 250 Main
Moore's Block, Main, opp. Masonic Temple
Morse's Block, State
N. H. Asylum for the Insane, Pleasant
N. H. Historical Society, 250 Main
Odd Fellows' Hall, Central Block
Phenix Block, Main, opp. Warren
Phenix Hall, Phenix Block
Phenix Hotel, Main, near Warren
Phenix Hotel Building, Main, near Warren
Police Station, Main, opp. Phenix Hotel
Post Office, School, near Main
Rumford Block, 176 Main
Sanborn's Block, 173 Main, corner Capital
Sherman House, Main, opp. Free Bridge Road
State Block, Main, corner School
State House, Main, between Capital and Park
State Prison, State, corner Tremont
Statesman Building, Main, corner Depot
Stickney's Block, Main, opp. Park
Tax Collector's Office, Police Station
U. S. Marshal's Office, 134 Main
White's Block, Capital
Whittredge's Hall, 6 Main

## CALENDAR.



| 1867. | Sunday. | Monday. | Tuesday. | Wednesday. | Thursday. | Friday. | Saturday. |
|---|---|---|---|---|---|---|---|
| JULY. | | 1 | 2 | 3 | 4 | 5 | 6 |
| | 7 | 8 | 9 | 10 | 11 | 12 | 13 |
| | 14 | 15 | 16 | 17 | 18 | 19 | 20 |
| | 21 | 22 | 23 | 24 | 25 | 26 | 27 |
| | 28 | 29 | 30 | 31 | | | |
| AUGUST. | | | | | 1 | 2 | 3 |
| | 4 | 5 | 6 | 7 | 8 | 9 | 10 |
| | 11 | 12 | 13 | 14 | 15 | 16 | 17 |
| | 18 | 19 | 20 | 21 | 22 | 23 | 24 |
| | 25 | 26 | 27 | 28 | 29 | 30 | 31 |
| SEPT. | 1 | 2 | 3 | 4 | 5 | 6 | 7 |
| | 8 | 9 | 10 | 11 | 12 | 13 | 14 |
| | 15 | 16 | 17 | 18 | 19 | 20 | 21 |
| | 22 | 23 | 24 | 25 | 26 | 27 | 28 |
| | 29 | 30 | | | | | |
| OCTOBER. | | | 1 | 2 | 3 | 4 | 5 |
| | 6 | 7 | 8 | 9 | 10 | 11 | 12 |
| | 13 | 14 | 15 | 16 | 17 | 18 | 19 |
| | 20 | 21 | 22 | 23 | 24 | 25 | 26 |
| | 27 | 28 | 29 | 30 | 31 | | |
| NOV. | | | | | | 1 | 2 |
| | 3 | 4 | 5 | 6 | 7 | 8 | 9 |
| | 10 | 11 | 12 | 13 | 14 | 15 | 16 |
| | 17 | 18 | 19 | 20 | 21 | 22 | 23 |
| | 24 | 25 | 26 | 27 | 28 | 29 | 30 |
| DEC. | 1 | 2 | 3 | 4 | 5 | 6 | 7 |
| | 8 | 9 | 10 | 11 | 12 | 13 | 14 |
| | 15 | 16 | 17 | 18 | 19 | 20 | 21 |
| | 22 | 23 | 24 | 25 | 26 | 27 | 28 |
| | 29 | 30 | 31 | | | | |

| 1868. | Sunday. | Monday. | Tuesday. | Wednesday. | Thursday. | Friday. | Saturday. |
|---|---|---|---|---|---|---|---|
| JAN. | | | | 1 | 2 | 3 | 4 |
| | 5 | 6 | 7 | 8 | 9 | 10 | 11 |
| | 12 | 13 | 14 | 15 | 16 | 17 | 18 |
| | 19 | 20 | 21 | 22 | 23 | 24 | 25 |
| | 26 | 27 | 28 | 29 | 30 | 31 | |
| FEB. | | | | | | | 1 |
| | 2 | 3 | 4 | 5 | 6 | 7 | 8 |
| | 9 | 10 | 11 | 12 | 13 | 14 | 15 |
| | 16 | 17 | 18 | 19 | 20 | 21 | 22 |
| | 23 | 24 | 25 | 26 | 27 | 28 | 29 |
| MARCH. | 1 | 2 | 3 | 4 | 5 | 6 | 7 |
| | 8 | 9 | 10 | 11 | 12 | 13 | 14 |
| | 15 | 16 | 17 | 18 | 19 | 20 | 21 |
| | 22 | 23 | 24 | 25 | 26 | 27 | 28 |
| | 29 | 30 | 31 | | | | |
| APRIL. | | | | 1 | 2 | 3 | 4 |
| | 5 | 6 | 7 | 8 | 9 | 10 | 11 |
| | 12 | 13 | 14 | 15 | 16 | 17 | 18 |
| | 19 | 20 | 21 | 22 | 23 | 24 | 25 |
| | 26 | 27 | 28 | 29 | 30 | | |
| MAY. | | | | | | 1 | 2 |
| | 3 | 4 | 5 | 6 | 7 | 8 | 9 |
| | 10 | 11 | 12 | 13 | 14 | 15 | 16 |
| | 17 | 18 | 19 | 20 | 21 | 22 | 23 |
| | 24 | 25 | 26 | 27 | 28 | 29 | 30 |
| | 31 | | | | | | |
| JUNE. | | 1 | 2 | 3 | 4 | 5 | 6 |
| | 7 | 8 | 9 | 10 | 11 | 12 | 13 |
| | 14 | 15 | 16 | 17 | 18 | 19 | 20 |
| | 21 | 22 | 23 | 24 | 25 | 26 | 27 |
| | 28 | 29 | 30 | | | | |

# GENERAL DIRECTORY.

---

### EXPLANATIONS AND ABBREVIATIONS.

The letter h. for house; b. or bds. boards; opp. opposite; r. rear; c. or cor. corner; wf. wharf; n. near; sq. square; pl. place; ct. court; ave. avenue; E. east; W. west; N. north; S. south; N. R. R., Northern Railroad; C. M. & L. R. R., Concord, Manchester, and Lowell Railroad; Con. R. R., Concord Railroad; P. & C. R. R., Portsmouth and Concord Railroad; B. C. & M, R. R., Boston, Concord, and Montreal Railroad; M. & C. Riv. R. R,. Merrimac and Connecticut River Railroad; after the name of the street the word "street" is omitted.

ABBOT DAVID J. house 27 Thompson
Abbot, Downing & Co. (*J. S. & E. A. Abbot and L. Downing & Sons*), coach and carriage manufacturers, 17 Main
Abbot Edward A. (*Abbot, Downing & Co.*), house South near Fayette
Abbot Frank D. clerk State Capital Bank, b. 27 Thompson
Abbot Jos. H. (*Abbot, Downing & Co.*), h. Main n. Fayette
Abbot Joseph S. 2nd, coachmaker, Abbot's, h. r. 37 Main
Abbot J. Stephens (*Abbot, Downing & Co.*), house Main
Abbott Amos S. springmaker, house West, near South
Abbott Albert J. printer, boards 11 Spring
Abbott Abial C. quarryman, boards Simeon Abbott's
Abbott Benjamin K. laborer, house Union, near Maple
Abbott Charles, farmer, boards G. Wheeler's, South
Abbott Charles H. blacksmith, Abbot's, h. State, c. Perley
Abbott Charles C. carpenter, bds. G. Wheeler's, South, near Wheeler's Corner
Abbott David 3rd, laborer, house 20 Rumford
Abbott Eleanor, widow of Elias, house Spring, near Cross
Abbott Eliza Mrs. widow of Joshua, house Pearl, n. State
Abbott Esther N. Miss, dressmaker, h. Spring, cor. Pleasant
Abbott Ezra W. physician, 9 Warren, house do.
Abbott Frank A. cabinet maker, house Merrimack, c. Center, Fisherville
Abbott George jr. painter, 9 Warren, house 38 Rumford
Abbott George, painter, 9 Warren, house 38 Rumford
Abbott George, carpenter, bds. J. J. Pillsbury's, North Arch
Abbott George W. house Brown's Hill, Fisherville
Abbott Hazen E. woodworker, Concord R. R. h. 58 Pleasant

Abbott Hiram R. lastmaker, boards 11 Spring
Abbott Horace S. carpenter, house Union, near Maple
Abbott Ira, laborer, house Washington, n. Main, Fisherville
Abbott Ira S. machinist, house 63 State
Abbott John, mayor of Concord, h. 278 Main, bet. Franklin and Pearl
Abbott Joseph, cooper, house Summer, Fisherville
Abbott Mary, widow of David, house Spring, near Pleasant
Abbott Mary Mrs. widow of Horace, house Summer, corner Center, Fisherville
Abbott Mary F. Mrs. wid. of Nathaniel, h. High, n. Summer, Fisherville
Abbott Nathaniel C. blacksmith, 11 Spring
Abbott Nathan, farmer, house Main, n. Summer, Fisherville
Abbott Rachael, wid. of Wm. A. bds. W. Abbott's, Huntingdon, near Warren
Abbott Rufus, lumberman, house West Concord
Abbott Seth E. peddler, h. Washington, n. Main, Fisherville
Abbott Simeon, farmer, house West Concord
Abbott Stephen, carpenter, bds. Charles H. Abbott's, State, corner Perley
Abbott Stephen F. farmer, boards Simeon Abbott's
Abbott Walter, house Huntingdon, near Warren
Abbott William, cabinet maker, house High, near Forest
Adams Anna L. widow of Stephen D. house 15 Monroe
Adams Benjamin O. boarding house, Main, corner Center
Adams Charles H. coachmaker, house 41 School
Adams Chas. G. (*G. H. & C. G. Adams*), bds. Railroad House
Adams Elisha, clergyman, house 205 State
Adams Frank, carpenter, house Rumford, c. Washington
Adams G. H. & C. G. (*George H. and Charles G.*), ale and porter, opp. Phenix House, Main
Adams George H. (*G. H. & C. G. Adams*), ale house, Main, opp. Phenix Hotel, h. Green, opp. Blake
Adams Wilson, carpenter, house 6 Chapel
Ager Herbert U. blacksmith, Abbot's, bds. 4 West
Ahern John, moulder, house Tremont, near State
Ahern John 2nd, moulder, house Tremont, near Franklin
Aherne John, watchman N. R. R. h. Walnut, n. Washington
Aherne Michael, machinist N. R. R. boards Walnut, near Washington
Aiken Edmund, silver plater, Smith & Walker's, h. 4 Pearl
Aiken Nancy Mrs. widow of Samuel, h. Center, c. Summer, Fisherville
Albin J. Henry, lawyer, Central Block, boards 100 State
Albin John, farmer, house 100 State, near Pleasant
Alden Albert, carpenter, house Spring, corner Pleasant
Alden Frank W. boards A. Alden's, Spring, corner Pleasant
Aldrich Henry H. upholsterer, School, n. Main, h. Center, near Spring
Aldrich Sewell, laborer, house Myrtle, near Thompson

Alexander Charles H. clerk, boards, J.G. Alexander's, South, corner Monroe [corner Monroe
Alexander James G. watchman C. M. & L. R. R. h. South,
Alexander Samuel, farmer, house East Concord [Hotel
Alexander William H. conductor C. M. & L. R. R. b. Phenix
Allen Asa M. wheelwright, house 37 State
Allen Christopher W. hairdresser, 145 Main, h. 227 State
Allen Daniel C. paymaster N. R. R. house 6 Center
Allen Edw. H. teacher, Main, cor. Depot, b. at Water Cure
Allen James B. bookbinder, Crawford's, b. Sherman House
Allen Walter C. blacksmith, 253 Main, h. Main, n. Penacook
Allen William H. merchant, Main, house 3 Webster Place, Fisherville
Allison Archibald, shoemaker, boards 34 Main [Block
Allison Catherine Mrs. widow of James, b. 30 Main, Tallant's
Allison Frederic, farmer, house 179 State
Allison James, blacksmith, boards 34 Main
Allison John, woodworker at Abbot's, house 16 Downing
Allison William H. wheelwright at Abbot's, h. 13 Downing
Allison William H. house 11 Pleasant
Ambrose Benjamin, laborer, b. Wm. Pecker's, East Concord
Ambrose Charles W. machinist, boards 13 Wall
Ambrose Thos. A. prop. Eagle Hotel, opp. State House, Main
Ames Charles A. ins. agent, Phenix block, bds. Elm House
Ames Fisher, house Summer, Fisherville
Ames Henry G. boards F. Ames', Summer, Fisherville
Ames Maria Mrs. widow of Albert, house 45 Warren
Amsden George H. cabinet manufacturer, boards Washington House, Fisherville [h. Elm, Fisherville
Amsden Henry H. (*Caldwell & Amsden*), furniture manuf.
Amsden Leroy, carpenter, b. Mrs. Mary Drown's, Merrimack, Fisherville [cor. Academy
Andrews Asa G. groceries, Wash. cor. Rumford, h. Wash.
Andrews Charles E. quarryman at the ledge, h. W. Concord
Andrews James G. clerk, Central block, bds. William G. Andrews [Rumford, near Short
Andrews William G. (*Gage & Andrews*), Central block, h. 19
Anderson William S. hairdresser, house Lane's block
Angier Samuel, machinist C. R. R. shop, house 54 Main
Annable Jehiel, upholsterer, 116 Main, h. 3 Monroe
Arlin Zachariah, fireman, C. R. R. boards Arlin's, State, junction Walnut
Arlin Zachariah C. stonecutter, State, junction Walnut
Arnold Michael, laborer, house rear Robert Woodruff's
Ash Charles W. clerk, N. R. R. office, house 54 State
Ash Sherburne T. blacksmith, house South, n. Downing
Ashton Elizabeth, widow of Daniel, nurse and seamstress, b. 39 State
Aspinwall Charles C. foreman N. R. R. machine shop, house Tremont, near Walnut

Atherton Alonzo, baker, J. S. Norris & Co. house 106 State, near Pleasant
Atkinson George W. farmer, house 65 South
Atkinson Mary C. widow of Henry, house 65 South
Atwell George P. stonecutter, boards Amos Bean's
Austin Charles, manuf. of melodeon and organ reeds, Railroad Depot Square, house Spring, near Pleasant
Austin Charles E. organ and melodeon manufacturer, Railroad Depot Square, house Spring, near Pleasant
Austin Harmon P. laborer, house Church, Fisherville
Avery Enoch, stonecutter, boards Columbian Hotel
Ayer Richard H. (*Stanley & Ayer*), jeweler, Phenix Hotel building, Main, boards Mrs. Coffin's, State, n. Penacook

BABB HENRY, blacksmith, Con. R. R. boards 13 Wall
Badger George A. (*Wilson & Badger*), optical instruments, Exchange block, house 47 Pleasant
Badger Benj. E. lawyer, Stickney's block, Main, house State, corner Montgomery
Badger George A. (*Wilson & Badger*), optical instruments, Exchange block, 47 Pleasant
Badger Stephen C. lawyer, Stickney's block, Main, house 181 State
Badger Warren, house Center, opposite Green
Badger William, gasfitter, office Gas Light Co. house 8 Maple
Baggs, Michael, laborer, at Ford & Kimball's, house Cross, n. Jefferson
Baker Charles E. carder, house 9 West Canal, Fisherville
Baker Charles P. wholesale and retail provision dealer, 1 Walnut, house do.
Baker Joseph, brickmaker, house Water, near the Bridge
Baker La Forest, teamster, boards 9 W. Canal, Fisherville
Baker Leonard H. blacksmith, N. R. R. house 5 Winter
Baker Osmon C. bishop M. E. Church, house 207 State
Baker Uriah, machinist, house Auburn, opposite St. John
Bailey Israel C. teamster, house Franklin, near High
Ballard John H. stoolmaker, Prescott Bros. h. 142 Spring
Ballard William, carpenter, house Court, near Main
Ballou Oliver, melodeon maker, house State, c. Thompson
Bancroft Jesse P. supt. and physician Insane Asylum
Barker Charles (*Wm. Hart & Co.*), market, 16 School, house Academy, near Washington
Barker William P. mason, house 29 Center
Barlow Mark, spinner, b. Edward Richardson's, Fisherville
Barnard John C. farmer, house High, near Franklin
Barnes Benj. J. marble worker, Clinton, n. Spring, house do.
Barnes George J. stonecutter, boards 2 Forest
Barnes Harriet E. widow of Jefferson, house 2 Forest
Barnett George, weaver, h. Summer, cor. High, Fisherville
Barrett Charles F. engineer Con. R. R. house 16 Thorndike

Barron, Dodge & Co. (*John V. Barron, Amos Dodge, Benj. Grover and Franklin Moseley*), flour and grain, Railroad Square

Barron John D. H. boards 54 School

Barron John V. (*Barron, Dodge & Co.*), wholesale flour dealer, Depot Square, house 54 School

Barry Ann, widow of Patrick, h. School, c. Huntingdon

Barry John, helper, N. R. R. house rear Rumford Hall

Barry John A. clergyman, house School, corner Huntingdon

Barter Lews (*Lewis Barter & Co.*), flour and grain, 6 Pleasant, house Spring, corner Warren

Barter Lewis & Co. (*Lewis Barter and W. W. Cochran*), flour and grain, 8 Pleasant

Bartlett Alonzo, laborer, bds. E. S. Gilman, W. Concord

Bartlett George W. blacksmith, boards J. F. Bartlett's, State, corner West

Bartlett John F. blacksmith, house State, corner West

Bartlett John F. jr. blacksmith, boards J. F. Bartlett's, State, corner West

Bartlett Sylvanus, farmer, house 4 Tremont

Bartlett Wm. H. lawyer and judge, Phenix block

Bartlett Wm. H. currier, house Penacook, n. the Tannery

Bartlett William H. house 25 Pleasant

Barton Cyrus N. blacksmith at Abbot's, boards 1 Downing

Barton George C. laborer at Abbot's, boards 1 Downing

Barton George M. watchman at Abbot's, h. State, c. Downing

Barton James W. watchman at Abbot's, house 1 Downing

Batchelder Addie, M. Mrs. widow of E. Frank, boards John Batchelder's, Fisherville [mack, opp. Orchard

Batchelder Albert F. fireman, Con. Railroad, house Merri-

Batchelder Albert L. grocer, boards 125 State

Batchelder Almira, widow, Peter H., house 60 South

Batchelder Charles F. clerk, house 1 Pleasant Avenue

Batchelder Clark W. moulder, Ford's Foundry, house Spring, near School [boards 8 Centre

Batchelder David, coach-maker, Harvey, Morgan & Co.,

Batchelder Francis, piano-forte maker, at Prescott's, boards L. D. Boynton's, Pleasant, near Fremont [near State

Batchelder Frank J. printer, Monitor Office, house Warren,

Batchelder Geo. H. boot & shoe manufacturer, Main, house Spring, cor. Lincoln Court

Batchelder Henry S. mechanic, at Prescott Bros'. Factory

Batchelder Jeremiah S. blacksmith, at Abbots, house Clinton, cor. Spring [mack, Fisherville

Batcheler John, grocers, Washington Square, house Merri-

Batchelder John T. (*N. S. Batchelder & Co.*), grocer, house 125 State [Spring, near Pleasant

Batchelder Jonathan P. switch tender, Con. Railroad, house

Batchelder Nathaniel, freight conductor, Con. Railroad, house 44 Spring

Batchelder Nathaniel S. (*N. S. Batchelder & Co.*), gro,cer house 42 Main
Batchelder N. S. & Co., (*N. S. & J. T. Batchelder*), grocers, wholesale and retail, 5 Statesman building [ing
Batchelder Peter H. blacksmith, at Abbot's, house 49 Down-
Batchelder J. & Co. (*John Batchelder & Orvel J. Evans*), groceries, Washington Square, Fisherville
Bates Edward E. clerk, 153 Main, bds. 8 Green
Bates Sidney T. compostor, house Thorndike, near State
Bates Walter, peddler, house Franklin, cor. Walnut
Beal Horace, carpenter, house Beacon
Bean Amos, house 4 Call's block, State
Bean Amos M. clerk, 155 Main, bds. 4 Call's block, State
Bean Charles C. carpenter, h. Summer, n. Cross, Fisherville
Bean Charles W. clerk, bds. 4 Call's block, State
Bean Edna A. Miss, cashier, 153 Main, bds. 55 Main
Bean Erastus, boot and shoe dealer, Main, h. Spring cor. Centre, Fisherville
Bean George W. painter, h. 26 Main
Bean Joel W. mason, house Lincoln Court
Bean John M. teamster, h. Washington, n. Warren, Fisherville
Bean John W. farmer, h. Spring, c. Center, Fisherville
Bean John, carpenter, h. Spring, c. Center, Fisherville
Bean Leonard W. mason, house 13 Union
Bean Moses, stonelayer, h. Elm, Fisherville [Fisherville
Bean Moses H. shoedealer, Mechanic's block, h. Brown's Hill,
Bean Sarah, widow of Abraham, house E. Concord
Bean William D. teamster, house Washington, near Warren, Fisherville
Beard William H. blacksmith, house West, near South
Beckett, Geo. C. pressman, boards Eagle Hotel
Beckwith Edson, assistant clerk, Phenix Hotel
Beede Francis C. clerk, house Union, corner Beacon
Beirne Barney, N. R. R. shop, boards Main, corner Centre
Beirne Thomas, N. R. R. shop, boards Main, corner Centre
Belile Andro Nigue, harness maker, 151 Main, b. Amos Bean's
Belisle Joseph, reedmaker, boards Amos Bean's
Bell John, farmer, boards 3 West
Bell Leonard, cooper, house 3 West
Bell Robert, stonecutter, bds. George Virgin's, East Concord
Bell William H. jeweller, Main, b. Mrs. Kilburn's, Fisherville
Belrose Louis, moulder, at Ford & Kimball's, h. 6 Jefferson
Bennett George, shoemaker, 240 Main, h. rear 34 Main
Bennett John, carpenter, bds. Mrs. Julia A. Carr's
Bennett Wm. H. road master, Con. Railroad, h. 28 Monroe
Benson Luke, laborer, h. Railroad Square, Hill's block
Bentley George E. quarryman, h. West Concord [n. South
Berry George W. freight conductor, Con. Railroad, h. Monroe,
Berry Jefferson, N. harness-maker, h. Walnut, n. Franklin
Betts Peter, spring-maker, h. Spring, n. Clinton

Betts William, spring-maker, h. lower end of Spring
Betts Wm. M. spring-fitter, h. Spring, n. Clinton
Bickford Alvah H. overseer at Prison, h. 183 State [Beaver
Bickford Benj. carriage-trimmer, at Abbot's, h. Cross, opp.
Bickford Bradbury G. clerk, E. G. Killburn's, h. Centre
Bickford Israel P. painter, at Abbot's, h. 20 West
Bickford Jerome, machinist, N. Railroad, h. 22 Downing [Sq
Bickford Nathan B. machinist, C. R. R. Shop, h. 1 Railroad
Bickford William, woodworker, house Perley, near State
Bickford William S. machinist N. R. R. bds. 22 Downing
Biddle Baruch, depot master, house 87 State
Bixby Eliza Mrs. widow, house 11 Elm
Bixby Phineas P. house State, near Fayette
Blackinton Fisher, house Elm, Fisherville [South
Blackstone Daniel, shoemaker, h. Downing, between State and
Blaisdell Andrew J. machinist, boards Washington House, Fisherville
Blaisdell Arthur, carpenter, boards 5 Jefferson [Washington
Blaisdell George E. machinist N. R. R. house Union, corner
Blaisdell James D. engineer N. R. R. house 32 School
Blaisdell Justus, dentist, Exchange block, house 58 Pleasant
Blaisdell Timothy K. master blacksmith N. R. R. house Union, corner Washington
Blake Enos, farmer, house 105 State
Blake James M. house Church, near Jackson
Blake J. Mallon, leather dealer, rear 105 State, h. 44 Centre
Blake Joseph C. blacksmith, house West, near State
Blake Mansel M. wood-worker, N. Railroad, h. Hill's Ave.
Blake Mansel, carpenter N. R. R. house Hill's Avenue
Blake Robt. P. brakeman C. M. & L. R. R. b. Sherman House
Blake Roxanna Mrs. widow of Samuel, boards Samuel Alexander's, East Concord
Blake Samuel, butcher, house 50 Main
Blake Sarah Mrs. widow of Sanborn, house East Concord
Blakely William J. blacksmith, house 46 West
Blanchard Charles G. clerk at Coffin's, boards F. Webster's, State, cor. Thompson
Blanchard Charles P. (*Porter Blanchard & Sons*), churn manufacturers, 211 Main, house do.
Blanchard David, stonecutter, house West Concord
Blanchard George S. lawyer, Sanborn's block, house Spring, on Academy Hill
Blanchard John, clerk, boards 33 Green
Blanchard John S. clerk at Harris & Co.'s, bds. F. Webster's, State, corner Thompson [Cross
Blanchard Moses W. teamster, bds. P. S. Ham's, South, cor.
Blanchard Thomas S. (*Porter Blanchard & Sons*), churn manufacturer, 211 Main, house Centre, near Spring
Blanchard Porter (*Porter Blanchard & Sons*), churn manuf., 211 Main, house do.

Blanchard Porter & Sons (*Porter, Charles P., and Thomas S. Blanchard*), churn manufacturers, 211 Main
Blaney Stephen K. coach painter, h. 93 Spring
Bliss John W. carriage-maker, at Abbot's, h. 8 Thorndike
Blodgett Elias, cabinet-maker, h. Summer, n. Cross, Fisherville
Blodgett Eliza Miss, boarding-house, 18 Centre
Blodgett James T. carriage-maker, h. 10 Maple
Blodgett John H. physician, 18 Centre, h. do
Blodgett John S. carpenter, h. 9 Maple
Blood Benjamin A. (*Gardner & Blood*), Soap and Candle manufacturer, Free Bridge Road, h. near Fair Grounds
Blood Samuel, crockery and picture-frame dealer, 132 Main, house 174
Boardman Geo. L. carriage-maker, bds. H. H. Holt's, school, n. Tahanto
Boardman John, stone cutter, bds. O. B. Adams'
Bodwell Susan, Mrs. widow Moses, house 14 West
Bogler William, furniture dealer, house 248 Main
Bond Asa M. butcher, Pleasant, n. Main, house do
Boody Lucinda W. Mrs. widow of Samuel H. bds. Ira E. Kenneys, Fisherville
Booth Betsy, widow, Geo. A. house, Centre, n. Washington
Bott Priscilla, widow of James, bds. 104 Spring [bds. 11 Wall
Bouchie Frederick, wheelwright, at Harvey Morgan & Co's.
Bouchie Isaac, blacksmith at Howey, Morgan & Co's. bds. 11 Wall
Bouchie Lewis W. Wheelwright, at Harvey Morgan & Co's. bds. W. Wall
Boulley Peter, helper, N. Railroad, house rear Hill's block
Bourke Joseph, N. reed-maker, house Washington, n. Walnut
Boutelle Wm. moulder at Ford & Kimball's, bds. 11 Wall
Bouton Nathaniel, clergyman, house Main, opp. City Hall
Boutwell Adelbert D. turner, bds. Washington House, Fisherville [ington House, Fisherville
Boutwell James E. overseer, Colwell & Amsden's, bds. Wash-
Bowers Joseph R. brick-maker, Turnpike, house do. near the brick-yard
Bowers Reuben C. house Turnpike, n. the brick-yard
Bowers Roxanna, widow, Benj. house Merrimack, Fisherville
Boynton Charles M. clerk, 153 Main, house 20 Green
Boynton John Y. carriage-maker, at Abbot's, bds. 4 West
Boynton Lyman D. bootmaker, house 40 Pleasant [Fremont
Boynton Lyman M. painter, bds. L. D. Boynton's, Pleasant, n.
Brackett Mary A. widow of George, h. Summer, cor. Winter
Bradbury F. C. & J. Y. confectioners, Stickney's new block, Main [Stickney's new block, bds. 1 Cedar
Bradbury Francis C. (*F. C. & J. Y. Bradbury*), confectioner,
Bradbury Joseph Y. (*F. C. & J. Y. Bradbury*), confectioner, Stickney's new block, bds. 1 Cedar
Bradbury Sophronia, widow, James G., house Cedar

Bradford James, quarryman, bds. D. Fish's, West Con. road
Bradford Oliver K. painter, Washington Square, bds. Washington House, Fisherville
Bradley Moses H. farmer, house Penacook, cor. State
Bradley Richard, farmer, house Penacook, cor. State
Bradley Sara Mrs. widow, house West. near South [son, h. do.
Brainerd Duane D. carpenter and joiner, State, cor. Thomp-
Bray Coleman, laborer, house 78 Warren
Brennen Patrick, moulder, bds. Joseph E. Phelps'
Bresnahan Patrick, laborer, house Cross n. Myrtle
Bridges Caroline O. Mrs. widow of Martin R. house Elm, corner Wall
Bridgeman C. C. teacher, Main, corner Depot
Briggs William A. bootmaker, house Prince, near Green
Bright J. Evesson, clerk, Eastman & Co.'s, bds. Phenix Hotel
Brine, John H., Lee's block, Chandler
Brock Charles, coachman, Eagle Hotel
Brockway George W. carriage smith, rear of the Depot, West Concord, house do.
Brook Henry, stonecutter, boards Water Cure building
Brooks Samuel, house 278 Main
Brooks Samuel R. laborer, house rear Robert Woodruff's
Bryant Charles, coachman, Phenix Hotel, boards do.
Bryant John A. house 218 Main
Brown Albert A. teamster, b. Ezekiel S. Reed's, Fisherville
Brown Betsy A. widow of Cotton S. house 75 Spring
Brown Charles, carmaker, Con. R. R. house 14 Fayette
Brown Daniel B. quarryman, b. D. Fish's, W. Concord Road
Brown D. Arthur (*D. Arthur Brown & Co.*), machinists, house Webster Place, Fisherville
Brown D. Arthur & Co. (*D. Arthur Brown and John S. Brown*), machinists, Fisherville
Brown David A. stable keeper, West Canal, h. Elm, Fisherville
Brown David F. house 6 Hanover [School, c. State
Brown Frank E. bookkeeper E. P. Prescott & Co.'s, boards
Brown Fred. J. boards H. H. Brown's, Fisherville
Brown George A. wheelwright at Abbot's, b. 65 Spring
Brown Harlan L. clerk at Remick's, boards Mrs. Bean's, Call's block
Brown Harry N. salesman, boards Phenix Hotel
Brown Henry F. (*Brown & Linehan*), grocer, Main, house Elm, Fisherville
Brown Henry H. (*H. H. & J. S. Brown*), manuf. cotton goods, house Elm, corner Webster Place, Fisherville
Brown Horace A. pressman at Statesman office, h. 36 Centre
Brown H. H. & J. S. (*Henry H. Brown and John S. Brown*), manufacturers cotton goods, Fisherville
Brown Ira E. butcher, house 27 Warren
Brown Jeremiah, superintendent of streets, house 65 Spring
Brown John, laborer, house 13 Wall

Brown John (*J. Brown & Co.*), furniture, Stickney's block,
house 4 Tahanto [Stickney's block, Main
Brown J. & Co. (*John Brown and William Vogler*), furniture,
Brown J. L. stonecutter, boards Sherman House
Brown John F. bookkeeper at Abbot's, house 65 Main
Brown John F. 2nd, blacksmith, house Walnut, n. Tremont
Brown John P. assistant physician Insane Asylum
Brown John L. T. carriage maker at Abbot's, h. 4 Perley
Brown John S. (*H. H. & J. S. Brown*), manuf. cottons, house
2 Webster Place, Fisherville
Brown John & Co. furniture, Stickney's block, opp. State
House, house Tahanto
Brown Joseph, coffin warehouse, 286 Main, h. 25 Franklin
Brown Jos. E. coffin finisher, b. Joseph Brown's, 25 Franklin
Brown Josiah, farmer, house 6 Tremont
Brown Lewis L. clerk at Wyatt's, boards 13 Wall
Brown Lorenzo D. house State, corner School
Brown Mary Mrs. widow of William, boards 64 Warren
Brown Samuel N. machinist, D. A. Brown & Co.'s, boards
John S. Brown's, Fisherville [House, Fisherville
Brown Samuel F. merchant tailor, Main, boards Washington
Brown Stephen Mrs. widow, house School, near State
Brown Stewart I. bookkeeper H. H. & J. S. Brown's, boards
John S. Brown's, Fisherville
Brown Theodate H. millinery and dry goods, 4 Statesman
building, Main, house Fayette, corner State
Brown William, machinist, house 28 School
Brown William H. farmer, house West Concord
Brown & Linehan (*Henry F. Brown and John C. Linehan*),
grocers, Main, Fisherville [Fisherville
Buckley Dana, overseer in mill, boards Ezekiel S. Brown's,
Burbank Wm. P. foreman Con. R. R. h. Allison, n. Turnpike
Bulleigh Peter, blacksmith, house rear Hill's block
Bullock Elizabeth, widow of Aaron, boards 36 Green
Bullock Gilbert, house Green, between Warren and School
Bunker Andrew, sash, door and blind manuf. Union Steam
Mill, house 2 Hanover street
Bunnell Lucius D. carpenter, house East Concord
Buntin William H. city marshal, house 62 Warren
Bunton David, A. stone-cuttor, honse 164 State
Burbank Betsy J. Miss, bds. Isaac Cilley's Fisherville
Burgess Abraham, laborer, house West, cor. South
Burgin Hall, house Fayette, cor. South
Burgum John, artist at Abbot's. house 39 State
Burke John, laborer at Gas Works, house 26 Downing
Burke Peter, picker, bds. Mrs. C. Clark's, High, cor. Spring,
Fisherville
Burke William, laborer, house Depot, near Railroad Square
Burleigh Henry, carpenter, house Spring, near Pleasant
Burnham Franklin W. carpenter, house 7 Rumford

Burnham Jabez W. express messenger, house 44 Green, near North Arch
Burns Cornelius, laborer, house rear Hill's block
Burns George, painter at Abbot's, bds. Mrs. Mary N. Neal, Ash, cor. Fayette [Pleasant
Burns Hannah R. Miss, clerk, 108 Main, bds. Mrs. Boynton's,
Burpee Jeremiah, stationary engineer, C. M. & L. Railroad, house 4 Railroad Square [Square
Burpee Sylvanus M. fireman, C. Railroad, bds. 4. Railroad
Burpee John C. conductor, bds. 33 Green
Burt Joseph, harness-maker, 151 Main, bds. Myrtle street
Burt Randall, engineer, N. R. Railroad, house Railroad Sqr.
Burton Robert, machinist N. Railroad, bds. Winter
Bushey Alfred H. carriage-maker, Harvey, Morgan & Co's. bds. Wall, cor. Elm
Bushey Isaac W. blacksmith, bds. Wall, cor. Elm
Bushey Lewis, wheelwright, Harvey, Morgan & Co's, bds. Elm, cor. Wall [near State
Buswell George F. carriage-maker, at Abbot's, house Perley,
Buswell Judith D. Mrs. widow of James, house Franklin cor. State
Buswell Wm. L. laborer, house Washington, n. Centre
Butterfield J. Ware, lawyer, Stickney's block, rooms do
Butterfield William, publisher, N. H. Patriot, Sanborn's block, house State, cor. of Capitol
Butterfield Wm. A. F. carpenter, house 21 State
Butters Charles, farmer and surveyor. house 13 Turnpike
Butters Charles H. laborer at Gas Works, bds. 13 Turnpike
Butters George F. machinist at Abbot's, bds. 13 Turnpike
Butters Sarah F. Miss milliner, Sanborn's block, bds. 16 Green
Butters Thomas, wheelwright, house 16 Green [Court
Button Reuben, pump-maker, Warren, n. Main, house Lincoln
Buzzell Gilbert H. carpenter, house Tremont, n. State
Buzzell Granville B. carpenter, house Henry, n. church
Buzzell Miles, carpenter, house 70 Franklin
Byrnes Barney, laborer, N. Railroad, bds. 83 Warren
Byrnes Thomas, laborer, N. Railroad, bds. 83 Main
Byron Chester, porter, Eagle Hotel

CAHILL MICHAEL, stone-cutter, bds. Moses Davis'
Caldwell Benj. F. (*Caldwell & Amsden*), cabinet-maker, Fisherville, house Merrimack, n. school [near school
Caldwell Dura P. carpenter, bds. B. F. Caldwell's, Merrimack,
Caldwell William H. cabinet-maker, house Elm, Fisherville
Caldwell & Amsden, (*Benj. F. Caldwell and Henry H. Amsden*), furniture manufacturers, Main, Fisherville
Calef Joseph W. hair-dresser, Main, house Main, Fisherville
Calef Rachael, Mrs. widow Benj. house Union, Fisherville
Call Horace, carpenter, house Auburn, cor. Chestnut
Call Levi, pump-repairer, house Rumford, n. Centre

Call Silas W. tinman, bds. Reuben C. Danforth's, Fisherville
Callaghan John, laborer, house State, n. Main
Callahan Michael, laborer, house Tremont, n. State [Lane
Callahan Michael, switchman, N. Railroad, house Herbert's
Calley Nahum, stone-cutter, bds. Joseph Hook's [ren
Cameron Andrew B. musical instrument-maker, bds. 29 War-
Campbell Alonzo, cabinet-maker, house High, Fisherville
Campbell Henry J. (*Campbell & Hall*), insurance agent, 6 State block, Main, house Liberty, near Asylum
Campbell Samuel W. cabinet-maker, house Elm, Fisherville
Capen Henry E. engineer, Con. Railroad, house Clinton, near Asylum
Cardenas M. hairdresser, bds. 4 Call's block, State
Carlile Charles, clerk, bds. Eagle Hotel
Carleton Arthur, laborer, Fayette, n. Main
Carleton James M. farmer, house East Concord
Carlton Elijah W. blacksmith at Abbot's, bds. T. Gawler's, Cross, near South
Carpenter David M. farmer, house Penacook, cor. Walnut
Carpenter Joseph, carpenter, house 19 Union
Carpenter Preston J. house-painter, house West Concord
Carroll Edward, laborer, house near 34 Main
Carroll Henry, clerk, bds. Phenix Hotel
Carroll John N. bds. American House
Carroll Lysander, H. stoves, tinware, &c., Main, near Elm House, bds. M. Blake's, Hill's Avenue
Carr Benjamin, phot. artist, 108 Main, house 2 Green
Carr Hial, laborer at Abbot's, house Turnpike, n. the brick-yard
Carr Julia A. Mrs. widow, William F. h Pleasant, near Main
Carr Lyman, watchmaker, house Warren, cor. Merrimack
Carr Norman G. watches, clocks, &c., Statesman block, house 20 Thompson
Carr William, (*Jewett Leg Co.*), Central block, house 15 Elm near Pleasant
Carrick Patrick, stone-cutter, house State, n. the new cemetery
Carter Albert E. upholster, bds. Henry H. Aldrich's [Cross
Carter Andrew B. clerk, 2 Phenix block, house Beaver, cor.
Carter Bradbury G. blacksmith, house 118 Spring
Carter Charles E. laborer, house West Concord
Carter Elbridge G. express-man, house 17 Warren
Carter Ezra, physician, house 249 Main
Carter Geo. W. clerk at Express Office, house 27 School
Carter George T. carriage-trimmer at Harvey, Morgan & Co's. house 20 Monroe
Carter Hiram J. harness-maker, house Prince, near Spring
Carter Jacob, jeweler, house 24 School
Carter John, engineer, N. Railroad, house Spring, n. Centre
Carter John, director, Union Store, house High, Fisherville
Carter Laura, widow of Wm. M. house 19 South [State
Carter Lewis C. harness-maker, 151 Main, bds. 4 Call's block,

Carter Nathan M. provision dealer, School, opp. P. O., house 21 South [house South, n. Thompson
Carter Nathan M. (*William Hart & Co.*) Market, 16 School,
Carter Orin T. clerk, 2 Phenix block, bds. C. C. Webster's
Casavaint Michael, painter,, house Union, n. Maple
Casey Martin, cleaner, C. M. & L. Railroad, house Spring, n. Warren
Casey Martin, laboror, house Spring, n. Pleasant
Casey Richard, laborer, house rear Hill's block
Casheen John, stone-cutter, bds. Joseph E. Phelps'
Casheen Michael, machinist, bds. Michael Mulcahy's
Cass Cyrus R. blacksmith, bds. 11 Washington
Cass Nancy J. Mrs. widow of Cyrus, house 11 Washington
Cassidy Michael, currier at Blake's, bds. Joseph E. Phelps'
Caswell Charles F. shoe-maker, house 109 Spring
Caswell George W. machinist, house 207 Main
Caswell John H. painter at Abbot's, house 20 Thorndike
Caswell Melinda P. Mrs. widow, Thos. J. house 13 Fayette
Cate Daniel T. lantern maker, bds. 163 State
Cavanaugh Arthur, laborer, house 14 Downing
Cerley Robert, laborer, house Church, near State
Cerley Thomas, laborer, house Church, near State
Chadwick Hale, dry goods, Main, boards Mrs. A. Pervier's, Warren, near Charles, Fisherville
Chambers William, stonecutter, boards Patrick Larkin's
Chandler Abiel, horticulturist, h. 78 South [opp. Beaver
Chandler Charles F. baggage master, Con. R. R. house Cross,
Chandler David S. book and newspaper dealer, Main corner School, house Spring, near Pleasant [ville
Chandler Frank, clothing dealer, Main, h. Merrimack, Fisher-
Chandler Frank, tinsmith, boards 83 State
Chandler Frank P. tinman, boards State, corner Warren
Chandler Isaac H. conductor C. M. & L. R. R. boards Phenix Hotel
Chandler Jeremiah, carpenter, h. St. John, opp. Vernon
Chandler John F. readymade clothing, Main, h. Merrimack, Fisherville
Chandler Luther, bookseller, Main, corner School
Chandler Mary Ann Mrs. widow of Nathan S. 9 Centre
Chandler Samuel, engineer, house Union, Fisherville
Chandler Sophia W. widow of Samuel A. h. 28 Pleasant
Chandler Susan, widow of Joshua, h. Washington, n. School
Chandler William, harness maker, at Hill's, b. Mrs. Mary J. Flanders', State, near Pleasant
Chapman Joshua, carpenter and surveyor, h. 12 Tremont
Chapman Phylester, farmer, house 14 Montgomery
Chaquette Joseph, house 7 W. Canal, Fisherville
Charter Oak Life Ins. Co., Lon. Weston, general agent N. H. and Vt., Central block, Main
Chase Dexter, collecting agent, Main, opp. State House, bds. Phenix Hotel

Chase Ellen M. Mrs. widow of Warren, boards 50 Pleasant

Chase George R. student, boards 15 Centre

Chase James H. stoves and tinware, opp. Statesman's building, Main, house Huntingdon, opp. Garden

Chase Perley S. lawyer, house 15 Centre

Chase Samuel H. painter, house Downing, near South

Chase William M. (*Marshall & Chase*), 2 and 3 State block, house Merrimack, opp. Orchard [n. Court

Cheney Edward J. painter, boards E. G. Cutting's, Summer

Cheney Frank B. machinist N. R. R. boards 33 Green

Cheney John, stonecutter, house 12 Tremont

Cheney Lyman K. currier, house Washington, Fisherville

Cheney & Co., now United States & Canada Express Co., Depot R. R. Square

Chesley Charles C. carpenter, boards 94 State

Chesley Curtis C. fishpeddler, house 94 State

Chesley James, proprietor Sherman House, Main, opposite Free Bridge Road [opp. Rumford

Chesley James G. carriagesmith at Abbot's, house Pleasant,

Chesley John, carriagesmith, bds. G. W. Brockway's, West Concord

Chesley Josiah C. blacksmith, house East Concord

Chesley Samuel M. blacksmith Union Steam Mill, house 183 State, near Methodist church

Chesley William A. coachmaker at Abbot's, h. 52 South

Chickering Henry F. freight agent Con. R. R. h. 18 Thompson

Child James B. baggage master N. R. R. h. Lincoln court

Childs Enoch L. house South, near Pleasant

Choate Gerrish J. painter, boards Mrs. Sarah G. Choate's, Summer, corner Centre, Fisherville

Choate Sarah G. Mrs. widow of George W. boarding house, Summer, corner Centre, Fisherville

Churchill Frank, quarryman, house West Concord

Churchill Henry (*Churchill, Kilburn & Co.*), dry goods, Main, opp. State block, boards Phenix Hotel

Churchill, Kilburn & Co. (*Henry Churchill and Gilbert T. Kilburn*), dry and fancy goods, Main, opposite P. O.

Cilley Isaac, farmer, house Walnut, Fisherville

Cilley James A. mason, bds. S. F. Cilley's, Downing, n. State

Cilley John G. lawyer, boards 54 Green

Cilley Jonathan L. (*Moore & Cilley*), hardware, h. 54 Green

Cilley Luther F. peddler, b. S. F. Cilley's, Downing, n. State

Cilley Stephen F. laborer, house Downing, near State

City Fire Ins. Co., Hartford, Ct., Webster & Smith, agents, State block, Main [Main, opposite Elm House

Clapp Henry W. foreman Ford & Kimball's foundry, house

Clark Benmore, farmer, h. East Concord [Fisherville

Clark Caroline, widow of Jonathan G. h. High, cor. Spring,

Clark Cady, farmer, house Spring, near Cross

Clark Charles C. farmer, house Clinton, near Asylum

Clark Charles M. machinist N. R. R. h. Main, c. Centre
Clark Charles, N. R. R. shop. house Main, corner South
Clark Charles W. engineer N. R. R. house South Arch
Clark Frederick, carver, boards Mrs. Sarah G. Choate's, Summer, corner Centre, Fisherville
Clark Harrison G. railroad agent, h. Wash. next to School
Clark Hiram, shoemaker, 71 South, house do.
Clark Myra A. Miss, boards 1 Cedar
Clark Stephen, farmer, house East Concord
Clark William W. blacksmith, house South, opp. Thorndike
Clarke Charles W. clerk, 5 Exchange block, b. 14 Fayette
Clarke David E. dry goods, 5 Exchange block, h. 74 Pleasant, corner Pine
Clarke Silas B. clerk, boards D. E. Clarke's
Cleaves Asenath, widow of Perley, house 68 Pleasant
Cleaves George P. (*Warde, Humphrey & Co.*), hardware, &c. 1 and 2 Exchange, boards Mrs. P. Cleaves's, 68 Pleasant
Clement Almina, widow of Jonathan C. house 46 Rumford
Clement Francis H. expressman, boards 163 State
Clement Isaac. farmer, house Clinton, corner Asylum
Clement John, laborer, house Summer, n. Church, Fisherville
Clement Jonathan H. house 163 State
Clement Zenas, lawyer, house 6 Call's block, State
Clifford Daniel (*Clifford & Currier*), carpenters, r. Stickney's block, house 52 Green
Clifford John, house West Concord road, near C. R. R.
Clifford Joseph E. boot and shoe dealer, Stickney's new block, Main, boards A. B. Sanborn's, Centre
Clifford Josiah S. (*Dow, Kenney & Clifford*), masons, house 13 Union, near Centre
Clifford & Currier (*Daniel Clifford & Erastus C. Currier*), carpenters, near Stickney's block
Clifford Sumner C. quarryman, house West Concord, near C. Railroad crossing
Clinton James, stone-cutter, house 18 Fosterville
Clisby Edmond, machinist, C. M. & L. Railroad-shop, boards Main, cor. Centre
Clisby Edmond H. B. machinist, house W. Canal, Fisherville
Clisby Orin T. engineer at Tannery, house Penacook
Cloud William W. carpenter, house Main, opp. Abbot's fact.
Cloudman Elizabeth, widow of Thomas, house Cedar
Cloudman Harriet N. Miss, boards with Mrs. Betsy F. Fife
Clough Charles H. spoke-maker, house 24 Green
Clough D. Ansel, artist in ink, oil and water colors, Exchange block, bds. Elm House
Clough Edwin D. (*Rowell & Clough*), groceries, Washington, near Rumford. bds. C. P. Rowell's, Rumford
Clough George, house 67 Warren
Clough George P. boards 67 Warren
Clough Henry W. clerk, boards 24 Green

Clough Jacob, boards 20 Union
Clough Jeremiah P. conductor, boards 24 Green
Clough John C. carpenter, house Spring, cor. Lincoln Court
Clough Joseph T. plaster-mill E. Concord, house do.
Clough Lawrin, depot-master, bds. J. T. Clough's, E. Concord
Clough Leonidas H. carpenter, house 20 Union
Clough Mahlen, shoe-dealer, house Prince, near Spring
Clough M. B. (*Piper & Clough*), boots and shoes, house 11 Prince
Clough Orin C. wheelwright at Abbot's, house 12 Downing
Clough Phillip C. blacksmith, house Washington, cor. Walnut
Clough William, carpenter, boards Charles B. Knight's, West Concord
Clough William A. clerk, house 16 Franklin, cor. Union
Coburn Elizabeth Mrs. nurse, house Liberty, cor. Warren
Coburn James, quarryman, boards D. Fish, West Concord road
Coburn John A. harness-maker, Main, house Merrimack, Fisherville
Cochran Annie, widow, Joseph, boards 9 Rumford
Cochran Joseph A. (*French & Cochran*), flour and grain, Main, cor. Pleasant, house 6 Green [near Cross
Cochran Jesse C. blacksmith, opp. Phenix Hotel, house State
Cochran Joseph C. blacksmith, boards Jesse C. Cochran's
Cochran Walter W. (*Lewis Barter & Co.*), 6 Pleasant, house 9 Rumford, near Pleasant [Beaver
Cochlan Patrick, laborer, boards H. Nason's, Monroe, near
Cochlin Wm. house Myrtle, near Thompson [Centre
Codman John M. wood contractor, N. R. Railroad, house 26
Coffin Benjamin Jr. house Centre, cor. Hanover [Hanover
Coffin Charles G. clerk, boards Benj. Coffin's, Centre, corner
Coffin Edward G. painter, house 17 Green
Coffin Frank (*S. Quimby & Co.*), flour and grain, 6 Pleasant, house Centre, corner Hanover
Coffin Frederick, melodeon keymaker, boards 50 Green
Coffin Harriet F. Mrs. wid. of Samuel, h. State, n. Penacook
Coffin John L. house 17 Green [31 Warren
Coffin Oliver C. hats, caps, &c. Stickney's new block, house
Coffin William, keymaker at Prescott Bros'. house 50 Green
Cofran Western, woodturner, house Union, near Washington
Cogswell James M. hostler at Norton's, bds. Eagle Hotel
Cogswell Lewis, engineer, boards Columbian Hotel
Cogswell P. Brainard, printer and publisher, Monitor office, Main, 32 School
Colbath Chas. A. bookkeeper, Hutchins & Co.'s, h. 2 Chapel
Colburn Luther, carpenter, house Spring, n. Lincoln court
Colby Charles, switchman C. R. R. house near 30 Main
Colby Charles S. switchman, house 8 Cross
Colby Frank P. teamster, boards 68 Warren
Colby James B. baggage master, house 125 State
Colby Timothy, carpenter, house 4 Wall

Colby Warren M. clerk, Remick's, h. 25 South, c. Thompson
Colby Willabey jr. blacksmith, h. 227 State, c. Main
Cole Alonzo B. wheelwright at Abbot's, house 1 Turnpike
Cole Benjamin, blacksmith, house East Concord
Cole Oliver C. (*Abbott & Cole*), painter, 9 Warren, house 55 State
Cole Richard, stonecutter, boards Columbian Hotel
Coleman Betsy Mrs. widow of Michael, house rear 34 Main
Coleman William, printer, Patriot office, h. Warren, n. Asylum
Collins Augustine W. carpenter, house Lincoln court
Collins George A. foreman Con. R. R. h. Fayette, n. Main
Collins Henry, track repairer Con. R. R. boards William P. Burbank's, Allison, near Turnpike road
Collis Nahum, stonecutter, boards Joseph B. Hook's
Colston Henry N. restaurant, 99 Main, h. Warren, c. Tahanto
Colston William, saloon keeper, b. Warren, c. Tahanto
Colston William H. clerk, 99 Main, b. Warren, c. Tahanto
Colwell John, moulder, h. R. R. Sq. r. Barron, Dodge & Co.'s
Comery Alex. harness maker, 3 Warren, house Depot square
Comstock C. E. hostler, boards Eagle Hotel
Conditt William B. roadmaker, boards Amos Bean's, State
Cone Julius, apothecary, boards Eagle Hotel
Coney Ellen, widow of Stephen, h. Washington, n. Warren, Fisherville
Conn Granville P. (*Gage & Conn*), physician, Stickney's block, house 22 Main
Connecticut Fire Ins. Co., Hartford, Stickney's new block, [Main
Connell Honora Miss, house 14 Main
Connell John, Assistant Marshal, house 2 Fremont
Connell Patrick, laborer, house West Concord
Conner Charles G. house 54 South
Conner Jerome B. boards 54 South
Conner Lawrence, spinner at Holden's mill, h. W. Concord
Conner Timothy H. carpenter, h. Centre, opp. Rumford
Conner William H. tinsmith at Carroll's, house 9 Wall
Connor Jacob, stonecutter, boards Columbian Hotel
Connor John E. stonecutter, boards Sherman House
Connors Thomas, helper C. R. R. h. Lee's block, Chandler
Converse Nathaniel P. clerk, house 16 Spring
Converse R. A. Mrs. dressmaker, Central block, Main, b. do.
Cook Aldrich B. baggage master C. M. & L. R. R. house Fulton, near South
Cooke Howard M. melodeon and organ maker, Exchange block, house 56 State
Cooke Samuel, clergyman, house 56 State
Cook Solomon, moulder, house 4 Montgomery
Cooper John A. clerk, 2 Phenix block, house 39 Warren
Cooper Josiah, stone-cutter, house 7 Turnpike
Cooper Levi, stone-mason, house 3 Turnpike
Corey George W. teamster at Ford & Kimball's, house 16 [Washington

Corey Nancy, widow John C. house 16 Washington
Corning Cyrus N. farmer, house 13 Green [Green
Corning Mary L. Mrs. widow Robert N. house Pleasant, cor.
Corning Warren H. hair-dresser, under Phenix Hotel, house State, cor. Warren
Cote Frank, laborer, house 3 Fosterville [Myrtle
Cotter Jeremiah, coach-trimmer at Abbot's, house Cross, near
Cotter Patrick, quarryman, boards Baldwin Humphrey's, West Concord
Cotton John F. book-keeper, Concord Railroad, house 19 Elm
Cotton Jonathan T. clerk, C. M. & L. freight depot, h. 19 Elm
Coty Thomas, blacksmith at Abbot's, house 6 Cross
Couch Benj. H. carpenter, house 10, Rumford [cor. Essex
Couch Calvin P. silversmith, at Durgin's, house Washington,
Couch John, clergyman, house Rumford, near Cambridge
Couch Mahala, widow of Hiram M. dress-maker, 83 State, house do.
Craigue George, blacksmith at Ford & Kimball's, boards 71 Spring
Craigue Geo. W. moulder at Ford & Kimball's, h. 71 Spring
Craigue Wm. moulder at Ford & Kimball's, h. 8 Warren
Crain Frank M. (*Eastman & Co.*), druggist, house 7 Call's block, State
Crane Roxie A. Mrs. widow of Calvin, house Fayette, corner South [Washington
Crapo Lucretia H. widow of Ezra B., house Academy, near
Crawford Frederick S. book-binder, Statesman building, Main, house 29 School
Crawford Jane L. Miss milliner, boards at F. S. Crawford's
Critchett Charles H. (*M. Critchett & Son*), soap and candle manufacturer, Walnut, near Washington, house Rumford, near Washington
Critchett Moses, (*M. Critchett & Son*), soap and candle manufacturer, Walnut, near Washington, house Rumford, cor. Washington
Critchett Moses B. tailor, City Block, h. Centre, opp. Tahanto
Critchett M. & Son, (*Moses Critchett and Charles H. Critchett*), soap and candle manufacturers, Walnut, near Washington
Crocker Ann M. Mrs. widow of Joseph S. bds. Jeremiah C. Elliott's, East Concord
Crockett George W. (*Jas. S. Norris & Co.*), confectioner, 85 Main, house 87 Main
Crockett Hannah, widow of Wm., house 2 Call's block, State
Crockett James S. (*Crockett & Pillsbury*), piano-forte and melodeon key-maker, 16 Wall, house 39 South
Crockett Zachariah J. teamster, house 65 State
Crockett & Pillsbury, (*James S. Crockett and Frank J. Pillsbury*), piano-forte and melodeon key-makers, 16 Wall
Cronan Dennis, melter, house Church, near State
Cronin Patrick, stone-cutter, bds. Mrs. Spaulding's, Pearl st.

Crosby Albert H. physician, Stickney's block, bds. J. P. Stickney's, Main

Crosby Jackson, spoke-maker, house Cambridge, near Academy

Cross Joseph, card-stripper at mill, bds. Ezekiel S. Brown's, Fisherville

Crow Charles, carriage-maker at Abbot's, house 33 Thompson

Crowley Daniel, blacksmith, house Church, near State

Crowley Dennis, laborer, house Penacook, near the Tannery

Crowley Jeremiah, laborer, house Penacook, n. the Tannery

Crowley John, harness-maker, 151 Main, house Main, near Washington

Crowther James S. carpenter, house Summer, cor. High, Fisherville

Crowther Richard, overseer of spinning-room, at Brown's, house Union, Fisherville

Crowther Robert, spinner, house Summer, cor. High, Fisherville

Crowther William H. spinner, boards R. Crowther's, Union, Fisherville

Crummett George E. machinist, house 35 Thompson

Crummett John, quarryman, boards Baldwin Humphrey's, West Concord

Crummett John B. tinsmith, opp. Statesman building, house Thompson, near South

Crummett Robert B. farmer, house 39 Pleasant

Culbertson Nathaniel A. laborer, house 75 Spring

Cull Roger, carriage trimmer at Abbot's, house 4 Jefferson

Cummings Eben E. clergyman, house 23 Green

Cummings Eben G. (*Cummings & Young*), dentist, Phenix block, house 5 Monroe

Cummings George A. marble worker, 89 Main, h. Huntingdon, corner Garden

Cummings James, stonecutter, b. David Silver's, E. Concord

Cummings Milon D. marble worker, bds. Geo. A. Cummings', Huntingdon, corner Garden

Cummings & Young (*E. G. Cummings and G. A. Young*), dentists, Phenix block

Cunningham George C. blacksmith, house 290 Main

Currier Albert A. (*Eastman & Currier*), dry goods and groceries, W. Concord, house do.

Currier A. L. hackdriver, 6 Warren, house 6 do.

Currier Cyrus C. melodeon tuner Parker & Secomb's, house Centre, corner Huntingdon

Currier Erastus C. (*Clifford & Currier*), carpenter, rear Stickney's block, house State, near Franklin

Currier George, fireman, boards Columbian Hotel

Currier Harriet, widow of James C. h. Spring, n. Warren

Currier Herman J. photographer, Washington square, house Main, Fisherville

Currier John A. cabinet maker, bds. S. H. Currier's, Charles, Fisherville

Currier Joseph H. bootmaker, h. 15 Montgomery, n. State

Currier Lyman, stonecutter, house 25 Union

Currier Samuel A. carpenter, bds. S. L. Currier's, Merrimack, opposite Orchard
Currier Samuel L. teamster, h. Merrimack, opp. Orchard
Currier Stephen H. shoemaker, house Charles, Fisherville
Curtice Amos H. peddler, house State, n. the new Cemetery
Curtice William S. farmer, house Clinton
Curtis George H. melodeon maker at Parker & Secomb's, house East Concord
Curtis Nancy D. widow of Samuel, house 112 State
Curtis Perry G. laborer at Abbot's, house South, n. West
Curtis Silas, clergyman, house Rumford, near Washington
Curtis William S. engineer, house West, near State
Curtis William S. jr. fireman, bds. William S. Curtis's, West, near State [bds. Mrs. Neal's, Fayette
Cushing George H. telegraph operator, Depot, R. R. Square,
Cushon Joel A. machinist, house Spring, near Church
Cutler Israel P. harness maker, Prescott's block, h. Spring, near Warren
Cutler Laura A. Mrs. wid. of Henry D. house 16 Thompson
Cutting Asa D. painter, Academy, n. Washington, house do.
Cutting Daniel, painter, house East Concord
Cutting Eben E. painter, Summer, near Court, house do.
Cutting Gilman, painter C. M. & L. R. R. house Academy near Washington [c. Huntingdon
Cutting Mary E. widow of John O. boards J. Evans', Short,
Cutting Rodney G. lumber dealer, Union Steam mill, house Main, corner Ferry

DADMUN JOHN H. shoemaker, house 3 Summer
Dadmun John J. blacksmith N. R. R. h. Church, n. Union
Dadmun Josiah A. tinplate worker, house 18 Union
Dakin John R. blacksmith, b. Mrs. N. Dakin's, West, n. South
Dakin Nancy, widow of Samuel, house West, near South
Damon Benjamin, painter, house 65 South
Dana Sylvester, lawyer and judge of police court, Rumford block, Main, house 6 Washington
Danforth Elizabeth, widow of John, house 6 Concord
Danforth Joel C. clerk at City Book Store, h. 5 Merrimack
Danforth Reuben C. tinman, Main, house Summer, c. High, Fisherville
Danforth William F. confectioner, house Hill's avenue
Darcy Mathew, laborer, house Warren, near Liberty
Darling James P. cooper, boards Baldwin Humphrey's, West Concord [Columbian Hotel
Davis Alamando W. clerk at 3 Moore's block, boards at
Davis Albert, painter at Abbot's, boards 1 Downing
Davis Alfred (*Davis & Morgan*), reed manuf. h. at Worcester
Davis Almond, carriage maker at Abbot's, boards Mrs. J. N. Flanders's, Perley, near State
Davis Ann Mrs. house rear Hill's block

Davis Benjamin B. (*Davis & Morey*), music teacher, Masonic Temple, house do.
Davis Chas. C. provision dealer, 1 Moore's block, h. at Jail
Davis Charles W. (*Davis & Giles*), carriage painter, rear Eagle Hotel, house 6 Monroe [Spring
Davis Daniel, carpenter, bds. J. S. Batchelder's, Clinton, cor.
Davis George H. printer, Patriot office, h. Centre, n. Union
Davis Geo. H. (*Donagan & Davis*), stonecutter, State, near Fosterville, house Walker, corner Union
Davis Henry C. machinist N. R. R. house State, n. Church
Davis James, tailor and repairer, Main, opp. School, house 101 Spring
Davis Jas. R. C. carriage maker at Harper's, h. E. Concord
Davis Job S. blacksmith, h. Main, n. Washington, Fisherville
Davis Lydia, widow of Simon, house 10 Rumford
Davis Moses, carpenter, house 254 Main
Davis Nelson, teamster, house Summer, Fisherville
Davis Rebecca, widow of Robert, house 170 State
Davis William R. machinist, boards H. C. Davis's, State
Davis William S. blacksmith, house 19 Washington
Davis & Giles (*Charles W. Davis and Andrew J. Giles*), carriage painters, rear Low's block
Davis & Morey (*Benjamin B. Davis and John H. Morey*), music teachers, Masonic Temple
Davis & Morgan (*Alfred Davis and John J. Morgan*), melodeon and organ reed manufacturers, Union Steam Mill
Day Alonzo, clerk, Cyrus Peaslee's, bds. Warren, cor. Rumford
Day William, house Union, near Centre
Dean Nathan B. painter, house High, cor. Spring, Fisherville
Dearborn Charles C. bds. Giles', 45 Pleasant
Dearborn Mary L. widow of Andrew P. h. 45 Pleasant
Dearborn William, hostler, Eagle Hotel
Delaney John, laborer, house West, n. South
Demers Joseph, carriage-smith at J. Welcome's, bds. J. Welcome's, Centre, opp. Hanover [the new Cemetery
Dennen John, stone-cutter, bds. J. M. Gallagher's, State, near
Dennett Charles, wheelwright at Abbot's, h. 17 Thorndike
Dennett Dixi C. machinist, h. Main, cor. Summer, Fisherville
Dennett Geo. S. carpenter, house 15 Thorndike
Dennett Harriet Mrs. widow of Joseph C., bds. J. H. Foss, Merrimack, Fisherville
Derby Henry J. carpenter, bds. Brown's, Wall
Derby Henry W. wood-worker, Con. Railroad, bds. 13 Wall
De Rome Edward, blacksmith, bds. Columbian Hotel
Derry Joseph, blacksmith, house 13 1-2 Centre
Desmond Daniel, laborer, bds. Patrick Larkin's
Desmond Patrick, laborer, house West Concord
Devereux Laurence, telegraph agent, bds. Mrs. Mary J. Flanders', State, near Pleasant

Dewey Hiram K. claim agent, Phenix block, house 4 Hanover
Dewey Lyman F., house Fayette, cor. South
Dickerman George O. clerk, N. Railroad office, bds. 15 Fayette
Dickerman Moses W. master, car depot, C. M. & L. Railroad 15 Fayette
Dickerman Silas B. book-keeper, Ind. Press Association, bds. [15 Fayette
Diedritch Miss, tailoress, rooms 2 Park
Dimond Waterman, stone-mason, Penacook, near Walnut
Dixon Edward, carpenter, bds. Mrs. Mary Drown, Merrimack, Fisherville
Doane Geo. H. clerk, J. H. Pearson & Co's. house 10 Green
Dodge Amos, (*Barron, Dodge & Co.*), house 70 Pleasant
Dodge Howard A. clerk at Warde, Humphrey's & Co's. bds. 70 Pleasant
Doffe Roy, harness-maker, 151 Main, bds. 19 Short
Doherty James, laborer, house 213 Main
Doherty Timothy, laborer, house Ferry, near Railroad
Dole George, painter, Abbot's fact., bds. Mrs. Julia A. Carr's
Dole Mary A. Mrs. widow of Seth J., bds. 43 Pleasant
Dole Seth R. coach-trimmer at Abbot's, house 43 Pleasant
Dolan James, carpenter, at Abbot's, house 25 Thompson
Dolan Michael, stone-cutter, bds. 25 Jefferson
Dolan Michael, laborer at Abbot's, bds. 25 Thompson
Donagan James A. (*Donagan & Davis*), stone-cutter, State, near Fosterville, house do.
Donagan & Davis, (*James A. Donagan and George Davis*), stone-cutters, State, near Fosterville
Donn John, harness-maker, 151 Main, house Cross, n. Main
Donahue Patrick, laborer, house Lee's block, Chandler
Donahoe Michael T. conductor, Con. Railroad, house rear 37 Main
Donovan Mary, widow of Daniel, house Cross, near Main
Donovan Nancy Mrs. widow of Michael, h. Cross, n. Beaver
Dooley Martin, laborer, house 10 State
Dorcey Michael, laborer, house Warren, near Pine
Dow Augustus, carpenter, boards Mrs. Julia A. Carr's
Dow Charles J. jeweller, boards Geo. W. Drew's
Dow Edward, architect, Masonic Temple, h. Pleasant, opp. Asylum
Dow Frank, restaurant, Main, bds. W. B. French's, Union
Dow George A. (*Dow, Kenney & Clifford*), masons, house 58 Centre
Dow Hiram, carpenter at Dow's, house Hopkinton road
Dow Horace P. carpenter, house 4 Charles, Fisherville
Dow Isaac, house Merrimack, corner Centre, Fisherville
Dow Judith W. Mrs. wid. of Enoch H. h. Church, Fisherville
Dow, Kenney & Clifford (*Geo. A. Dow, William H. Kenney, and Josiah S. Clifford*), masons, Main, opp. Columbian Hotel
Dow Lorenzo, carpenter, State, n. Cross, h. 19 Thorndike

Dow Margaret E. widow of Furber, house 111 Spring
Dow Maria L. widow of Andrew A. h. Summer, Fisherville
Dow Martha Mrs. house West Concord [Fisherville
Dow William, overseer at cabinet shop, boards 9 West Canal,
Dow William, hostler, 6 Warren, house do.
Downing Alonzo (*Abbot, Downing & Co.*), house 116 State
Downing George, engineer N. R. R. h. Washington, n. State
Downing George C. laborer, house Main, n. Penacook
Downing Geo. D, engineer N. R. R. house 16 Washington
Downing Lewis jr. (*Abbot, Downing & Co.*), coach manufacturer, Main, house 15 Pleasant
Downing Lewis, house 19 Main
Doyen Edward N. wheelwright, house 40 Green
Doyen Frank, laborer, house 1 Call's block, State
Doyle John G. moulder at Ford & Kimball's, h. 2 Water
Doyle Morris, foundry man, house Water, near Main
Drake Alfred, engineer, boards Sherman House
Drake George W. teamster, house 99 Spring
Drake Henry, fireman N. R. R. boards 59 Main
Draper William, boards Sherman House
Drew Curtis D. stonecutter, house West Concord road, near C. R. R. crossing
Drew Frank P. harness maker, 151 Main, b. Columbian Hotel
Drew George W. (*George W. Drew & Co.*), Main, opposite State House, house Centre, corner Tahanto
Drew George W. & Co. jewellers, opp. State House, Main
Drew John W. clerk at Lincoln & Shaw's, house 9 Union, corner Maple [Tremont
Drew Oliver J. moulder Ford's foundry, house Franklin, near
Drew Susan M. Mrs. house 6 Winter
Drew Walter S. compositor, boards Columbian Hotel
Driscoll Cornelius, laborer N. R. R. h. Walnut, n. soap factory
Driscoll Daniel, fireman N. R. R. boards 81 Warren
Driscoll John, woodsawyer N. R. R. house 8 Chapel
Driscoll Michael, laborer, house 29 Warren
Driscoll Michael, wood-sawyer, N. Railroad, house 81 Warren
Drown Albert H. overseer at D. Arthur Brown & Co's. house Elm, Fisherville [erville
Drown Mary Mrs. widow of Leonard, house Merrimack, Fish-
Ducey John, laborer, house Cross, near South
Dudley Charles, house 2 Montgomery
Dudley George M. clerk, house Summer, Fisherville
Dudley Hollis O. house Main, opp. City Hall
Dudley Lucien N. blacksmith, bds. W. Johnson's, Washington, near Main, Fisherville [151 State, cor. Centre
Dudley Peter, (*P. Dudley & Co.*), Phenix Hotel Stable, house
Dudley P. & Co. (*Peter Dudley and James H. Rowell*), props. Phenix Hotel stable, Main
Dumas Stebbins H. house State, cor. Penacook
Dunklee Ben F. (*Dunklee & Tilton*), house 16 Merrimack

Duncklee Chas. H. (*Stevens & Duncklee*), stoves and tinware, house 20 Green
Dunklee Benjamin F. farmer, h. Pleasant, cor. Merrimack
Dunklee Carolina E. widow of Wm. house 25 Green
Dunklee Jacob C. farmer, house 85 State
Dunklee & Tilton, (*Benj. F. Dunklee and Samuel J. Tilton*), machinists, 60 Main
Dunlap Daniel, carpenter, house 12 Montgomery [Main
Dunlap Henry S. sash and blind-maker, steam-mill, house 272
Dunlap Morrill, turner, Union Steam-Mill, house 5 Pearl
Dunn John, harness-maker at Hill's, house 23 Cross [Hotel
Dunning Michael, harness-maker, 151 Main, bds. Columbian
Duran Wm. brakeman, Con. Railroad, house Pleasant Avenue
Durgin Abner F. saloon, Main, opp. Washington House, bds. J. S. Durgin's, Main, Fisherville
Durgin Daniel C. freight conductor, bds. Columbian Hotel
Durgin Isaac P. machinist, house Summer, Fisherville
Durgin Jerry S. auctioneer, house Main, Fisherville [erville
Durgin J. Scott, cabinet-maker, bds. J. S. Durgin's, Main, Fish-
Durgin Luther P. printer, house 28 Union [Union
Durgin Luther W. book-keeper at Ford & Kimball's, bds. 28
Durgin Wm. B. silver-smith, School, near Main, house 40 Rumford
Durrell John P. carriage-maker, Harvey, Morgan & Co's. bds. Columbian Hotel
Dutton Jacob S. proprietor, Elm-house, Main, opp. Pleasant
Dwight Josiah E. (*James R. Hill & Co.*), 151 Main, house 70 Main
Dwyer Joseph, blacksmith, bds. Mrs. Julia A. Carr's [Pleasant
Dwyer Peter, blacksmith Harvey, Margan & Co.'s. boards 6
Dwyer William, blacksmith, house Lee's block, Chandler [dry
Dwyer William, machinist, N. Railroad, house Main, n. Foun-
Dyer Merrill, stone-cutter, house Walker, cor. Union
Dyer William O. dresser, house East Canal, Fisherville

EAGAN PETER, mason, h. r. Holden's mill, W. Concord
Eames J. H. D.D., rector of St. Paul's Church, h. 33 Main
Earle Horace A. moulder, Ford's foundry, house Church, near State [103 Spring
Eastman Alleyne B. reed-maker, bds. Mrs. Mary E. Eastman's
Eastman Chandler, wheel-wright, West Concord, house do.
Eastman Charles S. (*Eastman & Co.*), druggist, Hill's block, house 2 Franklin
Eastman Charles F. boards Spring, corner Short
Eastman Charles L. machinist Con. R. R. h. Pleasant avenue
Eastman Dudley L. carpenter, house Spring, c. Pleasant
Eastman Ebenezer, farmer, house East Concord
Eastman Edson C. bookseller and stationer, 160 Main, house 15 School
Eastman Elizabeth, widow of Mellen C. house E. Concord

Eastman Frank A. reedmaker, boards 103 Spring
Eastman George F. shoemaker, boards 227 State
Eastman George H. baker, boards 85 Spring
Eastman Ira A. lawyer, Central block, Main, house 43 Main
Eastman James H. teamster, house Spring, corner Short
Eastman John I. gunsmith, 236 Main, house 26 Washington
Eastman John M. farmer, house East Concord
Eastman John M. tinman, boards 19 Union
Eastman Jos. (*Eastman & Currier*), dry goods and groceries, West Concord, house do.
Eastman Judith, widow of George J. house 227 State
Eastman Mary E. widow of Benjamin C. house 103 Spring
Eastman Lowell, machinist, house 11 School
Eastman Mary P. Mrs. widow of Amos, h. Cross, c. Beaver
Eastman Ora, wheelwright, b. C. Eastman's, W. Concord
Eastman Samuel, farmer, house East Concord
Eastman Samuel C. (*S. & S. C. Eastman*), lawyer, office Rumford block, Main, house 122 State
Eastman Seth (*S. & S. C. Eastman*), insurance agent, Rumford block, Main, house 119 State
Eastman S. & S. C. lawyers and insurance agents, Rumford [block, Main
Eastman & Co. (*Charles S. Eastman and Frank M. Crane*), drugs, oils, &c., Hill's block, Main
Eastman & Currier (*Jos. Eastman and Albert A. Currier*), dry goods and groceries, W. Concord
Eaton Albion, carver, bds. Mrs. Sarah G. Choate's, Summer, [c. Centre, Fisherville
Eaton Calvin, woodworker N. R. R. house 7 Maple
Eaton Climena B. Mrs. widow of John W. house Mechanics' block, Fisherville
Eaton Henry J. clerk Phenix Hotel
Eaton Hilliard L. woodworker at Abbot's, house 11 Elm
Eaton Hiram, clock repairer, boards 57 State
Eaton John, farmer, house 9 Tremont
Eaton Joseph C. engineer at Abbot's, house 3 Rumford
Edgerly Alpheus C. farmer, h. High, c. Spring, Fisherville
Edgerly Ira C. proprietor of Washington House, Washington Square, Fisherville
Edmunds Andrew J. merchant tailor, Eagle Hotel block, h. [38 Green
Edmunds Susan H. wid. of Sam'l, h. Allison, n. Turnpike road
Egan Richard, currier, house 8 Fosterville
Ela Robert L. boards Eagle Hotel
Elden Lorenzo C. teamster, b. D. Fish's, West Concord road
Elkins Dolly, widow of David E. h. 109 Spring
Elkins Joseph, laborer, house Lincoln court
Elliot John G. car repairer C. M. & L. R. R. h. 5 Jefferson
Elliott Charles H. farmer, house East Concord
Elliott E. Fred. supt. clerk C. M. & L. R. R. b. Elm House
Elliott George, upholsterer, b. J. J. Pillsbury's, North Arch
Elliott Henry M. painter, house 17 Merrimack, Fisherville
Elliott Jeremiah C. farmer, house East Concord

Elliott John H. clerk C. M. & L. R. R. house Pleasant, near Merrimack
Elliott Lorenzo K. clerk Phenix Hotel, Main
Ellis Frank B. stationary engineer, boards 100 Spring
Ellis Joseph B. teamster, house 100 Spring
Ellsworth Smith N. clerk, 114 Main, boards 36 Green
Elwell Charles, overseer at prison, house State, cor. Wash.
Elwell Isaac (*Isaac Elwell & Son*), house State
Elwell Isaac N. (*Isaac Elwell & Son*), house State
Elwell Isaac & Son (*Isaac and Isaac N. Elwell*), furniture manufacturers, near freight depot
Elwell Timothy R. works at the prison, h. State, cor. Wash
Emerson Frank A. dresser at the stone-mill, house Summer, cor. Washington Square, Fisherville
Emerson Frank P. carpenter, house State, cor. Thorndike
Emerson Isaac L. carpenter, house Walnut, near Washington
Emerson Joseph F. blacksmith, N. Railroad, house Sullivan
near State [Square
Emerson Orlando S. machinist, C. Railroad, house 3 Railroad
Emerton Geo. W. stone-cutter, Walker, cor. Union, house 235 State
Emery Elbridge, carpenter, bds. Timothy W. Emery's, East
Concord [Main, house Auburn, cor. St. John
Emery George H. (*J. R. Hill & Co.*), harness-maker, 151
Emery Isaac, farmer, house East Concord
Emery John, freight conductor, N. Railroad, bds. 83 State
Emery Joseph W. stone-cutter, bds. 17 Franklin
Emery Nathaniel K. farmer, house High, near Franklin
Emery Timothy W. carpenter, house East Concord
Engel John P. dyer, Holden's Mills, house West Concord
Equitable Mutual Fire Ins. Co., Sanborn's block, Main
Erwin John, baker, house rear 54 Main [Centre
Estabrook Aaron G. painter, opp. Phenix Hotel, house 31
Estabrook Geo. W. painter, house 35 Green
Estabrook Hannah, widow of Aaron, house 35 Green [rimack
Esther Otis, mason, bds. John H. Elliott's, Pleasant, near Mer-
Evans Albertus, farmer, house 2 Bowery Avenue [ingdon
Evans Augustus W. printer, bds. J. Evans', Short, cor. Hunt-
Evans Elias, house 12 Union [Main
Evans Franklin, grocer, Main, south of Pleasant, house 79
Evans Franklin A. clerk F Evans', bds. 79 Main
Evans Ira C. printer, house Spring, near Pleasant
Evans Jonathan, engineer, house Short, cor. Huntingdon
Evans J. Orvel, (*J. Batchelder & Co.*), groceries, Washington Square, house Summer, near Cross, Fisherville
Evans Ralph, machinist, N. Railroad, bds. Mrs. Flander's, State, near Pleasant
Everett David E. harness-cutter, 151 Main, house 114 State
Everett Elkanah P. harness-maker, house Walnut, Fisherville
Eves John, plumber, 5 Fremont, house do.

FAGIN EDWARD, laborer, house Pleasant, n. Washington
Fagin Wm. laborer, house Pleasant, near Washington
Fairbanks Eliza W. widow of Winsor, house 23 Franklin
Fairbanks Frederick A. brakeman C. M. & L. Railroad, bds. Mrs. E. W. Fairbank's [banks', house E. Concord
Fairbanks John E. clerk, F. A. Fisk's, bds. Mrs. E. W. Fair-
Fairfield William B. boot and shoe-maker, Main, opp. Pearl,
Faneuf George A. cabinet maker, bds. R. J. French's, West Canal, Fisherville [West Canal, Fisherville
Faneuf Theophilus W. cabinet maker, boards R. J. French's,
Farley George B. (*H. N. Farley & Co.*), boards 74 Main
Farley H. Nelson (*H. N. Farley & Co.*), house 57 State
Farley H. N. & Co. (*H. N. and George B. Farley*), marble workers, Main, corner Depot
Farley Isaac N. machinist C. M. & L. R. R. h. 29 Thompson
Farley John, moulder at Ford & Kimball's, house Cross, near Jefferson
Farley Nathan, marble worker, Main, c. Depot, h. 74 Main
Farmer Chas. cabinet maker, boards Mrs. Sarah G. Choate's, Summer, corner Centre, Fisherville
Farmer George, cabinet maker, bds. Mrs. Sarah G. Choate's, Summer, corner Centre, Fisherville
Farmer Miles F. blacksmith, boards 6 Pleasant
Farnam Charles A. clerk Farnam & Osgood's, house Spring, corner Fulton
Farnam Henry S. M. (*Farnam & Osgood*), groceries and dry goods, Main, cor. Free Bridge road, house Spring, cor. Fulton
Farnam & Osgood (*Henry S. M. Farnam and Daniel Osgood, Jr.*), grocers, Main, corner Free Bridge road
Farnum Abner D. (*Farnum & Martin*), lumber dealer, West Concord, house do.
Farnum Benjamin, farmer, house West Concord
Farnum Ebenezer, carpenter, house 254 Main
Farnum Frank B. farmer, boards Moses H. Farnum's
Farnum Hazen K. house West Concord
Farnum Isaac H. carpenter, house West Concord
Farnum Mary M. Miss, house West Concord
Farnum Moses H. farmer, house West Concord
Farnum Hiram, farmer, house West Concord
Farnum Phebe Mrs. widow of Peter C. house W. Concord
Farnsworth Samuel N. packer at Abbot's, house 11 Main
Farrand Robt. O. tinsmith, h. Summer, n. Centre, Fisherville
Farrand Squire, laborer, h. Cross, n. Summer, Fisherville
Farrand William, spinner, b. S. Farrand's, Cross, n. Summer, Fisherville
Farrar Porter, card stripper, boards 9 W. Canal, Fisherville
Farrar Cyrus, silkdyer, East Concord, house do.
Farrington Hiram, house 23 Merrimack
Farrington James M. machinist N. R. R. bds. Elm House

Farrington Martha P. Mrs. widow of Samuel, h. 71 Main
Favor Laura P. widow of J. B. h. Church, c. Walnut
Faunce Daniel W. clergyman, house 29 Green
Fay Joseph P. house 5 Wall
Fay William W. clerk, Central block, boards J. P. Fay's
Fellows Albert H. trimmer at Abbot's, house 68 South
Fellows Howard, printer, boards 83 State
Fellows James B. blacksmith at Abbot's, h. West, n. State
Fellows John, physician, 13 West, house do.
Fellows Lyman R. mason, house Pleasant, near Main
Fellows Orra H. printer, Patriot office, b. c. State and Warren
Feltch Almira, widow of Jacob, house Tremont, n. Union
Feltch Hosea, carpenter, house Tremont
Fernald William J. carriage painter, boards 29 Downing
Ferrin Alvin C. mason, house Centre, opposite Union
Ferrin Charles, cabinet maker, house Main, cor. Washington,
Fisherville [Summer, Fisherville
Ferrin Ezekiel C. cabinet maker, b. H. Simpson's, Centre, c.
Ferrin John W. melodeon maker at Austin's, house 78 Spring,
near Pleasant
Fessenden H. carpetbag maker, Spring, cor. Pleasant, h. do.
Field Abbie C. Miss, boards Isaac Cilley's, Fisherville
Fife Betsey F. widow of Reuben, house 46 Main
Fifield Frank P. hostler, Brown's stable, b. Moses H. Fifield's,
Fisherville
Fifield Moses H. teamster, h. High, n. Summer, Fisherville
Fifield S. A. O. Mrs. widow of Rev. Winthrop, h. E. Concord
Finegan Richard, hostler, boards 83 State
First National Bank, Stickney's block, Main
Fish Dan'l, foreman at Concord Granite Works, house West
Concord road [27 Centre
Fisher Elisha P. jeweller at Knight's, Stickney's block, bds.
Fisk Francis N. house Main, near Penacook
Fisk Francis A. grocer, house Main, near Penacook
Fiske Albert W. clergyman, house Summer, opp. Church,
Fisherville
Fitch Everett, baggage master N. R. R. house 26 Centre
Fitch George E. horseshoer, opp. Phenix Hotel, h. 43 Centre
Fitts Dexter, conductor, house School, corner Spring
Fitzgerald Martin, marble cutter, house State, corner Cross
Fitzgerald Thomas, helper N. R. R. house lane north Ivory
Hall's, rear 228 Main
Flanders Charles, carpenter, boards 26 Thompson
Flanders Charles C. house 26 Thompson
Flanders George H. machinist, bds. Mrs. Mary J. Flanders',
State, near Pleasant [Perley, n. State
Flanders Jane N. Mrs. widow of Samuel H. boarding house,
Flanders John B. woodworker at Abbot's, h. 5 Downing
Flanders Kimball, stonecutter, boards Amos Bean's
Flanders Mary D. dressmaker, boards 157 State

Flanders Mary Jane Mrs. widow of Timothy P. boarding house, 102 State

Flanders Philip, pattern maker Con. R. R. house 3 Tahanto

Fletcher Arthur, lawyer, Main, h. Warren, c. Rumford, opp. School

Fletcher Eliza M. widow of Daniel H. house 6 South

Fletcher William W. dentist, Stickney's block, house Elm, near Pleasant

Fletcher William B. farmer, house East Concord

Fletcher William W. dentist, 210 Main, house 17 Elm

Flint Edward, farmer, b. J. C. Barnard's, High, n. Franklin

Flores Michael, laborer, house Main, Fisherville

Floyd Margaret, widow of Mark, house 3 Union

Floyd Mark, fireman N. R. R. boards 3 Union

Flynn James, marble cutter, house Lee's block, Chandler

Fogg Edward, farmer, boards John Wheeler's, Green, corner Centre

Fogg Edwin N. clerk at Smith & Newhall's, house Green, [c. Centre

Fogg George G. Hon. lawyer, house Main, opp. Court House

Foley Daniel J. machinist, house 79 South

Foley John, laborer, house rear 54 Main

Fookes William G. carriage spring maker at Palmer's, boards 3 Call's block, State

Follansbee James W. sash and blind maker, boards F. H. Locke's, Pleasant, corner Fremont

Folsom Asa, machinist N. R. R. house 7 Pearl

Folsom Lawrence, house 20 Monroe

Fonten Frank, shoemaker, house Fayette, near Main

Foote Robert M. sash and blind maker, boards S. E. Straw's, Washington, near Union

Ford Jerome, boards 223 State

Ford Thomas, granite cutter, house East Concord

Ford Theodore H. (*Ford & Kimball*), iron foundry, R. R. Sq. house 223 State

Ford William P. (*William P. Ford & Co.*), 235 Main, house 18 Franklin

Ford William P. & Co. (*William P. Ford and George H. Marston*), iron foundry, office 235 Main

Ford Winthrop H. stove mounter, house 290 Main

Ford & Kimball (*Theo. H. Ford and Benj. A. Kimball*), iron founders, Railroad Square, rear freight depot

Forister Mary, widow of Levi, boards 136 Spring

Forta Levi, tailor, house Main, near the gas works

Foss James M. master mechanic C. M. & L. R. R. bds. Elm House

Foss John, farmer, house Franklin, near Henry

Foss John H. provision dealer, under Washington House, house Merrimack, Fisherville

Foss William R. blacksmith, boards Dexter Fitz's, School, corner Spring

Foster A. & G. A. (*Albert Foster and Geo. A. Foster*), livery and hack stable, 6 Warren
Foster Albert (*A. & G. A. Foster*), 6 Warren, house 15 do.
Foster Geo. A. (*A. & G. A. Foster*), 6 Warren, bds. 15 do.
Foster Henry B. apothecary, 129 Main, house 29 Pleasant
Foster Ira, job wagon, house State, cor. Thorndike
Foster Wm. L. (*Foster & Sanborn*), lawyer, Sanborn's block, Main, house 160 State
Foster & Sanborn, (*William L. Foster and Charles P. Sanborn*), lawyers, Sanborn's block, Main
Fountain Frank, shoe-maker, house Fayette, near Main
Fowler Asa, (*A. & F. A. Fowler*), lawyer, Merrimack block, house 312 Main
Fowler A. & F. A. lawyers, Merrimack block, Main
Fowler Cephas H. (*J. S. Rollins & Co.*), druggists, h. Summer, cor. Centre, Fisherville
Fowler Frank A. (*A. & F. A. Fowler*), lawyer, house 312 [Main
Fowler Geo. R. lawyer, house 312 Main
Fox Betsy A. widow of Wm. house 103 State
Francis John G. blacksmith at Abbot's, house Cross, opposite [Myrtle
Frawley Daniel, blacksmith, house Church, above State
Frazier Loren, brakeman, N. Railroad, bds. 25 Franklin
Frazier John, fireman, N. Railroad, bds. 83 State, cor. Warren
French Augustus J. C. carder, house Merrimack, near Centre, Fisherville
French Benj. carpenter, house 5 Tahanto
French John, hostler, boards Elm House
French John L. coach-maker at Abbot's, house 4 Monroe
French Joseph, boot and shoe-dealer, School, opp. Post Office, house 11 Franklin
French Lewis L. stone-cutter, house 7 Washington
French Moses D. laborer, house Walnut, near Church
French Oliver N. tailor, house Spring, n. Main, Fisherville
French Oscar F. hair-dresser, bds. O. N. French's, Spring, near Main, Fisherville
French Reuben E. (*French & Cochran*), flour and grain, house [at Hopkinton
French Richard J. boarding-house, West Canal, Fisherville
French Ruth P. widow of Levi, bds. 19 Thorndike
French Samuel S. piano-tuner, bds. at J. H. Landers', Short, near Rumford
French Sarah C. widow of Henry S. G. house 179 State
French Theodore, house 67 Main
French Theodore J. dry goods, State block, Main, boards 6 South
French Thomas C. cabinet-maker, house W. Canal, Fisher- [ville
French William B. house 12 Union
French Wm. H. machinist, bds. O. N. French's, Spring, near [Main, Fisherville
French & Cochran, (*R. E. French, and Joseph A. Cochran*), flour and grain, Main, cor. Pleasant
Frost Lucy J. H. widow of Henry, bds. 10 Downing

Frost Wm. farmer, house East Concord
Frye James, farmer, house East Concord
Frye Orin G. carpenter, house 39 Pleasant
Frye Robert, express messenger, depot Railroad Square
Fuller Charles H. master, car department, Con. Railroad, h. 18 South
Fuller David G. house Pleasant, cor. State [Main
Fuller George C. proprietor of the Columbian Hotel, 165
Fuller Henry, upholsterer, house South, cor. Fulton
Fuller Hilton, blacksmith, West, cor. Turnpike, bds. 11 West
Fuller Luther P. blacksmith at Abbot's, house 11 West
Fuller Oliver, blacksmith at Abbot's, house South, near Wheeler's corner [Water
Fulton Thomas, wheelwright at Abbot's, house Hall, corner
Fury James, blacksmith, bds. Columbian Hotel
Fyler Lincoln, quarryman, bds. at D. Fish's, West Con. road
Fyler Moses, quarryman, bds. at D. Fish's, West Con. road

GAGE BENJ. (*Gage & Andrews*), boot and shoe-dealer, Central block, Main, house 61 Spring
Gage Charles P. (*Gage & Conn*), physician, Stickney's block, house 2 Montgomery
Gage Samuel, wheelwright at Abbot's, house 5 Main
Gage Walter, wheelwright at Abbot's, bds. 5 Main
Gage Wm. commercial-broker, house 92 State
Gage & Andrews, (*Benj. Gage and William G. Andrews*), boot & shoe dealers, Central block, Main
Gage & Conn, (*Charles P. Gage and Granville P. Conn*), physicians, Stickney's block, Main [Clinton
Gagnon John, carriage-maker at Abbot's, house Spring, near
Gahagan Rose, widow of Thomas, house W. Canal, Fisherville
Gahagan Thomas, laborer, house Church, Fisherville [ville
Gahagan Vincent, overseer at the Mill, house Church, Fisher-
Gale Ahira J. conductor Portsmouth Railroad, h. 19 Fayette
Gale Albert W. restaurant at depot, house 7 Railroad Square
Gale Augustus L. brakeman, boards 19 Fayette
Gale Benj. F. land-surveyor and farmer, house 59 Pleasant
Gale Henry C. house 237 State [State, near Pleasant
Gale Isaac R. (*Mitchell & Gale*), Central Market, house 76
Galon Solon S. express-man, boards 19 Fayette [Cemetery
Gallagher John M. quarryman, house State, near the New
Gallagher Wm. melter at Ford & Kimball's, house Downing, near South
Gallinger Jacob H. physician, house 153 State
Galloway James, clock and watchmaker, 159 Main, house Centre, cor. Merrimack
Gannon Darby, switchman, N. Railroad, house 83 Warren
Gannon Dominick, car-repairer, N. Railroad, house East side Railroad-track, rear Herbert's

Gannon Michael, stone-cutter, boards Dominick Gannon's
Gannon Patrick, laborer, house rear 211 Main
Gardner Christopher C. photographer, 108 Main, boards Elm House
Gardner Theodore O. (*Gardner & Blood*), soap and candle manufacturer, Free Bridge road, house n. Fair Grounds
Gardner & Blood (*Theodore O. Gardner and Benjamin A. Blood*), soap and candle manufacturers, Free Bridge road
Garle Perkins Mrs. widow, house State, corner School
Garter John, cabinet maker, house High, Fisherville
Garvey Bridget, widow, Luke, h. Merrimack, Fisherville
Garvin George F. mechanic, Prescott Bros. bds. 12 South
Garvin George W. farmer, house Hall
Garvin Mary R. wid. of Nathaniel, b. G. M. Judkins's, Hall
Garvin William H. casemaker Prescott Bros. bds. 12 South
Garvin Wilson D. laborer, house South, opposite Fayette
Gary Eugene F. boards Edwin Gary's, Plains
Gatley Richard, bootmaker, 7 Warren, house 171 State
Gauthier Joseph, harness maker, 151 Main, bds. Myrtle, near Cross
Gauthier Odilon, harness maker, 151 Main, b. Frank Leroques
Gawler George, engineer at Barter & Co.'s, h. 45 Pleasant
Gawler Robert A. hairworker, Low's block, School, house do.
Gawler Thomas, laborer, house Cross, near South
Gawler William, springmaker at Abbot's, boards T. Gawler's, Cross, near South
Gay Charles B. currier, house 17 Fayette
Gay Daniel, machinist at Abbot's, house Gay, cor. Allison
Gay G. Henry, clerk at W. B. Stearns's, boards 17 Fayette
Gay William, quarryman, house West Concord
Gear Jacob B. painter, bds. J. Gear's, Union, corner Maple
Gear John, dealer in patent machines, h. Union, c. Maple
Geavers Frank, collar maker, house R. R. Sqr. rear Barron, Dodge & Co.'s
Geavers Joseph, harness maker, house R. R. sq. rear Barron, Dodge & Co.'s
Geldert Edward B. house Prince, near Green
Gendron Joseph, laborer, house 1 Fosterville
George W. A. farmer, house State, near the new cemetery
George John, lawyer, Sanborn's block, boards 54 Green
George Hermon S. painter, house Spring, near Washington
George John H. lawyer, Sanborn's block, Main, h. 271 Main
George Martha, widow of Erastus B. h. State, opp. the prison
George True, house State, opposite the prison
Gerald Edward F. blacksmith at Harvey, Morgan & Co.'s, house 12 Cross [12 Cross
Gerald Frank E. blacksmith at Harvey, Morgan & Co.'s, bds.
Gerow John S. tinman, house West Canal, Fisherville
Gerrish Benjamin jr., N. R. R. office, boards Phenix Hotel
Gerrish Calvin, machinist at Ford & Kimball's, h. 7 Fayette

Getchell John C. carver, b. A. Campbell's, High, Fisherville
Gibney Margaret Mrs. widow of Patrick, house Lee's block, Chandler
Gibson Ruth C. Mrs. widow of John, house 7 Montgomery
Gilbert Emily L. Mrs. widow of Charles, boards Miss A. Lang's, East Concord
Gilbert Priscilla H. Mrs. widow of John H. h. 3 Washington
Giles Andrew J. (*Davis & Giles*), painter, rear Eagle Hotel, house 4 Monroe
Giles John B. stonecutter, house 2 Fosterville
Giles Nicholas, bookbinder, Stickney's block, b. Amos Bean's
Giles Sarah J. widow of William, boards 54 State
Gill Bradbury, blacksmith, r. Stickney's block, h. 120 Spring
Gill Samuel K. farmer, boards 120 Spring
Gillis Joseph, fruit and confectionery, 14 School, house do.
Gilson Charles E. cabinet maker, b. Paul Jarvis', Fisherville
Gilson James, stonecutter, bds. J. B. Giles's, 2 Fosterville
Gilman Ephraim S. farmer, house West Concord
Gilman Nathaniel, house 13 Monroe [n. Main, Fisherville
Gilman Samuel jr. carpenter, b. W. Johnson's, Washington,
Gilman William, boot and shoe manuf. opp. Statesman building, house 24 Centre [Square, house 47 Green
Gilmore Charles L. asst. manager telegraph office, depot, R.R.
Gilmore Edward C. harness maker, boards J. A. Coburn's, Merrimack, Fisherville
Gilmore Mitchell, Sec'y of Equitable Mutual Fire Ins. Co. 173 Main, Sanborn's block, house 47 Green
Gilmore Walter L. machinist, boards William W. Cloud's
Ginty John, at Con. R. R. h. Cross, c. Jefferson
Glennan Patrick, laborer, house rear Fisk's store
Glines Alonzo, moulder at Ford & Kimball's, b. 59 Main
Glover Artemas, clerk at C. C. Webster's, house Cross, corner Beaver
Glover George A. tinman, boards Artemas Glover's
Glover George P. painter, house 6 Montgomery
Glysson Loren W. machinist N. R. R. house 79 Spring
Godfrey Orlando I. mason, boards Green, corner Centre
Goldsmith John B. provision dealer under the Washington Hotel, h. Main, cor. Summer, Fisherville
Gonzalor Arguy H. mason, house Washington, n. Pleasant
Goodhue John G. reedmaker at Morgan's, boards 4 West
Goodman John, moulder at Ford & Kimball's, boards Joseph E. Phelps'
Goodman Michael, moulder, boards Joseph E. Phelps'
Goodrich James H. painter at Abbot's, boards 31 Main
Goodrich Mrs. h. Lee's block, Chandler
Goodrich Emily Mrs. widow of J. house 31 Main
Goodwin Benjamin S., Indian physician, house 4 Centre
Goodwin Hiram S. carpenter, boards R. Goodwin's, High, Fisherville

Goodwin Joanna, widow of Nathan, house 45 School
Goodwin Joseph, hostler, b. R. Goodwin's, High, Fisherville
Goodwin Reuben, farmer, house High, Fisherville
Goodwin William F. house 45 School
Goodwin Sarah Mrs. widow, house State, cor. Wall
Goold Nathan, machinist, Concord Railroad, bds. Elm House
Gordon Augustine W. mason, house 204 State
Gordon George, printer, boards 23 Pleasant
Gordon James, house 36 Rumford
Gordon James M. case-maker, Prescott Bros., house Main, opp. North Church [road Square
Gordon James T. machinist, Concord Railroad, house 2 Rail-
Gordon John L. farmer, house South, near Wheeler's Corner
Gordon L. N. brakeman, bds. Columbian Hotel
Gordon Wm. E. carpenter, house Union, near Washington
Goss Hannah A. widow of Jacob C. house 8 Hanover
Gould Lydia M. widow of Hiram M., house rear 211 Main
Gove Charles H. blacksmith at Abbot's, bds. 3 Main
Gove Laura L. Miss, artist, boards 3 Main
Gove Maria L. Mrs. widow of Jesse A. house 32 Pleasant
Gove Nathan W., Assistant Secretary of State, h. 3 Main
Graham Harry E. tobacco and cigars, bds. Phenix Hotel
Grant Albert G. harness-maker, house Green, near School
Grant Andrew M. engineer, N. Railroad, house 155 State
Graves Frank W. physician, house Walker, near State
Graves Geo. A. foreman, Statesman Job Office, bds. at O. Turner's, 34 Main
Graves Wm. house Walker, near State
Gray Calvin, carpenter, house 55 State
Gray Daniel, quarryman at the ledge, house West Concord
Gray John C. clerk, bds. 8 Green
Gray Joseph H. jeweller, 149 Main, bds. George W. Drew's
Greeley Stephen D. insurance agent, house 3 Wall
Green Charles H. machinist, house Main, near Washington, Fisherville
Green J. K. cabinet-maker, bds. Columbian Hotel
Green John R. blacksmith, bds. Mrs. Fairbanks', Franklin
Green John S. carriage-maker at Abbot's, house 5 Turnpike
Green Timothy, quarryman, bds. Baldwin Humphrey's, West Concord
Green Wm. J. silver-smith at Durgin's, bds. 40 Rumford
Greene Abigal L. widow of Sherburne, house 18 West
Greene Benj. machinist at Abbot's, house 31 Main
Greene Geo. H. painter, house 204 State
Greene Mary L. widow of William E., house 20 Pleasant
Greere Mary J. Mrs., widow of John, house rear Hill's block
Greenleaf Seth, bds. Eagle Hotel
Grenier Francis, harness-maker, 151 Main, house 6 Green
Griffin Benjamin F. wood-worker, N. Railroad, house Cross, near State

Griffin Henry J. moulder at Ford's foundry, bds. at Oliver J. Drew's [255 Main
Griffin Samuel M. carriage-manufacturer, 253 Main, house
Griffin Patrick, marble-worker, house rear of Phenix Hotel
Griffin Patrick, laborer, house rear Hill's block [cord
Grindell Norris, blacksmith, bds. G. W. Brockway, W. Con-
Grover Benj. (*Barron, Dodge & Co*), flour wholesale, Railroad Square, house 17 Pleasant
Grover Loring, boot-maker, 5 Warren, house Do.
Groves Frank, fireman, N. Railroad, bds. 7 Summer [Winter
Groves Lucius F. engineer, N. Railroad, house 7 Summer, n.
Guernsey Darius L. (*D. L. Guernsey & Co.*), State block, house 42 Green
Guernsey D. L. & Co. book-sellers, State block, Main
Guevin Baptiste, shoe-maker, house Cross
Guild Charles F. laborer, house Thorndike, near Main
Guild John, laborer, house Fulton
Gunn James, car-maker, N. Railroad, house 22 Cross
Gurley James, laborer, house rear 18 School
Gurley Michael, laborer, house rear Stickney's block

HACKETT EPHRAIM, moulder, Ford's foundry, house Church, near State
Hackett Patrick, laborer, house Chandler, near Main
Hadley Amos, Editor and Law Reporter, Ind. Democrat and Monitor Office, house State, near Meth. Institute
Hadley Moses C. stone-contractor, house 21 Franklin
Hadley Sidney B. carpenter, bds. 21 Franklin [cor. Cross
Hagar John C. cook at Smith & Newhall's, house, 49 Main,
Hagerty John, stone-cutter, bds. Joseph E. Phelps'
Haggerty Patrick, laborer, house 6 Cross
Haines John M. clerk at Adj. General's office, house Monroe, near Beaver
Haines Joseph A. porter, Phenix Hotel [Allison
Haines Lewis M. silver-smith at Durgin's. bds 1 State, cor.
Hale Wm. H. machinist, house 19 State
Haley James, laborer, bds. at 9 W. Canal, Fisherville
Haley Thomas, weaver, bds. at 9 W. Canal, Fisherville
Hall A. J. (*Campbell & Hall*), insurance agent, 6 State block, Main, house Centre, near Spring
Hall Frank, laborer, house Main, cor. East Canal, Fisherville
Hall Frank P. watch-maker and jeweller, house 262 Main
Hall Ivory, watch-maker and jeweller, house 262 Main,
Hall Joseph, laborer, house 1 Fosterville
Hall Lyman K. (*Putnam & Hall*), merchant, Main, Fisherville, house Boscawen
Hall Thomas, blacksmith, boards 45 Pleasant
Hall Thomas B. helper, bds. Pleasant, near Spring [Main
Hallett Geo. W. hoop-skirts and corsets, Statesman block,
Halloran Dennis, blacksmith, house 14 South

Halloran John, laborer, Chandler, near Railroad [Hall
Hallowen Jerry, helper, N. Railroad, house rear Rumford
Halpin Patrick, laborer, house 80 Warren
Halpin Patrick, laborer, house Cross, near South
Halpin Philip, teamster at Hutchins', house Cross, near South
Ham Paul S. teamster, house South, cor. Cross
Hammer Philip, laborer, house Main, near the gas works
Hamilton John H. laborer, house Spring, near Warren
Hammond Edgar A. F. carriage maker at Abbot's, house 24 State
Hancock John C. carpenter, house 22 South
Hannaford John, watchman, house Spring, Fisherville
Hanrahan Michael, tanner, house East Concord
Hanson Eli, laborer, house Cross, Fisherville
Hanson Susan Mrs. house 21 Spring
Hardie George, florist, house 78 South
Hardy John, laborer, house rear 211 Main
Hardy Lydia Mrs. widow William P. house 12 Fayette
Harlow Jas. P. moulder Ford's foundry, h. State, n. Church
Harper Charles S. carriage manufacturer, E. Concord, h. do.
Harradin Caroline A. Mrs. widow of Timothy A. house 15 Montgomery
Harrington George, machinist N. R. R. house 43 Warren
Harrington John, laborer, house W. Concord
Harriman James W. cabinet maker, 9 W. Canal, Fisherville
Harris Augustus G. (*Harris & Co.*), State block, h. 263 Main, corner Franklin [House
Harris Henry L. (*Harris & Co.*), State block, bds. American
Harris John A. (*Harris & Co.*), dry goods, State block, boards Phenix Hotel
Harris & Co. (*John A., Augustus G. and Henry L. Harris*), dry goods, State block, Main
Harrold William, boltcutter C. M. & L. R. R. h. r. 6 Main
Hart Christopher, saloon, Depot, near R. R. Sq. house do.
Hart Patrick, laborer, boards Patrick Larkin's
Hart Sarah, widow of William, boards 9 South
Hart Thomas, saloon, Depot, n. R. R. Square, house do.
Hart Wm. (*William Hart & Co.*), market, 16 School. house 9 South [*M. Carter*), market, 16 School
Hart William & Co. (*Wm. Hart, Charles Barker and Nathan*
Hartford Fire Ins. Co., Webster & Smith, agents, State block, Main
Hartford John, blacksmith, house Cedar, near State
Hartford John H. blacksmith, boards Columbian Hotel
Hartley Charles W. spinner, house West Concord
Harvey Charles W. life insurance agent, house 20 South
Harvey George P. (*Harvey, Morgan & Co.*), carriage manuf. Main, house 7 Thorndike
Harvey James R. woodturner, Water, near R. R.
Harvey John, blacksmith, house South, near Thorndike

Harvey Jonathan C. (*Harvey, Morgan & Co.*), carriage manuf. Main, house 43 State
Harvey M. boards Eagle Hotel
Harvey, Morgan & Co. (*Jonathan C. Harvey, Rufus M. Morgan, Geo. P. Harvey and Chas. P. Moore*), carriage and wagon manufacturers, 58 Main
Harvey Stephen C. carpenter, h. High, n. Summer, Fisherville
Haskell Nathaniel H. painter at Abbot's, house 11 Perley
Haskins Emily L. Mrs. (*Piper & Haskins*), bds. State, corner Warren
Hatch Byron S silversmith, house 9 Prince, near Spring
Hatch Jabez W. janitor at State House, house Hall, n. Water
Hatch Josiah P. stonemason, house Prince, near Spring
Hatch Robinson Mrs. clairvoyant, Prince, near Spring, h. do.
Hayes Charles H. painter, house South, near Downing
Hayes Francis W. carpenter, house 8 Tahanto
Hayes Francis W. jr. clerk, boards Francis W. Hayes'
Hayes Timothy, blacksmith, boards Moore's, Main
Haynes Arvilla, widow of James H. house High, c. Valley
Haynes Francis W. carpenter, house 8 Tahanto
Haynes Frank S. clerk, boards 8 Tahanto
Haynes George P. clerk, Pearson's, R. R. Sq. h. 80 Main
Haynes John, lasts and boot trees, house 6 Maple
Haynes Martin, printer, boards 34 Main
Haynes Michael, blacksmith, house 4 Main
Haynes Thomas, stonecutter, boards Michael Haynes'
Haynes Timothy, physician, house 8 Park
Haynes William B. laborer, boards Dr. Timothy Haynes'
Hazeltine Ann A. Miss, milliner at Mrs. T. H. Brown's, Main boards Mrs. Brown's
Hazeltine Charles W. master painter N. R. R. h. 25 Spring
Hazeltine Life A. wholesale boot and shoe dealer, 240 Main, house 17 School
Hazelton James, dry goods and millinery, 158 Main, house 13 School
Hazelton John, painter N. R. R. house Penacook, west State
Hazelton John A. painter, bds. D. M. Carpenter's, Penacook, corner Walnut
Hazelton Lydia Mrs. widow of Rufus, house 254 Main
Healey James, laborer, house 4 Main
Heath Byron C. wheelwright, house 9 Warren
Heath Ira, fireman No. R. R. boards 59 Main
Heath Joshua, carpenter, h. Downing, bet. State and South
Hebert Antonia, carriage maker at Abbot's, h. 14 South
Hemenway Rebecca, widow of Joseph, boards 3 Downing
Hemminway Joseph, cabinet maker, bds. G. Morrill's, Washington, Fisherville
Herbert Albert, farmer, boards Main, opp. Washington
Herbert Charles H. farmer, house 185 State road
Herbert Nancy B. Mrs. widow of Samuel, h. Main, c. Ferry road
Herbert Sarah O. Miss, h. Main, opposite Washington

Hern William A. laborer, house State, north of Franklin
Hersey Jeremiah N. carbuilder C. M. & L. R. R. house 46 Prince
Hersey Jeremiah N. carpenter, house Spring, below Fulton
Heselton Richmond, cabinet maker, h. Church, Fisherville
Hibbard Charles H. hostler, Dr. E. G. & J. M. Moore's, bds. Mrs. Sawin's, Warren, corner State
Hichborn Philip, baker, house Spring, corner Short
Hickey James, stonecutter, boards Barney Dumot's
Hicks James, laborer, house 15 Spring
Hildreth Charles F. P. physician, 9 State block
Hill Byron C. stone-cutter, house 4 Walnut
Hill Calvin B. stone-cutter, boards at Amos Bean's
Hill Cavis S. stone-cutter, bds. at William Smith's [3 Centre
Hill Charles E. clerk, Austin & Co's, rear Sherman House, bds.
Hill Chase, shoe-findings, 147 Main, house 147 1-2 Main
Hill Daniel A. furniture-dealer, 238 Main, h. 22 Montgomery
Hill Cyrus, house 16 Centre
Hill Edwin, painter, 238 Main, bds. Washington, cor. State
Hill Eliot A. furniture, Stickney's block, Main, h. 124 State
Hill Geo. F. furniture, Stickney's block, Main, bds 124 State
Hill George H. varnisher, Prescott Bros'., bds. at M. G. Mead's, 167 State
Hill Howard F. law student, bds. 18 Montgomery
Hill Isaac A. Register of Probate, City Hall, house Rumford, cor. Cambridge [Hill's
Hill Isaac William, collector, for Gas Co., bds. at William P.
Hill James, blacksmith, 253 Main, house 29 Franklin, near State [Main, house 70 Main
Hill James R. (*James R. Hill & Co.*), harness-makers, 151
Hill James R. & Co. (*James R. Hill, George H. Emery and Josiah E. Dwight*), harness and trunk-makers, 151 Main
Hill John H. merchant tailor, 118 main, house Rumford, cor. Centre [ery
Hill John M. agent Concord Gas Light Co., h. 18 Montgom-
Hill John N. truck-repairer, bds. at W. Hill's, East Concord
Hill Joseph G. house 3 Centre
Hill Oliver, carpenter, house 68 Franklin [h. 189 State
Hill Samuel, furniture-manufacturer, and dealer, 238 Main,
Hill Samuel, teamster, house State, cor. Washington
Hill Susan A. Mrs., widow of Isaac, house 7 1-2 School
Hill Thos. B. book-binder at Crawford's, bds. 6 1-2 Call's block
Hill Thomas P. harness-maker, 151 Main, bds. Mrs. Harriet Sawin's, 83 State
Hill Washington, farmer, house East Concord
Hill William P. reporter, house 7 1-2 School
Hilliard Mercy, widow of Samuel, bds. 32 Warren
Hills George L. wheelwright, house 113 Spring
Hillson Henry, coach-maker, house 35 Warren
Hillson Henry W. carriage-maker, house 7 Pearl

Hinkley Stillman, blacksmith at Harvey, Morgan' & Co's., bds. 8 Thorndike [Spring
Hobart Hiram, laborer, bds. at J. S. Russ's, School, corner
Hobbs John F. freight conductor, C. M. & L. Railroad, bds. Mrs. Flanders', State, uear Pleasant
Hoben Michael, overseer at Holden's, house West Concord
Hodgdon Ruth M. widow of Chas. C., bds. Wm. E. Webster's, Spring, near Washington
Hodgdon William A. (*Hodgdon & Merriam*), insurance agent, 9 State block, house 282 Main, opp. Franklin
Hodgdon & Merriam, (*William A. Hodgdon & Joseph A. Merriam*), insurance agents, 9 State block, Main
Hodgkinson William, stone-cutter, bds. 24 Franklin
Hoit Amos E. machinist, house Church, Fisherville
Hoit Elisha, cabinet-maker, house Summer, cor. Washington Square, Fisherville
Hoit J. Frank, (*J. F. Hoit & Co.*), grocer, Masonic Temple, house School, cor. Huntington [grocers, Masonic Temple
Hoit J. F. & Co. (*J. Frank Hoit and Charles A. Robinson*),
Hoit Lewis B. clerk of J. F. Hoit & Co.), bds. 26 Thorndike
Hoit Nancy, widow of James, bds. J. F. Hoit's, School, cor. Huntingdon
Hoit Sewell, confectioner, Main, house 171 State
Hoit Walter, mason, bds. Mrs. Julia A. Carr's [coln court
Hoit Wm. B. painter, Con. Railroad, house Spring, opp. Lin-
Hoit William P. photograph artist, Exchange block, h. State, opp. the Prison [Concord, house do.
Holden Benjamin F. (*B. F. & D. Holden*), woolen mill, West
Holden B. F. & D. (*Benjamin F. and Daniel Holden*), woolen mill, West Coneord [cord, house do.
Holden Daniel, (*B. F. & D. Holden*), woolen mill, West Con-
Holden George E. clerk, B. F. & D. Holden, h. W. Concord
Hollidan Jeremiah, striker, house rear Rumford block
Hollis Abijah, (*Hollis Bros.*), granite dealer, W. Concord, house do. [house do.
Hollis Thomas Jr., (*Hollis Bros.*) granite dealer, W. Concord,
Holman Sullivan Rev. clergyman, bds. Eagle Hotel [erville
Holmes George, cabinet-maker, bds. Washington House, Fish-
Holmes John A. farmer and surveyor, house Summer, near Cross [School
Holt Abel B. land and lumber dealer, house Merrimack, cor.
Holt Abner C. lumber dealer, house 4 Franklin
Holt Emily, widow of Franklin F., house 8 Spring
Holt Horace H. house School, near Tahanto
Holt James E. silver-plater, bds. Pillsbury's, Call's block, 15 State
Holt Leonard, carpenter, bds. 12 Thompson [ville
Holt Mary M. widow of Timothy, house Merrimack, Fisher-
Holt Moses A. carpenter, house 7 Chapel
Holt Nathaniel, farmer, house West, near South

Holt Samuel W. painter, house Charles, Fisherville
Wood William E. bds. William L. Hood's
Hood William L. carpenter, house 5 Rumford
Hook Eliza, widow of Charles G., house 3 Winter
Hook Harriet N. widow of Asa J., house 17 Franklin
Hook John G. farmer, house Auburn, near Chesnut [City Hall
Hook Joseph B. boarding-house, Main, first door north of
Hooker Alonzo, teamster at Barter & Cochran's, bds. L. Barter's, Spring, cor. Warren
Hopkins Laura K. widow of Wm. H., house 12 Thompson
Hopkins Seth, railroad contractor, house 70 State
Horner Elias, farmer, house Cedar [Fisherville
Hosmer Wm. H. physician, Merrimack, cor. Centre, house do.
Houston Edwin H. blacksmith at Abbot's, house 3 Fremont
Houston Mary S. widow of Henry, house Elm, cor. Wall
Howard Samuel A. engineer at Ford & Kimball's, h. 51 Main
Howe Calvin, cashier Barron, Dodge & Co.'s, h. 115 State
Howe Caroline J. Miss, tailoress, house 7 Washington
Howe Isaac G. blacksmith, house 33 Green
Howe Joseph, boards 4 Pearl
Howe Joseph M. coachman, house 263 Main
Howe Lucretia L. Miss, tailoress, house 7 Washington
Howe Miss, milliner Geo. W. Wadleigh's, Central buildings, boards Phenix Hotel
Howe Morgan, laborer, house State, near the new cemetery
Howe William H. wheelwright at Abbot's, h. Thordike, near South
Hoyt Charles H. carriage maker at Abbot's, boards 4 West
Hoyt Daniel, truckman, house 31 Green
Hoyt John, cooper, near Steam Mill, house 238 Main
Hoyt Lydia A. Mrs. wid. of Seth B. h. Main, c. Washington, Fisherville
Hoyt William, house Pleasant avenue
Hughes David, stonecutter, boards 4 Pearl
Hughes John, painter, bds. E. G. Cutting's, Summer, n. Court
Humiston Edwin N. tuner at Prescott Bros.' b. 39 Pleasant
Humphrey Abner, cooper, house West Concord
Humphrey Baldwin, boarding house, West Concord
Humphrey Moses, mackerel kit manufactory, West Concord, house 59 Warren
Humphrey Stillman (*Warde, Humphrey & C*[illegible] &c. 1 and 2 Exchange, house 63 Warr[illegible]
Hunt Albion, peddler, house Court, opp. Summer
Hunt Daniel, mason, house South, corner Wall [Main
Huntress Henry L. clerk Warde, Humphrey & Co.'s, b. 218
Hurlburt A. C. engineer, boards Columbian Hotel
Hurlburt George N. harness maker, house Church, n. State
Hurd Oscar P. clerk Harris & Co's. b. Jonathan W. Sleeper's, Tremont street
Hurd William B. farmer, house East Concord

Hurd William H. painter, State, rear Enos Blake's, 105 State
Hurley William H. tailor, boards Sherman House
Huse John, farmer, house Warren, near Washington
Hutchins Abel (*Hutchins & Co.*), Dept Square, house South, opp. Fayette
Hutchins Charles, house 35 Main
Hutchins Ebenezer, watchman B. C. & M. R. R. h. 228 Main
Hutchins Ephraim, house South, near Wall
Hutchins George, house 37 Main
Hutchins George H. (*Hutchins & Co*), grocer, Depot Square, [h. 37 Main
Hutchins Jacob E. blacksmith at Abbot's, house 11 Main
Hutchins John, B. C. & M. R. R. house East Concord
Hutchins John, machinist at Abbot's, house 10 Downing
Hutchins John C. engineer C. R. R. house East Concord
Hutchins John E. blacksmith at Abbot's, h. Downing, n. State
Hutchins & Co. (*George H. Hutchins and Abel Hutchins*), grocers, wholesale, Depot square
Hutchinson Augustus P. farmer, house Thorndike, n. Main
Hutchinson Ebenezer B. carpenter, house 55 Main

INDEPENDENT DEMOCRAT, Independent Press Association, 176 Main
Independent Press Association, Rumford block, 176 Main
Ingalls Charlotte A. widow of Joshua, h. Tremont, n. State
Ingalls Frank E. clerk, 103 Main, boards 145 State
Ingalls George E. clerk R. Mayers', house 11 Tremont
Ingalls Gustavus W. reedmaker, house 5 Call's block, State
Ingalls Josiah S. city messenger and lamplighter, house 33 Thompson
Ingalls Melvin L. painter N. R. R. house 4 Monroe
Ireland Henry A. jr. carriage maker Harvey, Morgan & Co's. boards 6 Pleasant
Ivers Joseph, laborer, house rear Hill's block

JACKMAN LYMAN, insurance agent, 6 State block, house Centre, near Spring
Jackson Mary, widow of Forest, b. I. L. Emerson's, Walnut, [n. Washington
Jackson William, farmer, house Centre, junction Washington
Jackson Wm. cabinet maker, h. Main, c. Summer, Fisherville
Jacob Godfrey, laborer, house rear 209 Main
James Elizabeth, widow of Thos. h. Walnut, n. Washington
James Sarah J. widow of Samuel, bds. J. N. Berry's, Walnut, near Franklin
Jameson Edward C. b. J. W. Jameson's, Summer, n. Church, [Fisherville
Jameson Henry, printer, b. J. Evans', Short, c. Huntingdon
Jameson Jas. B. cabinet maker, b. 9 West Canal, Fisherville
Jameson Josiah W. shoemaker, house Summer, near Church, Fisherville
Jameson Samuel, boxmaker, boards 9 West Canal, Fisherville
Jameson T. Henry, compositor, boards J. Evans'

Jameson William E. shoemaker, house Main, Fisherville
Jarvis John, farmer, house East Concord
Jarvis Paul, laborer, house Main, Fisherville
Jenkins Jethro, stonecutter, boards 34 Main
Jenks Geo. E. (*McFarland & Jenks*), printers and publishers, Main, corner Depot, house School, corner Merrimack
John Hancock Mutual Life Ins. Co. Boston, Hodgdon & Merriam, agents, State block, Main
Johnson Albert, laborer, house 10 Tremont
Johnson Albert P. laborer, house Tremont, corner Union
Johnson Asa S. foreman Concord Granite Co. b. Amos Bean's
Johnson Chas. I. carriage maker at Abbot's, house South, near Pleasant
Johnson James A. painter, boards 5 Jefferson
Johnson Joel D. harness maker, 234 Main, h. 11 Centre [State
Johnson John P. dry goods, Stickney's block, Main, house 156
Johnson Joseph G. stonecutter, house Church, opp. Jackson
Johnson Lewis, quarryman, b. D. Fish's, West Concord road
Johnson Lorenzo, stonecutter, house 27 Union [Fisherville
Johnson Warren, blacksmith, house Washington, near Main,
Jones Abraham G. printer, Exchange building, h. Orchard
Jones Amos, engineer C. R. R. h. Turner's block, r. 26 Main
Jones Charles, fireman C. R. R. boards Mrs. M. J. Flanders'
Jones Charles, wood dealer, house 12 Chapel street
Jones Charles H. teamster, house 12 Chapel
Jones David B. currier, house 40 Green
Jones Elizabeth P. widow of Timothy L. h. 23 Pleasant
Jones Frank K. clerk 160 Main, boards 7 Merrimack
Jones Goodwin C. engineer Con. R. R. house 14 Monroe
Jones Harriet Mrs. widow, house Cross, near Summer, Fisherville [near Warren
Jones James M. conductor C. M. & L. Railroad, house Green,
Jones James M. teamster, house Summer, near Court
Jones John M. clerk, house 16 Union
Jones Joseph D. farmer, house Hall
Jones Joseph P. hostler, r. Eagle Hotel, bds. Columbian Hotel
Jones Sarah M. widow of Philip, bds. 25 Spring
Jones Seth K. house 7 Merrimack
Jordan George W. shoe-maker, house Liberty, near Pleasant
Joy Charles, (*J. L. Pickering & Co.*), grocer, 3 Masonic Temple, bds. at John E. Thompson's
Judkins Gilman M. farmer, house Hall
Judkins Henry, stone-cutter, bds. 17 Franklin

KALLEHER TIMOTHY, laborer, h. Main's bl'k, r. 40 Main
Kanah Timothy, stone-cutter, Myrtle, near Thompson
Kannar Patrick, blacksmith, house Low's building, Chandler
Kannar Wm. laborer, house Low's building, Chandler
Kayes Hazen G. insurance agent, Phenix Hotel block, house School, cor. Rumford

Keefe William H. currier, bds. James Morrill's
Keenan John C. laborer, house Franklin, near Walnut [ville
Keenan Laurence, cabinet-maker, house West Canal, Fisher-
Keenan Michael, laborer, house Franklin, near Walnut
Kegan Sylvester, laborer, house Washington, near Liberty
Keith Minnie, widow of Caleb, house 33 Green
Kellan John H. stone-mason, house West Concord
Kelley Charles, N. Railroad shop, bds. Joseph B. Hook's
Kelley James, quarryman, bds. Baldwin Humphrey's, West Concord
Kelley James, laborer, house near Harvey, Morgan & Co
Kelley James D. house 19 Spring
Kelley Jason A. carpenter, house North Arch
Kelley Patrick, machinist, house Walnut, Fisherville [Court
Kelley Michael H. machinist, N. Railroad, bds. Main, corner
Kelliher Michael, stone-cutter, bds. Timothy Kelliher's
Kellom Ruel, laborer, bds. at Stephen W. Kellom's, West Concord
Kellom Stephen W. farmer, house West Concord
Kemp Asa, picker, Holden's woolen mill, house W. Concord
Kempton Byron E. cooper, house West Concord [h. 80 Spring
Kendall Charles A. musical instrument maker at Austin's,
Kendall David, carpenter, house 21 Downing
Kendall Henry A. clergyman, house East Concord [roe
Kendall Joshua T. carriage-maker at Abbot's, house 2 Mon-
Kendall Phebe, widow of Jonathan, house 80 Spring
Kendrick James R. supt. C. M. & L. Railroad, house 98 State, near Pleasant
Kenna John, blacksmith, Concord Railroad, house Jefferson
Kenna Martin, laborer, house Monroe, near South
Kennedy Mary, widow of Duncan, house Wash. cor. Essex
Kenney Ira E. Rev. clergyman, house Elm, Fisherville
Kenney John F. marble-worker, house Cross, near Myrtle
Kenney William H. (*Dow, Kenney & Clifford*),masons, house Academy, near Washington
Keniston Wm. grave-digger, house Church, near State
Keniston Wm. H. tin-peddler, house Church, near State
Kerley Timothy, clerk, 1 Moore's block, bds. C. C. Davis'
Kayes Hazen G. insurance agent, Phenix Hotel building, h. 47 School
Kayes Niram M. pump-repairer, house 92 Warren
Keyes Frank L. house 12 Tahanto [turer, house 12 Tahanto
Keyes Frank Mrs. (*N. Quimby & Co.*), Hoop Skirt Manufac-
Keyes Sewell, farmer, house East Concord
Kibby Clark O. wheelwright at Abbot's, house 24 State
Kierley Thomas, laborer, house 80 Warren
Kierley William, farmer, 80 Warren
Kiernan Bernard, tailor, bds. Joseph E. Phelps'
Kilburn E. G. & Co. (*Enoch G. Kilburn and Moses K. Sawyer*), grocers, 2 Moore's block, opp. Masonic Temple

Kilburn Enoch G. (*E. G. Kilburn & Co.*), 2 Moore's block, house 12 Union
Kilburn Francis W. carpenter, house North Arch
Kilburn G. T. (*Churchill, Kilburn & Co.*), groceries, 242 Main, bds. 12 Union
Kilburn John C. clerk, 1 Moore's block, bds. C. C. Davis'
Kilburn Lucy D. widow of Milton, house Main, cor. Washington, Fisherville
Kiley Bridget, widow of James, house 25 Cross [ing, n. South
Kiley Mary, widow of Jeremiah, bds. D. Sweeney's, Down-
Kimball Albert D. carriage-maker, bds. 46 State
Kimball Anne Miss, house Main, opp. Church
Kimball Benj. A. (*Ford & Kimball*), Iron founders, Main, h. 61 Main, opp. foundry
Kimball Benj. F. teamster, house 6 West [State block, Main
Kimball Bros. (*Willis G. C. & Howard A.*) photographs,
Kimball David F. with E. G. Kilburn & Co. 2 Moore's block, Main, house 31 Spring
Kimball Hannah W. Mrs. widow, house 40 Warren
Kimball Howard A. (*Kimball Bros.*), photographic artist, Main, cor. School, bds. 7 Tahanto
Kimball Jeremiah, junk-dealer, house 36 Warren [118 State
Kimball John, collector internal revenue, Central block, house
Kimball John H. quarryman, house West Concord [ball's
Kimball John M. melodeon-maker, bds. Mrs. Sophia A. Kim-
Kimball John T. harness-maker, 151 Main, house Franklin, cor. Jackson
Kimball Jonathan, carpenter, house Franklin, near Walnut
Kimball Joseph S. farmer, house East Concord
Kimball Nathaniel O. brakeman, bds. 10 Chapel [10 Chapel
Kimball Robert P. book-keeper, Stevens & Duncklee's, house
Kimball Ruth A. widow of Benj. bds. 118 State
Kimball Sarah Miss, house Main, opp. Church
Kimball Sophia A. widow of Samuel, house 23 Washington
Kimball Tilden, shoe-maker, house West Canal, Fisherville
Kimball Wm. H. house 7 Tahanto
Kimball Willis G. C. (*Kimball Bros.*), photographic artist, Main, cor. School, house Rumford, near School
King Leander, blacksmith, house Main, cor. Centre [Phelps'
Kirwin John, moulder at Ford & Kimball's, bds. Joseph E.
Kittredge F. E. Rev. clergyman, bds. Eagle Hotel
Kittredge Henry H. baggage-master, N. Railroad, bds. Mrs. Julia B. Kittredge's [Church
Kittredge Julia B. Mrs. widow of Jonathan, house Main, opp.
Kittredge Perry, (*Underhill & Kittredge*), druggist, Main, cor. School, bds Mrs. Julia B. Kittredge's
Knee Catherine Mrs. widow of James, house rear Hill's block
Knee James Jr., hair-dresser, bds. Mrs. James Knee's, rear of Phenix Hotel
Knight Charles B. blacksmith, house West Concord

Knight Elijah, jeweller, Stickney's block, house 27 Centre
Knight Fred. E. blacksmith, bds. 245 Main
Knight Harry, clerk, bds. 42 Green
Knight Sarah D. widow of Thomas, house 157 State
Knight Wm. A. carriage-smith, Harvey, Morgan & Co.s, house 245 Main
Knowles Albert H. C. stone-cutter, house East Concord
Knowles Joseph, carpenter, house Church, Fisherville
Knowlton Abner L. civil engineer, Main, Concord, h. Main, Fisherville
Knowles Lyman, stone-cutter, house East Concord
Knowlton Charles T. B. painter at Abbot's, house 45 State
Knowlton Edward L. (*J. H. Pearson & Co.*), Railroad Square, house Main, opp. Winter

LABONTA FRANCIS W. shoe-cutter, house Washington, near Essex
Labonta Frank, blacksmith at Abbot's, house Myrtle, near Thompson [South
Labonta Joseph, blacksmith at Abbot's, house Downing, near
Labonta Mary A. Mrs. house Washington, cor. Academy
Labreche John, stone-cutter, bds. Main, cor. Centre
Labreche Roderick, stone-cutter, bds. O. B. Adams'
Lecasse Joseph, boot-maker, 3 Warren, house Centre, n. State
Ladd Moses, blacksmith, bds. at J. Rollins', 32 Pleasant
Ladd Wm. stone-cutter, bds. Elm-house [Warren, near Green
Ladd Wm. D. (*Walker & Co.*), iron-store, Railroad Square, h.
Ladue Peter, laborer, house Main, cor. East Canal, Fishervile
Layfaette Lawrence, stone-cutter, house 10 Fosterville
Lake George W. farmer, house East Concord
Lake Reuben, express-man, house 20 Fayette
Lamarche Sophie, widow of Leon, house 6 Cross
Lamper Abel, stone-mason, house West, near South
Lamprey Abel Jr., foreman at Gas Works, house State, near the Turnpike road
Lamprey Daniel, farmer, house south end of South [yard
Lamprey Ephraim, farmer, house Turnpike, near the brick-
Lamprey George, spring-maker, bds. 24 Spring [the brick-yard
Lamprey John H. gardener, bds. E. Lamprey's, Turnpike, nr.
Lamprey Levi, wood-worker, N. Railroad, house Washington, near Walnut
Lamprey Morris, stone-cutter, house Forest, cor. Valley
Lamprey Stephen, stone-cutter, bds. D. Law's, Washington, near Centre [Washington, cor. Rumford
Lamprey Stephen C. blacksmith, Warren, cor. Pine, bds.
Lancaster Augustus C. cabinet-maker, bds. at George C. Lancaster's, Main, cor. Spring, Fisherville [Fisherville
Lancaster George C. cabinet-maker, house Main, cor. Spring,
Landers James H. house Spring, near Rumford
Landrie Eli, harness-maker, 151 Main, bds. 19 Short

Lane Alexander, cabinet-maker, bds. W. Johnson's, Washington, near Main, Fisherville

Lane Andrew L. carriage maker, boards 15 Downing

Lane Charles T. carriage maker at Abbot's, house 76 Spring

Lane Cyrus T. route agent, boards Columbian Hotel

Lane John A. blacksmith at Abbot's, b. Mrs. S. H. Edmunds', Allison, near Turnpike

Lane Jonathan C. wheelwright, house 1 Fremont

Lane Joseph H. carriage builder, h. 30 Main, Tallant's block

Lane Joshua, silver plater, house 18 Monroe, corner Beaver

Lane Samuel G. lawyer and real estate agent, Hill's block, h. Rumford, corner Centre

Lang Abbie Miss, house East Concord

Lang Charles M. painter Con. R. R. house Blake, n. Green

Lang George K. carpenter, house Pleasant, cor. Washington

Lang John K. painter, house Centre, near Washington

Lang Thomas M. pattern maker, house Centre, cor. Spring

Lang Jonathan E. clerk H. G. Kayes', house 328 Main

Langley Andrew J. carriage maker at Abbot's, h. Perley

Langley Calvin F. blacksmith at Abbot's, house State, near the Turnpike road

Langley Frank G. express messenger, boards Elm House

Langmaid Albert, overseer of carshop at N. R. R. house 26 Pleasant

Langmaid Edward jr. carpenter, boards 19 Fayette

Larkin Frank, machinist N. R. R. house n. Rollins' drug store

Larkin James E. painter, house 59 Warren

Larkin Patrick, laborer, house rear Fisk's store [Larkin's

Larkin Patrick jr. bookkeeper F. A. Fisk's, boards Patrick

Larkin R. Mrs. widow of Henry, house 35 Warren

Larnare Tophile, harness maker, 151 Main, house 81 Spring

Lass Thomas F. marble worker, boards Franklin House

Lass Thomas, marble cutter, boards Joseph E. Phelps'

Lauder Jas. M. master mechanic N. R. R. h. 24 Washington

Laughlin John, moulder at Ford & Kimball's, house Myrtle, near Thompson

Lauthlin Frank, mechanic, house rear Stickney's block

Law Daniel, blacksmith C. R. R. h. Washington, n. Centre

Lawrence Elizabeth Mrs. widow Elijah, boards 53 Main

Lawrence Fred. compositor, b. Oliver Turner's, 34 Main

Lawrence James M. moulder Ford's foundry, h. 24 Franklin

Lawrence John L. painter, boards E. C. Cutting's, Summer, n. Court [5 Warren, h. 18 Thorndike

Lawrence Joseph E. (*Shallies & Lawrence*), harness maker,

Lawrence Luther, coachmaker at Abbot's, house 40 State

Lawrence Mich'l, shoemaker, h. Main, opp. Free Bridge road

Lawson Robert, shoemaker, house Herbert's lane

Leahy James, car repairer Con. R. R. h. Cross, c. Jefferson

Lear Edward H. foreman Norton's stable, b. Columbian Hotel

Lear George A. painter, house 2 Tremont

Lear Henry N. moulder, house Allison, near Gay
Lear John, sawfiler, house Turnpike
Lear John, carpenter Con. R. R. house Allison, near Gay
Leary James, laborer, boards John Leary's
Leary James, swtchman N. R. R. house Herbert's lane
Leary John, laborer, house Ferry, near R. R.
Leary John, harness maker, house 14 Main
Leaver Mary, widow of Thomas, house 6 Wall
Leaver William, carriage maker at Abbot's, house 6 Wall
Leavitt Benjamin F. painter at Abbot's, house 7 Perley
Leavitt Edward P. clerk J. S. Norris & Co.'s, bds. 87 Main
Leavitt Sarah, widow of Jonathan, boards 7 Perley
Leavitt Walter, carpenter, house Washington, near Centre
Leavitt William F. stonecutter, boards 17 Franklin
Lee Charles H. broommaker, boards 248 Main
Lee Helen, widow of Richard, house Warren, near Liberty
Lee John, laborer, h. John Lee's block, Chandler St. n. R. R.
Lee Michael, laborer N. R. R. house Monroe, near South
Lee Richard, laborer, house Lee's block, Chandler
Lee William, laborer, house Chandler, near R. R.
Leighton Alexander, painter at Harvey, Morgan & Co.'s, house 43 Downing
Leighton Betsy T. Mrs. widow of J. N. house 12 Wall
Leighton Calvin B. caterer, house 3 Chapel
Leighton James, butcher, house Walnut, near Washington
Leighton John W. blacksmith, house Spring, near Maple
Leighton Mary, widow of William, boards 43 Downing
Leroque Frank, pressman, house rear of James R. Hill's
Leslie Horace G. physician, house Washington, Fisherville
Lester James, coppersmith, house 207 Main
Lewis Cornelius, butcher, house rear 14 Main
Lewis Jerry, stonecutter, boards Joseph E. Phelps'
Libbey E. Walter, porter Phenix Hotel
Libbey Charles, carriage maker at Abbot's, boards 1 State
Lincoln Beza H. coachtrimmer, house 136 Spring
Lincoln J. G. (*Lincoln & Shaw*), hats, furs and clothing, Exchange block, house 33 School
Lincoln & Shaw (*John G. Lincoln and Wentworth G. Shaw*), hats, caps, clothing, &c., Exchange building
Linehan John, laborer, h. Warren, opp. W. Canal, Fisherville
Linehan John C. (*Brown & Linehan*), dry goods and groceries, Main, house Charles, Fisherville
Linehan Timothy, machinist, bds. J. Linehan's, Warren, opp. W. Canal, Fisherville
Little Henry, engineer, house Franklin, near Jackson
Little Enoch C., C. R. R. shop, house Pleasant, n. Main
Little John W. dentist, 176 Main, house Plesant, cor. South
Little Thos. B. bookkeeper Warde, Humphrey & Co's, h. 248 Main
Littlefield Charles H. moulder Fords foundry, bds. Joseph B. Hook's
Littlehale Langdon, Phenix Hotel, Main, near passenger depot

Littlehale W. S. clerk, Columbian Hotel
Locke Amos S. blacksmith, Harvey, Morgan & Co's., house 2 Liberty [Pleasant
Locke Benj. L. car-repairer, N. Railroad, house Spring, near
Locke Effie, widow of Benj., house Washington, near Walnut
Locke Franklin H. machinist, house Pleasant, cor. Fremont
Locke John P. farmer, house East Concord
Locke Levi, teamster, house Penacook, cor. Walnut
Locke Reuben, carriage-painter, bds. Mrs. Mary A. Brackett's, Summer, cor. Winter
Locke Reuben B. blacksmith, house East Concord
Locke Samuel, farmer, house Washington, near Walnut
Locke William, teamster, bds. Joseph B. Hook's
Locke Wm. T. police-officer, house 19 Franklin [h. 69 State
Lockerby Chas. A. physician and surgeon, Merrimack bld.
Long Daniel W. coach-trimmer, house Spring, n. Cambridge
Long Hannah C. widow of Stephen, house Centre, cor. Spring
Long Sylvester G. machinist, N. Railroad, house Centre, cor. Spring
Longfellow Abigail, widow of Hannibal, house 18 Green
Lorillard Fire Ins. Co. New York, Hodgdon & Merriam, agents, State block, Main
Loring Charles, house 27 Franklin
Lor Tertullien, painter, bds. Mrs. Lamarche's
Lossing Robert, boot-maker, house Ferry, near Railroad
Lougee B. H. letterer, Harvey, Morgan & Co's., bds. Elm House [Neal's, Ash, cor. Fayette
Lovejoy George N. painter at Abbot's, bds. Mrs. Mary N.
Lovejoy Judith C. widow of Samuel, house 156 State
Lovely Israel, painter at Abbot's, house 20 Cross
Lovely John, laborer, bds. Main, cor. Centre
Lovering Joseph F. clergyman, house 88 State
Low Franklin, Real Estate Agent, house 69 Main
Low Gracia Mrs. School, cor. Main
Lucy Martha Miss, tailoress, house Spring [Fisherville
Ludlow Leavitt M. carpenter, house Merrimack, near Centre,
Lull Charles A. moulder, bds. 14 Main
Lull Edwin F. blacksmith at Abbot's, bds. 31 Downing
Lull George U. laborer, house Downing, near South
Lull Henry, painter at Abbot's, bds. 31 Downing
Lull Jesse H. teamster, house 19 Monroe
Lull John E. teamster, bds. 31 Downing
Lull John M. engineer, house 14 Main [ning
Lull Leander C. watchman, cor. Railroad depot, h. 31 Dow-
Lull Leander F. Ford's foundry, bds. 14 Main [School
Lund Chas. C. (*Stevens & Lund*), lawyers, 67 Main, opp.
Lund Joseph K. express messenger, Railroad depot, Railroad Square
Lund Joseph S. house 71 Main [Washington
Lyman George, shoe-maker, bds. Mrs. E. James', Walnut, n.

Lynch Hugh, house South, near West
Lynch Jane, widow of Daniel, house East Concord
Lynch John, laborer, house Main's block, rear 40 Main
Lynch Timothy, laborer, 4 Main
Lyster James, coppersmith, N. Railroad, house 217 Main

MACAULY PATRICK, stonecutter, boards Main, c. Centre
Mace Joseph H. clerk, Sherman House, house State, near Thompson
Magoffin Michael, stone-cutter, bds. Moses Davis'
Mahagen Charles, laborer, house 283 Main
Mahan Barney, mason, house Cross, near South
Mahoney Michael, stone-cutter, bds. James Gurley's [tery
Mahoney Timothy, laborer, house State, near the new Ceme-
Main George, (*Main & Nutter*), nurseryman, 3 Merrimack, house do. [Merrimack
Main & Nutter, (*Geo. Main & E. S. Nutter*), nurserymen, 3
Makepeace Orson, cooper, house West Concord [Concord
Makepeace Henry, quarryman, bds. G. W. Brockway's, West
Manley John E. painter at Abbot's, bds. Mrs. S. H. Edmund's, Allison, near Turnpike
Mann Henry, carpenter, house 159 State
Mann Samuel R. machinist, house Merrimack, Fisherville
Mann Marion, widow of James, bds. S. R. Mann's, Merrimack, Fisherville [Avenue
Manning Augustus R. blacksmith at Abbot's, house Pleasant
Manning Orlando L. blacksmith, N. Railroad, bds. Mrs. Sarah E. Runnells', Union, cor. Washington [Centre
Mansur Amos, painter, bds. N. Mansur's, Washington, near
Mansur Amos O. painter, bds. J. N. McNeil, Warren, Fisherville [N. Mansur's, Washington, n. Centre
Mansur George, baggage master C. M. & L. Railroad, bds
Mansur Nathan, silver-smith at Durgin's, house Washington, near Centre [near Spring
Marcey Lucy, widow of Octavius, bds. P. A. Welcome's, Prince
Marden Alfred L. groceries, &c., West Concord, house do.
Marden Daniel, farmer, house West Concord
Marden Frank, carpenter, house West Canal, Fisherville [ton
Marden George W. stone-cutter, house Walnut, n. Washing-
Marden George W. tailor, house 11 Washington
Marden James, belt-maker, house Penacook [ville
Marsh David, shoe-maker, bds. William E. Jameson's, Fisher-
Marsh David S. cabinet-maker, bds. William E. Jameson's, Fisherville [Fisherville
Marsh George B. cabinet-maker, bds. William E. Jameson's,
Marsh George H. laborer, house Water, near Main
Marsh James, laborer, house 2 Tremont
Marshall Anson S. (*Marshall & Chase*), lawyer, 2 & 3 State block, house Pleasant, cor. Spring
Marshall E. H. Mrs. (*Mrs. E. H. Marshall & Co.*), milliner, Stickney's new block, house Park, near Main

Marshall E. H. Mrs. & Co. (*Mrs. E. H. Marshall and Miss Nellie F. Marshall*), milliners, Stickney's new block, Main
Marshall Gustine, milliner, Stickney's block, house Park, next to Episcopal Church
Marshall Nellie F. Miss (*Mrs. E. H. Marshall & Co.*), milliners, Stickney's new block, bds. Park, near Main
Marshall Wm. (*F. S. Peck & Co.*), clothing, 114 Main, bds. Phenix Hotel
Marshall & Chase, (*Anson S.Marshall and William M. Chase*), lawyers, 2 & 3 State block, Main
Marston Alfred A. clerk, bds. J. C. Dunklee's, State
Marston Anna, widow, house Cedar
Marston George H. (*Wm. P. Ford & Co.*), iron foundry, rear Merrimack County Bank, office 233 Main, house 20 Franklin, cor. Jackson
Marston Jeremiah, carpenter, house State, north of Franklin
Marston John, carpenter, house Jackson, cor. Church [Arch
Marston Joseph B. insurance agent, house Green, cor. North
Marston Samuel B. carpenter, house Walnut, near Franklin
Martin Addison F. machinist, house Millbury road
Martin Charles H. clerk, 103 Main, bds. 20 Pleasant
Martin Frank, shoe-maker, bds. Mrs. Bean's
Martin James, granite-cutter, bds. Columbian Hotel
Martin Jeremiah C. (*J. C. Martin & Son*), doors, sashes and and blind-maker, house Summer, Fisherville
Martin J. C. & Son, doors, sashes and blinds, Fisherville
Martin Joseph, laborer, h. Pleasant, n. Washington [n. Main
Mason Frank G. wood-worker, N. Railroad, house 2 Pearl,
Mason George A. carriage-maker, bds. 46 State
Mason James L. carriage-maker, house 46 State
Mason John, house Union, corner Centre
Mason John K. clerk, 129 Main, bds. Amos Bean's
Mason John P. machinist and engineer, N. Railroad, house 9 Union, cor. Maple
Mason John S. (*Mead, Mason & Co.*), carpenter, Main, house Centre, cor. Union [tre, near Spring
Mason Wm. G. carpenter, Union steam-mill, Main, house Cen-
Masten Archibald, house rear 211 Main
Mathews Horace, supt. of Shaker Farm, house Ferry road
May Thomas, laborer, C. Railroad, house rear 34 Main
Mayers Abraham, bds. 5 Elm [5 Elm
Mayers Richard, dry goods, Phenix Hotel building, Main, h.
McAleer George, laborer, house rear Rumford block
McAllister Alexander, carpenter, house Washington, n. Warren, Fisherville
McAulisse Patrick, stone-cutter, bds. Centre, cor. Main
McCardle Edward, laborer, house Merrimack, Fisherville
McCarthy Charles, laborer, house Cross, near Main [son
McCarty Mary, widow of Callahan, house Myrtle, n. Thomp-
McCarty Michael, dresser, bds. 9 West Canal, Fisherville

McCarty Timothy, laborer, house Ferry, near Railroad [South
McCauley Wm. painter, house Downing, between State and
McCaulley James, painter at Abbot's, house Spring, n. Clinton
McClay Harriet Miss, house 240 Main
McCuddy Jeremiah, blacksmith, bds. 24 Thompson [John
McCrilliss Moses O. bds. David B. Rowe's, Valley, cor. St.
McDaniel John, farmer, house 2 Winter
McDaniel Samuel, hostler, bds. 2 Winter
McDonald Daniel, farmer, house 9 Walnut [Main
McFarland Asa, (*McFarland & Jenks*), printer, house 278
McFarland Henry, (*McFarland & Jenks*), printer, Statesman building, house 241 Main
McFarland & Jenks (*Asa McFarland, George E. Jenks and Henry McFarland*), printers and publishers, Main, corner Depot
McIntire Harvey G. physician, School, cor. Tahanto, house do.
McKenzie Wm. machinist, house 35 Thompson
McKorne Patrick, currier, house East Concord
McLaughlin John, nail-maker, house Merrimack, Fisherville
McLean Abbie L. widow of James, house 37 Pleasant
McLear —— hostler, bds. Phenix Hotel
McMichael Charles, blacksmith, house Clinton, opp. Spring
McMichael Henry W. blacksmith, bds. C. McMichael, Clinton, opp. Spring
McNeil James, dresser, house Warren, Fisherville
McNeil John, clerk, house Warren, Fisherville
McNeil John, agent, Union Store, house Canal, Fisherville
McPherson Charles A. painter, Con. Railroad, house Pleasant, opp. Rumford [7 Wall
McQueston Greenough, clerk, C. M. & L. Railroad, house
McShane James E. blacksmith, house Thompson, near Spring
McShane James, blacksmith, house Spring, cor. Short
McVicar Alexander, carpenter, house Centre, cor. Merrimack
Mead Charles E. (*Mead, Mason & Co.*), carpenter, Union Steam Mill, house 143 State
Mead, Mason & Co. carpenters, office School, opp. P. O.
Mead Nathaniel J. (*Union Steam Mill*), Main, house Centre
Mead Nicholas G. (*Union Steam Mill*) Main, house 167 State
Mehan Patrick, machinist, Con. Railroad, h. Cross, n. State
Mellen Geo. K. clerk, A. T. Sanger's, Lowe's block, house 9 Thompson
Mentean Cyprian, teamster, house Railroad Square
Merriam Jonas, bds. Cambridge, cor. Academy
Merriam Joseph A. (*Hodgdon & Merriam*), ins. agent, house at East Concord
Merrill Darius, clerk in Pension Office, bds. 57 State
Merrill David B. house 23 Spring [Green, near Centre, h. do.
Merrill Dora L. Miss, family and day School for young ladies,
Merrill George W. teamster, house 6 West
Merrill John W. professor at Biblical Institute, h. 161 State

Merrill Joseph F. compositor, house West, corner South
Merrill Joseph S. trimmer at Abbot's, h. South, opp. Monroe
Merrill Joshua B. deputy sheriff, house 9 Franklin
Merrill Lyman, clerk J. A. West's, boards Joshua B. Merrill's
Merrill Nancy W. widow of Caleb, boards 23 Spring
Merrill Sarah, widow of Samuel, house Spring, near Clinton
Merrill Stephen A. wood turner, b. 9 West Canal, Fisherville
Meserve Geo. P. (*J. C. Martin & Son*), door, sash and blind maker, house Summer, Fisherville
Meserve Grant P. cabinet maker, house Summer, Fisherville
Meserve Joseph, cabinet maker, b. W. Johnson's, Washington, near Main, Fisherville [Beaver
Messe Francis, tuner at Prescott's, b. J. Lane's, Monroe, cor.
Messer Hezekiah, yard master N. R. R. house rear 228 Main
Meyers Peter W. trimmer at Abbot & Downing's, house 106 Spring [Pleasant
Miller Edwin A. carpenter and builder, Main, house Pine, n.
Miller George, blacksmith, house Washington, corner State
Miller George L. stonecutter, boards John Williams'
Miller George N. stonecutter, boards 8 Union
Miller James A. painter at Abbot's, house 11 Thompson
Miller James D. varnisher Parker & Secomb's, house Pine, near Warren
Miller John R. carpenter, house Warren, corner Merrimack
Miller Sally E. Mrs. widow of John, h. Warren, c. Merrimack
Milligen Elizabeth, widow of Thomas, house East Concord
Mills Clarissa, widow of Nathaniel, house south end South, near West
Mills George H. machinist, house 1 State
Mills George W. cabinet maker, bds. 9 W. Canal, Fisherville
Mills John, farmer, house West, near State
Mills John J. trimmer at Abbot's, house rear 6 Main
Mills Seba H. farmer, house 1 State
Minot Charles (*Minot & Co.*), banker, over P. O. h. 158 State
Minot James, cashier Minot & Co.'s, School, b. 158 State
Minot Josiah (*Minot & Mugridge*), lawyer, Hill's block, and (*Minot & Co.*), bankers, over Post Office, house Warren, corner Rumford
Minot Selina W. C. Mrs. widow of George, h. 16 Montgomery
Minot & Co. (*Charles and Josiah Minot*), bankers, over P. O. School
Minot & Mugridge (*Josiah Minot and John Y. Mugridge*), lawyers, Hill's block, Main [Fair Ground
Mitchell Andrew S. (*Mitchell & Gale*), Central Market, house
Mitchell Frank A. tinman, house 16 Washington
Mitchell Frank J. painter, boards 16 Washington
Mitchell Geo. carriage trimmer, 253 Main, b. 16 Washington
Mitchell Geo. cabinet maker, h. Main, c. Summer, Fisherville
Mitchell George A. lastmaker, boards 17 Spring
Mitchell George W. painter at Abbot's, house 17 Spring

Mitchell John E. silver plater, b. F. A. Mitchell's, 16 Wash.
Mitchell & Gale (*Andrew S. Mitchell and Isaac R. Gale*), meat market, opp. Depot, Main
Mixer Eliza Jane Mrs. widow of Charles T. h. 240 Main
Moffatt Alexander, fancy goods, boards Eagle Hotel, Main
Monitor, Concord Daily, Independent Press Association, 176 Main
Moody Charles, farmer, house Main, opposite Church
Moody Franklin G. clerk, 129 Main, boards 29 Pleasant
Moody George W. farmer, house East Concord
Moody Jane Mrs. widow of Nathaniel, h. Summer, Fisherville
Mooers Reuben D. house 12 Wall
Moore Abel F. roadmaster C. R. R. house 5 R. R. square
Moore Albert A. merchant, house Franklin, near Jackson
Moore Byron, bookkeeper Wm. P. Ford & Co's, 235 Main, boards 247 Main [Moore's
Moore Charles P. (*Harvey, Morgan & Co.*), boards Dr. E. G.
Moore Chas. W. ins. agent, Hill's block, Main, h. Chapel ct.
Moore Ebenezer G. physician and surgeon, house Main, cor. Pleasant
Moore Eugene D. carriage maker, house 235 State
Moore George H. boots and shoes, 5 Exchange block, house Franklin, near Jackson [State, n. Pleasant
Moore Harrison, fireman Con. R. R. b. Mrs. M. J. Flanders',
Moore Henry M. carpenter, house 177 State
Moore Henry O. carpenter, house Washington, Fisherville
Moore Henry P. artist, Henry, corner Church, house do.
Moore Irving, laborer C. R. R. boards 1 State
Moore James (*Moore & Cilley*), hardware, 212 Main, h. 247 Main, corner Washington
Moore James M. physician and surgeon, h. Main, c. Pleasant
Moore Nancy B. Mrs. widow of Thomas T. house Washington, Fisherville
Moore Orville, quarryman, b. D. Fish's, West Concord road
Moore Robert, laborer, house Merrimack, Fisherville
Moore Thomas, C. R. R. shop, house 6 R. R. square
Moore Thomas A. carpenter, house R. R. square
Moore Timothy, butcher, house 290 Main
Moore Van R. coffin maker, 188 Main, house 33 Franklin
Moore & Cilley (*Jas. Moore and J. L. Cilley*), hardware, 212 Main
Moores Albert H. butcher, house 254 Main
Moores Alfred H. marketman, Main, opp. Free Bridge road, house Main, opposite Washington
Moores Nathan W. marketman, Main, opp. Free Bridge road, house Washington, opposite Union
Moores Timothy G. butcher, house Main, nearly opp. Chapel
Moran Christopher, laborer, h. Fayette, n. Main
Moran Mary Mrs. widow of Michael, house 13 1-2 Centre
Morey John H. (*Davis & Morey*), music teacher, Masonic Temple, boards B. Biddle's

Morgan Alonzo, woodworker N. R. R. h. 269 Main, c. Franklin
Morgan Benj. A. clerk 103 Main, boards 101 State
Morgan Charles L. woodworker N. R. R. house 116 Spring
Morgan George, carpenter, boards 33 Green
Morgan Ira N. harness maker, 151 Main, boards Kilburn's
Morgan James (*James Morgan & Co.*), druggist, 103 Main, house 101 State
Morgan James & Co. druggists, 103 Main
Morgan Jesse, farmer, house Main, corner Union, Fisherville
Morgan John, photographic artist, Moore's block, Main, house Pleasant, corner Spring
Morgan John J. (*Davis & Morgan*), reed manufacturer, h. 134 Spring
Morgan Reuben B. carpenter, house Beacon
Morgan Richard F. clerk, 103 Main, boards 101 State
Morgan Rufus M. (*Harvey, Morgan & Co.*), carriage manufacturer, Main, opposite Thompson, house 31 Thompson
Morgan Schuyler W. organ reed maker, boards 25 South
Morgan Scott, cabinet maker, boards J. B. Goldsmith's, Main, corner Summer, Fisherville
Morrill Alpheus, physician, 82 Main, house do.
Morrill Asa H. house Summer, Fisherville
Morrill Charles, cabinet maker, house Main, Fisherville
Morrill Clara Miss, house 240 Main
Morrill Elisha, farmer, house Spring, opposite Cross
Morrill Frank P. cabinet maker, b. G. Morrill's, Washington, Fisherville
Morrill George M. farmer, b. E. Morrill's, Spring, opp. Cross
Morrill George S. carpenter, boards A. H. Morrill's, Summer, Fisherville
Morrill Gilman, farmer, house Washington, Fisherville
Morrill Hazen, house Water, near the bridge
Morrill James, shoemaker, house rear 310 Main
Morrill John B. farmer, b. E. Morrill's, Spring, opp. Cross
Morrill John F. (*S. F. Morrill & Co.*), jewellers, Central block boards Phenix Hotel
Morrill Joseph H. confectioner, Main, opp. State House, house 9 School
Morrill Lucius B. bookbinder, house 36 Green
Morrill Luther M. (*Morrill & Silsby*), bookbinder and stationer, Central block, Main, house 35 School
Morrill Luther S. student-at-law, boards 35 School
Morrill Mary Miss, milliner, b. Washington Hotel, Fisherville
Morrill Obadiah, clerk 12 State block, boards 163 State
Morrill Reuben, jeweller, house East Concord
Morrill Samuel F. (*S. F. Morrill & Co.*), jeweller, 119 Main, house State, corner Wall
Morrill Shadrach C. physician, 82 Main
Morrill S. F. & Co. (*Samuel F. and John F. Morrill*), jewellers, Central block, Main
Morrill Willis H. jobwagon, house 14 State
Morrill & Silsby (*Luther M. Morrill and Geo. H. H. Silsby*), bookbinders, stationers, &c. Central block, Main

Morrison Amos H. machinist N. R. R. house 5 Maple, n. Union
Morrison Charles H. melodeon maker, h. Centre, opp. Green
Morrison George A. painter N. R. R. boards Charles H. Morrisons', Centre, opp. Green
Morrison George P. upholsterer Prescott Bros. b. 5 Maple
Morrison James, blacksmith at Abbot's, h. Downing, n. South
Morrison John C. lumber dealer, house Centre, cor. Summer, Fisherville
Morrison Mary A. widow of Edward, house 4 Forest
Morrison Thomas, spring maker, house rear 211 Main
Morse Benj. F. machinist, b. Washington House, Fisherville
Morse Charles G. cabinet maker, house Union, Fisherville
Morse Eliza A. widow of Aaron, house 103 State
Morse Frank F. machinist C. R. R. b. S. F. Morse's, Spring, c. Cross
Morse Fred. S. carriagesmith, b. Chas. S. Harper's, E. Concord
Morse Ira F. (*Morse & Putnam*), gasfitter, School, house 32 Warren
Morse John H. gas and steam fitter, School, b. 32 Warren
Morse Nathan K. clerk E. G. Kilburn & Co's, h. 6 Chapel
Morse Oscar, conductor N. R. R. boards Eagle Hotel
Morse Stephen F. carpenter, house Spring, corner Cross
Morse & Putnam (*Ira F. Morse and Wm. T. Putnam*), gas and steam fitters, School, near Post Office
Morton Wilson E. teamster, house rear 11 Perley
Moseley Carlos B. clerk Barron, Dodge & Co. b. 14 Merrimack
Moseley Franklin (*Barron, Dodge & Co.*), flour dealer, house 14 Merrimack
Moseley John F. bookkeeper Barron, Dodge & Co. boards 14 Merrimack
Moulton Albanus K. clergyman, house Fayette, near State
Moulton Albert A. physician, house 1 Call's block, State
Moulton Edward A. painter, Union, n. Washington, house 21 Washington
Moulton Elizabeth S. widow of James, h. 25 Washington
Moulton Jacob S. boot and shoe dealer, house Main, opp. Free Bridge road
Mower Lewis L. printer, house 59 Main
Much Charles T. laborer, house Downing, near South
Much Thomas, tailor, house Spring, cor. Clinton
Mugridge John Y. (*Minot & Mugridge*), lawyer, Hill's block Main, house Main, opp. Church
Mulcahy Michael, fireman, Con. Railroad, house Myrtle, near Thompson
Mulike Patrick, laborer, bds. Mrs. Mary U. Scales', Clinton
Munroe John, house Green, near Pleasant
Munroe John P. telegraph operator, depot, Railroad Square, house Green, near Pleasant
Munsey Frank P. boot and shoe-dealer, City block, bds. Mrs. Bean's
Munsey James B. teamster, house State, near West
Murphy Barney, stone-cutter, bds. Joseph Ivers'
Murphy Eugene, harness-maker, house Short, near Rumford

Murphy Jeremiah, laborer, house Water, near Main
Murphy Jeremiah, stone-cutter, bds. Joseph E. Phelps'
Murphy Jeremiah Jr. stone-cutter, bds. Jeremiah Murphy's
Murphy John, laborer, house 9 Walnut
Murphy John, laborer, house 283 Main [bds. Eagle Hotel
Murphy John E. (*Murphy & Towle*), dentist, Masonic Temple,
Murphy John H. carriage-trimmer at Abbot's, house Main, n. the Gas Works
Murphy Michael, laborer, house Chandler, east of railroad
Murphy Peter, house Short, near Rumford
Murphy Thomas, stone-cutter, bds. Joseph E. Phelps'
Murphy Thomas, hostler, Eagle Hotel
Murphy Thomas, laborer, house 2 Water
Murphy Thomas, laborer, house West, near South
Murphy Thomas, laborer, house 211 Main
Murphy William, stone-cutter, bds. 3 Jefferson
Murphy & Towle, (*John E. Murphy and Charles N. Towle*), dentists, Masonic Temple, Main
Murray Elizabeth, widow of Henry J., house 16 Washington
Mutual Life Ins. Co. of New York, Stickney's new block
Muzzey John Jr., American House, Main
Myers Peter W. carriage-trimmer, 253 Main, h. 106 Spring

NASH ALBERT, stone-cutter, bds. G. T. Kilburn's, 12 Union
Nash Albert C. stone-cutter, bds. Elias Evans'
Nash George, stone-cutter, bds. Joseph B. Hooks'
Nash Moses, harness-maker, 151 Main, bds. Amos Beans'
Nash Robert H. stone-cutter, bds. Joseph B. Hooks'
Nason Henry, laborer, house Monroe, near Beaver
National State Capitol Bank, 11 State block, Main
Neal David L. clerk at C. C. Webster's, bds. Mrs. Mary N. Neal's, Elm, cor. Fayette [cor. Fayette
Neal Mary N. Mrs. widow of David, boarding-house, Elm,
Neal Wm. H. express-man, bds. Mrs. Mary N. Neal's
Nealy Nancy Mrs. widow, house Main, near Cross
Nelson Nathaniel C. watch-maker and engraver, house Henry, near Franklin
Nevens Phineas, teamster, house 4 Chapel
Newell Charles D. carriage-maker at Abbot's, house Turnpike, near the brick-yard
Newell Charles H. machinist, house 22 Thorndike
Newhall Daniel B. clerk, bds. T. Frank Newhall's
Newhall Lucinda B. widow of Thomas H. house 14 Monroe
Newhall T. Frank, (*Smith & Newhall*), saloon-keeper, Main, cor. Hutchins, house School, near Green
New Hampshire Bible Society, Room 5 State block, Main
New Hampshire Historical Society, Rooms 250 Main [Main
New Hampshire Missionary Society, Room 5 State block
New Hampshire Patriot and State Gazette, Sanborn's block, Main

New Hampshire Statesman, Main, cor. Depot
Newry John, shoe-maker, house Pleasant, near the Asylum
Niagara Fire Ins. Co. New York, Webster & Smith, agents, State block, Main
Nichols Alexander, stone-cutter, house West Concord
Nichols Charles F. clerk, repair-shop, N. Railroad, bds. Centre, cor. Spring
Nichols Charles H. fireman, Northern Railroad, bds. 83 State
Nichols Joseph B. agent for Butter's patent flat-irons, bds. L. W. Nichols, Centre, cor. Spring [cor. Spring
Nichols Luther W. time-keeper, N. Railroad, house Centre,
Nichols Richard, cabinet-maker, bds. 9 W. Canal, Fisherville
Nichols Timothy, painter, house Warren, opp. Tahanto
Nichols Timothy M. painter, house 61 Warren
Nichols Wm. T. stone-cutter, house Franklin, near Walnut
Niles Stephen W. fruit and confectionery, Chase's building, house South Arch, near State
Nolan James, watchman, Holden's Mill, house W. Concord
Nolan Mary Mrs. widow of Michael, house 285 Main
Norris James S. (*Jas. S. Norris & Co.*), confectioner and baker, 85 Main, house 83 Main
Norris Jas. S. & Co. (*James S. Norris and Geo. W. Crockett*), bakers and confectioners, 85 Main [block, Main
Northern Telegraph Co., J. W. Robinson, sup.'t, office State
Norton Abigail G. widow of John D. house 31 School [State
Norton Charles H. livery-stable, rear Eagle Hotel, house 107
Norton Charles H. jr. book-keeper, Norton's stable, bds. 107 State, cor. Warren
Norton John B. quarryman, bds. Baldwin Humphrey's
Norton Wm. K. hostler at Norton's stable, bds. 107 State
Nourse Eliza Mrs. widow of Benjamin, bds. 26 Main [ion
Noyes Clara A. Miss, dress-maker, 4 State block, bds. 24 Un-
Noyes Edward R. photograph artist, City block, h. 27 Union
Noyes Enoch R. clock-repairer, b. J. Noyes, Main, Fisherville
Noyes George, house 27 Rumford
Noyes George D. S. clerk, bds. 27 Rumford
Noyes Hannah Mrs. widow of George, bds. 11 School
Noyes James, clerk C. Railroad office, b. Geo. G. Sanborn's
Noyes Jefferson, house 24 Union
Noyes Jeremiah, wheelwright, house Main, Fisherville
Noyes Jeremiah S. farmer, house 76 South
Noyes Samuel G. fancy goods, books, &c., Main, bds. J. Noyes', Main, Fisherville [Union
Noyes Sarah H. Miss, dress-maker, 4 State block, bds. 24
Nutter Eliphalet S. (*Main & Nutter*), nurseryman, 3 Merrimack, house 5 Montgomery
Nutter Geo. L. clerk, house 163 State
Nutting Charles, granite dealer, house 51 State
Nutting Franklin, quarryman, house West Concord
Nye George S. job-wagon, Cross, near Jefferson, house do.

O'CONNELL PHILIP, laborer, house Spring, cor. Short
O'Connor Daniel, laborer, house Chandler, near Railroad
O'Connor Thomas, marble-worker, house 4 Tremont
Odell John A. stone-cutter, bds. Amos Beans'
Odlin John W. book-keeper, bds. 268 Main [268 Main
Odlin Woodbridge, U. S. Assistant Assessor Central block,
O'Donnahoe John, stone-cutter, bds. T. Doherty's [and South
O'Flanigan Patrick, laborer, house Downing, between State
O'Haran John, watchman, N. Railroad, house Walnut, near Washington
O'Herren Patrick, laborer, house State, near Main
O'Neill Francis, laborer, house Merrimack, Fisherville
Ordway Albert, mason, bds. Mrs. Mary J. Flanders', State, n. Pleasant
Ordway Annie P. Miss, artist, bds. Smith Moulton's
Ordway Harriet S. Miss, dress-maker, Stickney's new block, Main, bds. J. C. Ordway's
Ordway John C. farmer, house 17 Centre
Ordway John C. jr., telegraph manager, bds. 17 Centre
Ordway Lorenzo W. carpenter, bds. 9 Maple
Ordway Mary, widow of Ebenezer, house E. Concord
Ordway Richard M. (*Ordway & Robinson*), mason, 7 Warren, house 14 Montgomery [*inson*), masons, 7 Warren
Ordway & Robinson, (*Richard M. Ordway and Nahum Rob-*
Orne Wm. H. cooper, house W. Concord
Osgood Daniel jr., (*Farnam & Osgood*), grocers, Main, cor. Free Bridge road, house Rumford, cor. Short
Osgood Frank V. blacksmith, house E. Concord
Osgood Robert C. ins. agent, Stickney's new block, house Green, near School
Osgood True, printer, house 30 Warren
Otis Harrison G. machinist, bds. 29 State
Otis James M. wood-worker at Abbot's, house 29 State
Ouilette Benjamin, carpenter, bds. Amos Beans' [Concord
Owens Patrick, jack-spinner, house rear Holden's mill, West

PACKARD FRANK, moulder, bds. 83 State
Packard Wm. T. moulder at Ford & Kimball's, bds. at Sawin's, Warren, cor. State
Packard Zadock S. car-builder, house Green, cor. Warren
Packard Zebulon T. car-builder, house Warren, cor. Green
Page Benjamin F. teamster, house Downing, between State and South
Page James K. blacksmith, house West Concord
Page Jeremiah, farmer, house Hall
Page William, carpenter, house East Concord
Page William, farmer, bds. J. Page's, Hall
Paige Cyrus W. farmer, house 265 Main
Paige Laura J. Miss, bds. 265 Main
Paliquen Flavien C. blacksmith, house Myrtle, near Cross

Palmer Benj. F. carpenter, bds. B. Palmer's, 54 State
Palmer Brackett, house 54 State
Palmer Charles W. printer, house 54 State
Palmer Dudley S. house 12 Warren
Palmer Frank M. blacksmith, bds. Mrs. Julia A. Carr's
Palmer Harriet A. widow of Wesley B. h. Cross, c. Myrtle
Palmer James, stone-cutter, bds. Columbian Hotel
Palmer John B. printer, bds. at B. Palmer's, 54 State
Palmer Joseph (*Palmer, Ward & Co.*), spring manufacturer, Railroad Square, Call's block, State
Palmer Mary A. Mrs. widow of Moses D. house 15 Wall
Palmer Moses T. machinist, N. Railroad, house 60 Warren
Palmer Thomas N. printer, bds. 54 State
Palmer, Ward & Co. spring manufacturers, Railroad square
Palmer Wm. H. painter at Abbot's, house Cross, cor. Myrtle
Palmer William W. clerk, Eagle Hotel
Parker Asa, carpenter, house 7 West
Parker Benjamin, civil engineer, house 12 Centre
Parker Caleb, (*Parker & Secomb*), Phenix block, house 89 State, cor. Wall
Parker Charles O. bds. 7 West [Fayette, near South
Parker Harris M. tobacco and cigars, 101 Main, house 22
Parker Samuel G. conductor, Con. Railroad, bds. 7 West
Parker Trueman R. cabinet-maker, bds. 7 West
Parker & Secomb, (*Caleb Parker and Daniel F. Secomb*), manufacturers of organs, melodeons and pianostools, ware-rooms, Phenix block
Partridge Harrison, cooper, house West Concord
Patch Ira H. packer at Abbot's, house 6 Thorndike [ington
Patten David, professor in Biblical Institute, house 34 Wash-
Patten Richard M. blacksmith, 253 Main, house Walnut, near Washington
Patterson John, stone-cutter, house rear of the Depot, West Concord [cookville
Patterson J. N., U. S. Marshal, 134 Main, house at Contoo-
Patterson Samuel, engineer, house 187 State
Paul George A. key-maker at Crockett & Pillsbury's, bds. T. Pillsbury's, Thompson, cor. Elm [son, near Franklin
Paul Horace F. pattern-maker, Ford's foundry, house Jack-
Paul James L. key-maker at Crockett & Pillsbury's, bds. J. Monroe's, Green, near Pleasant
Peacock Charles H. machinist at Abbot's, bds. 42 State
Peacock Lorenzo K. foreman wheelwright-shop at Abbot's, house 42 State
Pearce Joseph H. stone-cutter, bds. Joseph E. Phelps' [son's
Pearson Charles C. (*J. H. Pearson & Co.*), b. John H. Pear-
Pearson Charles W. clerk, bds. John M. Pearson's, 79 State
Pearson John H. (*J. H. Pearson & Co.*), house 263 Main
Pearson J. H. & Co. (*Edw. L. Knowlton and Chas. C. Pearson*), flour and Western produce, Railroad Square

Pearson John M. groceries, State, cor. Downing, house 79 State, cor. Fayette
Pearson Joseph A. printer
Pease Edward H. laborer, bds. J. Pease, South, cor. Cross
Pease John, shoe-maker, South, cor. Cross, house do.
Peaslee Charles C. clerk, Central market, bds. Daniel C. Peaslee's, 145 Main [house Warren, cor. Rumford
Peaslee Cyrus, fish-market, Main, near Free Bridge road,
Peaslee Daniel C. salesman Jas. S. Norris & Co.'s, h. 145 Main, opp. Phenix Hotel [Salem, Mass.
Peck Freeman, (*F. S. Peck & Co.*), clothing, 114 Main, house
Peck F. S. & Co. (*Freeman S. Peck and Wm. Marshall*), clothing, 114 Main
Pecker George B. boards William Pecker's, East Concord
Pecker Jonas E. reporter for the *Boston Journal*, Statesman building, boards 18 Centre
Pecker Mary Mrs. widow of Jeremiah, house East Concord
Pecker Robert E. merchant, house 326 Main
Pecker William, farmer, house East Concord [117 State
Peirce Augustine C. cashier Union Bank, Central block, house
Pelissier Chas. harness maker, 151 Main, b. Frank Leroque's
Pelkey Philipye, harness maker, 151 Main, house 19 Short
Pelren Oliver, painter, house Church, near State
Pendergast Karn, spinner, house Church, Fisherville
Pendergast John, billiard saloon, Main, bds. K. Pendergast's, Church, Fisherville
Pension Agency, Central block, Main
Perkins A. F. machinist, house 10 Green, corner Warren
Perkins Charles, blacksmith at Harvey, Morgan & Co.'s, bds. 13 Wall
Perkins Edward, house Centre, opp. Green
Perkins Hamilton E. lawyer and judge of Probate, Stickney's block, house Penacook, corner Warren
Perkins Harriet E. widow, house 111 Spring
Perkins William W. painter, house 107 Spring
Perley Ira, attorney-at-law, house Spring, corner Cambridge
Perry Priscilla A. widow of Amos, h. Washington, n. Centre
Perry Sewall A. harness maker, house West, near South
Perry Willis A. assistant clerk, Eagle Hotel
Pervier Ann H. Mrs. widow of Asa L. house Warren, near Charles, Fisherville
Peters John F. express messenger, h. 73 State, c. Thompson
Pettengill Andrew J. laborer, house East Concord
Pettengill Charles B. machinist, house Penacook, n. Main
Pettengill Daniel H. laborer, house East Concord
Pettengill David, laborer, b. D. H. Pettengill's, E. Concord
Pettengill George B. W. bds. C. B. Pettengill's, Penacook, near Main
Peverly James, house School, corner Tahanto
Phelps Joseph E. house Hill's avenue

Phenix Mutual Life Ins. Co., Hartford, Conn., C. W. Moore, agent, Hill's block, Main
Philbrick Albert, farmer, boards 7 Fosterville
Philbrick George, farmer, boards 7 Fosterville
Philbrick Martha, widow of Ornando, house 7 Fosterville
Philbrick R. N. harness maker, 151 Main, house 46 Spring
Phillips Calvert, peddler, house 17 Fayette
Phipps George W. machinist, house 41 State
Pickering Hazen, house 86 State
Pickering J. L. & Co. (*Jonathan L. Pickering, Charles Joy and John E. Thompson*), grocers, 3 Masonic Temple, Pleasant [Masonic Temple, house 47 State
Pickering Jonathan L. (*J. L. Pickering & Co.*), grocers, 3
Pierce Charles, laborer, house Washington, near Centre
Pierce Franklin Genl. lawyer, house Main, near Cross
Pillsbury Frank J. (*Crockett & Pillsbury*), pianoforte and melodeon keymaker, 16 Wall, house Thompson, c. Elm
Pillsbury George A. wood agent, house 25 Rumford
Pillsbury Hannah, widow of Joseph, house 8 Spring
Pillsbury Joseph J. blacksmith, h. North Arch, near State
Pillsbury Parker, house 30 School
Pillsbury Thos. W. wood agt. No. R. R. h. Thompson, c. Elm
Pilsbury John C. stationary engineer N. R. R. house 14 Washington, corner State
Pilsbury Thos. A. machinist N. R. R. h. 14 Washington, c. State
Pinkham Charles H. blacksmith at Harvey, Morgan & Co.'s, h. Downing, near South
Pinkham Fred A. blacksmith, h. Washington, n. Centre
Pinkham Hazen, laborer, house Washington, n. Centre
Pinkham Nancy Mrs. house 22 Fayette
Piper Chas. H. (*Piper & Haskins*), fancy goods and eating-house, Central block, Main, house State, cor. Warren
Piper C. S. (*Piper & Clough*), boots and shoes, Low's block, Main, house 25 Merrimac, near School
Piper Henry, hack driver, house Centre, opposite Union
Piper Joseph H. carriage trimmer at Abbot's, house 25 South
Piper Mary S. Mrs. dress maker, 12 Tremont, house do.
Piper William C. carpenter, boards 6 Winter
Piper & Clough (*Chas. S. Piper and Mahlon B. Clough*), boot and shoe manfs. and dealers, opp. State Capital Bk. Main
Piper & Haskins (*Chas. H. Piper and Mrs. Emily L. Haskins*), fancy goods and eating-house, Central block, Main
Pitman John W. (*Pitman & Swain*), soda water and pop beer manufacturers, 17 Wall, house do.
Pitman Oscar V. (*O. V. & W. H. Pitman*), grocers, Main, cor. Free Bridge Road, boards 5 Centre
Pitman O. V. & W. H. (*Oscar V. & William H. Pitman*), grocers, Main, cor. Free Bridge road
Pitman Stephen J. clergyman, house 5 Centre [5 Centre
Pitman Stephen J. jr. clerk O. V. & W. H. Pitman's, boards

Pitman William H. (*O. V. & W. H. Pitman*), grocers, Main, cor. Free Bridge road, boards 5 Centre
Pitman & Swain (*John W. Pitman and William B. Swain*), soda water and pop beer manufacturers, 17 Wall
Plamondon Louis P. varnisher, Prescott Bros. h. 44 Centre
Plasterage Martin V. B. engineer Union Steam Mill, h. do.
Porter Albert A. assistant physician, Insane Asylum
Porter Benjamin S. clerk, boards 11 Prince
Pothier Louis, harness maker, 151 Main, bds. Amos Bean's
Potter Alvah K. lawyer, Stickney's blk. bds. East Concord
Potter Benjamin, clerk, bds. M. Clough's, Prince, n. Spring
Potter John, machinist Concord R. R. boards 59 Main
Powell Alvin C. farmer, house West Concord
Pranter Ellen Mrs. widow of Joy, house near Hill's block
Pratt N. R. Mrs. widow, house Washington, Fisherville
Prentiss Charles B., City market, house Old Fair Ground
Prentiss Edmund S. boards Charles B. Prentiss'
Prescott Abraham J. (*Prescott Brothers*), Exchange block, h. 47 Main, cor. Cross [melodeons, Exchange building
Prescott Brothers (*Abraham J. and George D. B. Prescott*),
Prescott Edward P. (*E. P. Prescott & Co.*) flour and groceries, wholesale, 42 Railroad square, house 83 State
Prescott E. P. & Co. (*Edward P. Prescott and Moses B. Smith*), groceries, wholesale, 42 Railroad square
Prescott Geo. painter, C., M. & L. R. R. house Washington, near Centre
Prescott Geo. D. B. (*Prescott Bros.*), melodeons, Exchange block, boards Phenix Hotel [block, house 39 Main
Prescott Joseph W. melodeon and organ manuf. Exchange
Prescott Mary E. Mrs. widow of James, h. 7 Centre
Prescott William, physician, house Elm, near Pleasant
Presenham John, laborer, house 13½ Centre
Pressey Carlos G. carpets, crockery ware, &c. 3 Moore's block
Pressey George H. clerk, 3 Moore's block
Preston James E. painter N. R. R. h. 22 South, op. Thompson
Price Bernard, hair dresser, boards State, corner Warren
Price James M. shoemaker, h. Washington, near Walnut
Priest George H. clerk Stanley & Ayers', Main, boards Geo. Batchelder's, Spring
Prince Cleophas, woodworker N. R. R. h. Myrtle, near Cross
Prince Clifford, carpenter, house Myrtle, near Cross
Proctor Charles H. hair-dresser, Masonic Temple
Proctor Mary E. Mrs. widow of Noah M. bds. 11 School
Proctor Solon, machinist, bds. Mrs. A. Pervier, Warren, near Charles, Fisherville [near Washington
Provancher Felix, melter at Wm. P. Ford & Co's. h. Walnut,
Provancher John L. moulder, bds. F. Provancher's Walnut, near Washington [Main, h. Charles, Fisherville
Putnam David (*Putnam & Hall*), dry goods and groceries,
Putnam Nehemiah, carpenter, house 68 South

Putnam William T. (*Morse & Putnam*), gas-fitters, School, boards D. Fitz's, School, cor. Spring
Putnam & Hall (*David Putnam and Lyman K. Hall*), merchants, Main, Fisherville
Putney John, merchant, East Concord, house do.

QUIMBY CHARLES Jr. teamster, h. Water, n. the bridge
Quimby Enoch J. stonecutter, house Franklin, near High
Quimby John, engineer Con. R. R. house Hall, near Water
Quimby Nicholas, (*N. Quimby & Co.*) hoop skirt and corset manufacturer, 232 Main, house 12 Tahanto
Quimby N. & Co. hoopskirt and corset manuf. 232 Main
Quimby Parkhurst P. painter, bds. E. E. Cutting's, Summer, near Court
Quimby Ransom S. farmer, house Walnut, near Tremont
Quimby Stephen (*S. Quimby & Co.*) flour and grain, 6 Pleasant, house Tahanto, cor. School [and grain, 6 Pleasant
Quimby S. & Co. (*Stephen Quimby and Frank Coffin*) flour
Quinn Jeremiah, dresser at the mill, house West Concord
Quinn John, overseer of card room at Holden's, h. W. Concord
Quinn Timothy, spinner, house West Concord

RAND DAVID, telegraph operator, house 9 Union
Rand Esther, widow of Daniel, house 9 Union
Rand Hamilton L. billiard hall, Hill's blk. Main, boards Mrs. Mary N. Neal's, Ash, corner Fayette
Rand H. B. house Pleasant, near Main
Rand Jacob B. house Court, corner Summer
Rand James E. police officer, house 48 Spring
Rand Mary Mrs. widow of Tobias, house Water, near R. R.
Randall Clarissa, widow of William, h. Franklin, cor. High
Randall Holman, stonecutter, boards 17 Franklin
Ranlet Henry W. (*H. W. Ranlet & Co.*), boards Elm House
Ranlet H. W. & Co. (*Henry W. and Noah Ranlet*), wood, coal and ice dealers, Hill's ave. cor. R. R. square
Ranlet Noah (*H. W. Ranlet & Co.*), house Hill's ave.
Ray Hiram M. wheelwright, house 96 State
Raymond Nancy Mrs. wid. h. Summer, n. Church, Fisherville
Reardon Bartholomew, stonecutter, boards 4 Pearl
Reardon Jeremiah, laborer, bds. Mrs. Mary U. Scales, Clinton
Reed Charles F. spring-maker, boards Charles H. Reed's
Reed Charles H. laborer, house Washington, near the jail
Reed Emily, widow Hiram, house 3 Tahanto
Reed Ezekiel S. miller, house Main, Fisherville
Reed George F. clerk, 8 Stickney's blk. boards 3 Tahanto
Reed George L. paper hanger, house 46 South
Reed Pamelia, widow of Orlin, house 37 State
Reiley John, blacksmith, boards Mrs. Julia A. Carr's
Remick Charles G. clerk Adj. General's office, bds. 39 Spring
Remick Granville L. grocer, Merrimack block, h. 39 Spring

Rice Harvey, house 30 Pleasant
Rich Wm. P. wheelwright at Abbot's, h. Perley, n. State
Richardson David W. tanner, h. Penacook, n. the tannery
Richardson Edward, overseer in mill, h. Walnut, Fisherville
Richardson George W. woodworker N. R. R. house 8 State, cerner Pearl
Richardson Hiram, carpenter C. R. R. house 7 Franklin
Richardson James, spinner, house Walnut, Fisherville
Richardson Loring S. clerk, boards 16 Green
Richardson Maria E. Miss, tailoress, boards 7 Franklin
Richardson Osborn T. mason, boards 12 Thompson
Richardson Thomas, jeweller, bds. Mrs. Mary N. Neal's, Ash, corner Fayette
Riley Barney, laborer, house 11 Monroe
Riley John, blacksmith, boards Mrs. Carr's, Pleasant
Riley William, laborer, house Lee's block, Chandler
Rines Nath'l P. dealer in hardware and old iron, 68 Warren, house do.
Ring James P. machinist Con. R. R. house 9 Fayette
Ripley George H. packer W. P. Ford & Co. h. 21 Thompson
Rix Eugene, trimmer at Harvey, Morgan & Co's, boards Mrs. J. N. Flander's, Perley, near State
Rixford Frank W. student, boards 4 West
Rixford William H. carpenter, house 2 Park [n. Turnpike
Roach Jeremiah P. W. harness maker T. P. Hill's, h. Allison,
Roach William S. tailor, house Elm, Fisherville
Robbins Charles E. machinist N. R. R. h. Spring, n. Centre
Robbins Edward A. moulder at Ford & Kimball's, boards 6 Pleasant
Robbins George W. painter at Abbot's, house 67 South
Roberts Alfred, quarryman, house West Concord
Roberts Calvin, cabinet maker, house Merrimack, Fisherville
Roberts Charles H. boards Eagle Hotel
Roberts Edgar, laborer, h. High, c. Spring, Fisherville
Roberts George W. woodworker N. R. R. bds. Amos Bean's
Roberts John, cabinet maker, h. High, cor. Spring, Fisherville
Roberts Lyman R., blacksmith, bds. B. E. Rogers', Spring, n. Main, Fisherville [ford, cor. Cambridge
Roberts Martha, wid. of Eben, boards Wm. W. Storrs', Rum-
Robertson Charles N. millhand, h. Merrimack, Fisherville
Robinson A. H. physician, house 1 Park [bds. 2 Park
Robinson Allen H. clerk, N. H. Patriot and Gazette Office,
Robinson Charles A. (*J. F. Hoit & Co.*), grocer, Masonic Temple, house 1 Franklin
Robinson Charles C. photographer, house 24 West
Robinson Charles E. (*C. Robinson & Sons*), tanners and curriers, Penacook, house 350 Main, near Penacook
Robinson Chester G. carriagesmith, Warren nr. Main, house 24 Thompson [Penacook, h. 15 Centre
Robinson Cyrus (*C. Robinson & Sons*), tanners and curriers,

Robinson Cyrus R. (*C. Robinson & Sons*), tanners and curriers, Penacook, house East Concord
Robinson Cyrus & Sons (*Cyrus, Cyrus R. and Charles E. Robinson*), tanners and curriers, Penacook
Robinson Edward B. ploughmaker, r. L. C. Stickney's Block, house 36 Washington
Robinson Frank W. hackdriver, boards Elm House
Robinson George C. ploughmaker, house 26 Union
Robinson George C. laborer, house 26 Union
Robinson Henry C. teamster, h. Church, n. Union
Robinson Henry M. painter, h. 25 Union [West Concord
Robinson Jennie Miss, weaver, bds. Baldwin Humphrey's,
Robinson John, laborer at Abbott's, house Cross, n. South
Robinson Jos. farmer, h. 10 West [Main, h. 15 Perley, n. State
Robinson Joseph W. supt. Northern Tel. Co. State Block,
Robinson Josiah S. cooper, house 24 West
Robinson Nahum (*Ordway & Robinson*), mason, 7 Warren, h. 40 Rumford
Robinson Thos. F. gilder, 132 Main, h. 114 Spring, n. School
Robinson Wesley, h. rear School, near Merrimack
Robinson Wesley J. spring bed manuf. State Block, house rear School, near Merrimack
Robinson William, laborer, house Chandler, near R. R.
Roby Harrison A. silver plater, boards William Roby's
Roby Luther, house 281 Main [Fisherville
Roby Samuel C. carpenter, house Summer, cor. High,
Roby William, farmer, house Washington
Rochette Gideon, currier at Blake's, boards Joseph Phelps.
Rochlow Louis, painter at Abbot's, house 6 Jefferson
Roger Williams Fire Ins. Co. of Providence, Stickney's new block [near Main, Fisherville
Rogers Brooks E. blacksmith, Main, opp. Spring, h. Spring,
Rogers Caleb S. house 38 State
Rogers Charles, laborer, house Downing, near South
Rogers Moses F. house Tremont, near Union
Rogers Wm. harness maker, house 26 Downing
Rolfe David J. painter at Abbot's, house 43 State [erville
Rolfe Enoch E. cabinet maker, bds. T. C. Rolfe, Church, Fish-
Rolfe Henry P. lawyer, Stickney's block, house 21 Green
Rolfe Hiram, foreman at Abbot's, house 49 State
Rolfe Horace, painter, boards D. Fitt's, School, cor. Spring
Rolfe Lucy, wid. of Saml. hoopskirt maker, bds. 12 Tahanto
Rolfe Mary, widow of Benjamin, boards 43 State
Rolfe Timothy C. carpenter, house Church, Fisherville
Rolfe Timothy E. cabinet maker, bds. T. C. Rolfe's, Church Fisherville [R. crossing
Rollins Albert S. teamster, house West Concord road, near R.
Rollins Edward H. (*Rollins & Co.*), druggist, Main, opposite State House, house 243 Main

Rollins Frank, house rear 30 Main
Rollins John, boots and shoes, Main, house 32 Pleasant
Rollins John E. harness maker, 151 Main, b. 32 Pleasant
Rollins John F. (*Rollins & Co.*), apothecaries, b. Eagle Hotel
Rollins John S. (*J. S. Rollins & Co.*), druggists, h. Summer, cor. Centre, Fisherville [druggists, Main, Fisherville
Rollins J. S. & Co. (*John S. Rollins and Cephas H. Fowler*),
Rollins & Co. (*E. H. Rollins and John F. Rollins*), apothecaries, opposite State House, Main [Cross, n. Jefferson
Ronan Richard, wheelwright, at Harvey Morgan & Co.'s, h.
Rooney James F. stonecutter, boards Dominick Gannon's
Ross Mrs. widow, house Fayette, corner State
Rounsefell James, painter, 9 Pleasant, house 17 Thompson
Rouney Owen, laborer, house Washington, near Warren
Rowe Daniel, carpenter, boards Main, corner Centre
Rowe Daniel, blacksmith, 253 Main, bds. Joseph Mayhew's
Rowe David B. carpenter, house Valley, cor. St. John
Rowe Edward W. clerk, boards 2 Winter
Rowe Elizabeth M. wid. of George, house Spring, n. Pleasant
Rowe John T. quarryman, house West Concord
Rowell Charles P. (*Rowell & Clough*), groceries, Washington, near Rumford, house Rumford, opposite Cambridge
Rowell Horace N. manager Western Union Telegraph, at Depot, h. School, n. Green
Rowell James H. (*Peter Dudley & Co.*), livery stable, near Phenix Hotel, house 21 School
Rowell Thompson, mason, house School, near Tahanto
Rowell & Clough, (*Charles P. Rowell and Edwin D. Clough*), groceries, Washington, n. Rumford [bds. do. E. Concord
Royce George Henry, carriage smith at Charles S. Harper's,
Runals John B carpenter, house Warren, near Spring
Runnells J. Dwight, upholsterer, bds. at Mrs. Sarah E. Runnell's, Union, cor. Wash. [nell's, Union, cor. Wash.
Runnells Lyman B. upholsterer, bds. at Mrs. Sarah E. Run-
Runnells Sarah E. wid. of Hazen, h. Union, cor. Washington
Russ John S. conductor, house School, corner Spring
Russell Moses W. physician, Central block, boards 28 School
Ryan James, laborer, house near Fiske's store
Ryan John, blacksmith, house 9 Walnut
Ryan Patrick, laborer, house West Concord
Ryder Jepthah M. ironmoulder, house 23 Washington

SAFFORD WILLIAM B. carriage trimmer, h. 104 Spring
Saltmarsh Aaron H. h. Pleasant, cor. Liberty [lin, cor. High
Saltmarsh Austin G. wood dealer, Free Bridge road, h. Frank-
Saltmarsh Sarah A. wid. of Andrew, house Tremont, n. State
Sanborn Abbie, wid. of Josiah H. house 26 Green
Sanborn Abraham B. (*A. B. Sanborn & Co.*), State block, Main, house Centre, near Merrimack

Sanborn A. B. & Co. (*Abraham B. and Charles H. Sanborn*), dry goods and groceries, South end State block, Main
Sanborn Alfred L. carpenter, boards N. Sanborn's, Centre, corner Spring
Sanborn Austin, pressman, 114 Main, boards 114 Main
Sanborn Benning W. (*B. W. Sanborn & Co.*), Sanborn's block, boards Eagle Hotel
Sanborn B. W. & Co. (*Benning W. Sanborn and Josiah B. Sanborn*), booksellers, Sanborn's block, Main
Sanborn Carroll, wheelwright, State, n. West, h. 42 West
Sanborn Charles H. (*A. B. Sanborn & Co.*), dry goods, &c. State block, Main, h. Spring near Washington
Sanborn Charles H. boiler maker, h. West, near South
Sanborn Charles P. (*Foster & Sanborn*), lawyer, Sanborn's block, Main, house 90 State
Sanborn Daniel, farmer, house East Concord
Sanborn Edwin, blacksmith, at Abbot's, boards 3 West
Sanborn Eliza, widow of Jacob, house 166 State
Sanborn Frank A. farmer, boards D. Sanborn's, E. Concord
Sanborn George E. wheelwright, Harvey, Morgan & Co.'s, house 80 Main
Sanborn George G. general ticket agent, Concord R. R. house Pine, opposite Orchard
Sanborn George W. teamster, h. Turnpike, n. the brick yard
Sanborn Heman, house East Concord
Sanborn Henry, blacksmith, boards Joseph B. Hook's
Sanborn Henry A. clerk, at Webster's, boards 4 West
Sanborn Henry C. collector and carrier, house 105 Spring
Sanborn Henry M. woodworker, boards 83 State
Sanborn James, farmer, house East Concord
Sanborn James, carpenter, house State, corner Wall
Sanborn John H. carpenter, house 17 Union
Sanborn Jonathan, carpenter, house State, corner Pleasant
Sanborn Josiah (*A. B. Sanborn & Co.*), Sanborn's block, Main, rooms Gustine Marshall's [bds. Eagle Hotel
Sanborn Josiah B. (*B. W. Sanborn & Co.*), Sanborn's block,
Sanborn Newell, carpenter, house Centre
Sanborn Peter, State Treasurer, house 63 Main
Sanborn Phineas G. stonecutter, boards Columbian Hotel
Sanborn Plummer W. salesman E. P. Prescott & Co. boards Mrs. Underhill's, Green [Washington, Fisherville
Sanborn Priscilla P. Mrs. widow of Joshua, b. L. K. Cheney's,
Sanborn Richard P. bedspring maker, house 111 Spring
Sanborn Thomas J. rooms W. H. Rixford's, 2 Park
Sanborn Thomas W. house 95 Spring
Sanborn William, carpenter, bds. H. Simpson's, Summer, cor. Washington square, Fisherville
Sanders Henry L. stonecutter, b. John Sanders, jr. E. Concord
Sanders Jacob P. clothing, Main, house Charles, cor. Warren, Fisherville

Sanders James H. painter at Abbot's, boards 18 West
Sanders John jr. house East Concord
Sanders Joseph, stonecutter, bds. John Sanders jr. E. Concord
Sanders Jos. E. carpenter, b. Washington House, Fisherville
Sanders Reuben L. farmer, house East Concord
Sanford Austin, clothes cleaner, h. 114 Main [9 Thompson
Sanger Austin T. hats, caps, &c. Low's block, opp. P. O. bds.
Sargent Amos B. casemaker Prescott Bros. h. 25 Green
Sargent Charles W. treas. N. H. Savings bank, 252 Main, house Hanover, corner School
Sargent Charles W. printer, house Jackson, near Church
Sargent David H. miller, house Merrimack, Fisherville
Sargent David P. eating saloon, 2 Depot, h. Centre, n. Tahanto
Sargent E. C. agt. Concord Granite Co. office Ferry, n. R. R.
Sargent Eli H. miller, house Summer, Fisherville
Sargent Flora, widow of James F. house 3 Union
Sargent Frank A. finisher Prescott Bros'. boards 25 Green
Sargent George J. foreman of stone yard, near Union Steam mill, boards Amos Bean's
Sargent James G. mason, house Cedar
Sargent Mehitabel, widow of David W. house 58 South
Sargent Sarah W. widow of John L. h. School, c. Hanover
Sargent Simeon, stonecutter, boards Joseph B. Hook's
Sargent Thomas, house 13 Centre
Sargent Wells, blacksmith at Abbot's, house 16 Monroe
Saul John W. trimmer at Abbot's, house 56 State
Saunders Charles H. foreman at Cummings' marble works, boards Elm House [Concord, h. do.
Saunders Daniel J. boot and shoemaker, r. of the Depot, West
Saunders Oral, peddler, b. Baldwin Humphrey's, W. Concord
Savage Isaac M. book-keeper Lewis Barter & Co. house 13 Fayette
Sawin Harriet Mrs. boarding-house, house 83 State
Sawyer Geo. brakeman, bds. 83 State [erville
Sawyer John, farmer, house Washington, cor. Warren, Fish-
Sawyer Joshua F. carpenter. house 15 Thompson
Sawyer Lyman, farmer, house West Concord
Sawyer Moses K. (*E. G. Kilburn & Co.*), grocer, 2 Moore's block, house South, cor. Fayette
Sawyer Thomas J. house West Concord [cor. Spring
Scales Charles F. laborer, bds. J. S. Batchelder's, Clinton,
Scales Mary U. Mrs. widow of John, house Clinton
Scales Royal jr. cabinet-maker, house High, Fisherville
Schuer Adolph, house 108 Spring
Scott George H. blacksmith, bds. Main, cor. Centre
Scott John F. carpenter, house 68 Franklin
Scribner Frank B. clerk, bds. J. W. Burnham's, 44 Green
Seavey Adoniram B. carpenter, house East Concord [erville
Seavey John, machinist, house Main, near Washington, Fish-
Seavey Nancy Mrs. widow of Samuel, house East Concord

Seavey Shadrach, carpenter, house 6 Washington
Secomb Charles, melodeon-maker, bds. 83 State, cor. Warren
Secomb Daniel F. (*Parker & Secomb*), melodeon and organ manufacturer, Phenix block, house 1 Rumford
Senter Charles J. machinist, house Mechanics block, Fisherville
Serett George, blacksmith, bds. Columbian Hotel
Sewall Geo. F. teamster, bds. 54 Warren
Sewall James E. teamster, bds. 54 Warren
Sewall Stephen, teamster, house 54 Warren
Sexton John, laborer, house Main, opp. Abbot's factory
Shackford James C. bds. William Shackford's
Shackford John L. overseer of carding-room at Brown's, house High, Fisherville
Shackford William, mill-wright, house State, cor. Penacook
Shaw Alfred, roofer, house 25 Union
Shaw Annie M. Miss, at G. W. Hallett's skirt-rooms, bds. at J. J. Pillsbury's, North Arch
Shaw Clinton, laborer, house Centre, cor. Spring
Shaw David, carpenter, 25 Monroe, house do.
Shaw Frank E. fireman, N. Railroad, house 2 Pearl, near Main
Shaw Joseph D. artist, 108 Main, house 37 Pleasant
Shaw Josiah C. steward, Insane Asylum
Shaw Judson W. book-agent, 160 Main, house 7 Monroe
Shaw Lauren A. carpenter, bds. 25 Monroe
Shaw Nathaniel, wood-worker at Abbot's, house 9 West
Shaw Samuel J. stone-cutter, house High, near Franklin
Shay John C. painter at Abbot's, bds. 39 State
Shea John B. harness-maker, bds. Main, cor. Centre
Shehan William, carriage-trimmer, house near 14 Main
Sheldon Oliver E. agent, Granite Railway Co. stone-cutter, near Union Steam Mill, house Milton, Mass.
Shenks Edward, blacksmith at Abbot's, house Downing, near South
Shepard Edwin F. blacksmith, N. Railroad, house Walnut, near Tremont
Shepard James M. laborer, house Main, near Union, Fisherville
Shepard Omar L. clerk, bds. Joseph Eastman's, W. Concord
Sherburne Alden P. jeweller, 149 Main, house 19 Green, near Warren
Sherburne Joseph, bds. 32 Pleasant
Sherburne Robert H. house 32 Pleasant
Sherman Lovell, carpenter, bds. 45 Pleasant
Shute Aaron, bds. S. L. Currier's, Merrimack, opp. Orchard
Shute Hannah K. widow of John, bds. George W. Garvin's, Hall
Shute Henry P. wheel-wright at Abbot's, bds. Mrs. Jane N. Flanders', Perley, near State
Shute John, farmer, house 28 West
Shute Mary L. widow of Edmund W. house 21 Green
Shute Samuel, carpenter, house 20 West
Shallies Augustus D. harness-maker, 151 Main, house 44 Rumford
Shallies Ira B. carpenter, bds. A. D. Shallies', 44 Rumford

Shallies Joseph J. (*Shallies & Lawrence*), harness-maker, 5 Warren, house 44 Rumford

Shallies & Lawrence, (*Joseph J. Shallies and Joseph E. Lawrence*) harness-makers, 5 Warren [Depot, h. 164 State

Sharpe Wm. H. principal of the Business College, Main, cor.

Sharples Ralph, laborer, house Spring, n. Clinton [Rumford

Shattuck Henry S. conductor, N. Railroad, house School, cor.

Shattuck Samuel W. auctioneer and dealer in furniture, Moore's block, up stairs, house 1 Bowery Avenue

Shaw Wentworth G. (*Lincoln & Shaw*,) hats, cloth, furs, &c., Exchange building, house 44 School

Sherman House, James Chesley, proprietor, Main, opp. Free Bridge road

Silloway David F. cabinet-maker, house Church, Fisherville

Silsby Almira Miss, bds. 326 Main

Silsby George H. H. (*Morrill & Silsby*), book-binder, Central block, Main, house 27 Pleasant

Silver David D. stone-cutter, house East Concord

Silver Henry H. moulder at Ford & Kimball's, bds. 11 Wall

Silver Roswell, farmer, house Thorndike, near South

Silver Wm. C. blacksmith, Warren, cor. Pine, house Washington, near Rumford

Silver Wm. P. stone-mason, house Washington, near Centre

Simons Andrew, house Summer, Fisherville

Simons Joseph, cabinet-maker, bds. Mrs. Mary Abbot's, Summer, cor. Centre, Fisherville [Railroad Square

Simons William F. transportation clerk, N. Railroad, bds. 5

Simpson Andrew, clergyman, house Liberty, cor. Pleasant

Simpson Charles, laborer, house Washington, opp. School

Simpson Hamilton F. stone-cutter, bds. Calvin Worth's, Franklin, near Walnut

Simpson Henry, carder, h. Summer, corner High, Fisherville

Simpson John, gunsmith, boards 26 Washington

Simpson S. L. F. physician, house Main, near Pleasant

Sinclair Henry M. house 35 Centre

Sinclair Mary W. widow of Moses H. house 35 Centre

Sinclair Nelson B. jeweller, Stickney's block, house 54 Centre

Sleeper Charles W. harness maker, boards D. Fitts', School, corner Spring

Sleeper Jas. P. melodeon maker at Union Steam Mill, h. Hall

Sleeper Jeremiah D. painter at Harvey, Morgan & Co.'s, h. Hall, near Water [the Prison

Sleeper Jonathan W. harness maker, house 12 Tremont, near

Sleeper Joseph T. merchant tailor, Stickney's block, Main, house 49 Pleasant [State, near Pleasant

Sleeper Sherman, brakeman, boards Mrs. Mary J. Flanders',

Sleeper William A. harness maker, h. Walnut, n. Washington

Sloane John D. machinist, N. R. R. boards 60 Warren

Smart Abial, teamster, house 15 Merrimack

Smart Albert H. blacksmith, N. R. R. boards 6 Pearl

Smart Calvin, watchman, N. R. R. house 6 Pearl, n. Main
Smart Charles H. currier, boards 6 Pearl
Smart Charles S. woodworker, N. R. R. house North Arch
Smart Frank, driver steam fire engine, boards 15 Merrimack
Smart George, painter, house 23 1-2 Green
Smart Hannah, widow of Caleb, boards 15 Merrimack
Smart Herman F. boards 73 Main
Smart Joseph B. mason, house 10 Maple
Smart Joseph B. jr. printer, boards 10 Maple
Smart Mary Mrs. wid. of Chas. h. Main, nearly opp. Church
Smart William H. physician, 73 Main, house do.
Smith Albert W. clerk, H. G. Kaye's, boards D. E. Smith's, Prince, near Green
Smith Arum B. marbleworker, house Spring, near Pleasant
Smith Christopher, laborer, house rear 211 Main
Smith Daniel E. insurance agent, house Prince, near Green
Smith David A. hostler, house Asylum, near Pleasant
Smith David O. blacksmith, house 30 Centre
Smith Dudley, horse dealer, boards Eagle Hotel
Smith Ezra D. house 77 South
Smith Francis F. stone cutter, boards Columbian Hotel
Smith Fred. dresser, boards Mrs. C. Clark's, High, corner Spring, Fisherville
Smith George F. clerk, boards Philip Flanders'
Smith Geo. W. (*Webster & Smith*), ins. agt. 12 State block
Smith Henry, laborer, rear Robert Woodruff's
Smith James M. house 216 Main
Smith Jeremiah, blacksmith, house East Concord
Smith John, spring polisher, house Spring, cor. Clinton
Smith John, stonecutter, boards Joseph Hook's
Smith John, mechanic, house Spring, Boat Road
Smith John, blacksmith, b. C. F. Guild's, Thorndike, n. Main
Smith John K. blacksmith, Concord R. R. boards George H. Emery's, Auburn, cor. St. John [254 Main
Smith Joseph M. boots and shoes, wholesale, 164 Main, house
Smith Leland A. (*Smith & Walker*), silverplaters, Depot, house 68 1-2 Main
Smith Mahala D. Mrs. wid. of Jer. H. boarding house, 11 Wall
Smith Margaret Mrs. widow Wm. house E. Concord
Smith Milo, express messenger, boards Columbian Hotel
Smith Moses B. (*E. P. Prescott & Co.*), wholesale flour dealer, 42 Railroad Sq. house 16 Fayette, cor. Elm [Merrimack
Smith Preston S. cashier State Capital Bank, Main, house 9
Smith Richmond (*Smith & Newhall*), restaurant, b. Eagle Hotel
Smith Selden A. pianoforte maker, bds. D. E. Smith's, Prince, near Green
Smith Thomas, laborer, house E. Concord
Smith Thomas Jr. laborer, house E. Concord
Smith Thomas, currier, house Penacook, near the Tannery

Smith William, machinist, C. M. & L. R. R. h. West, n. South
Smith William, carcleaner, N. R. R. honse Cross, near South
Smith William, stonecutter, house Franklin, cor. High
Smith & Newhall, (*Richmond Smith and Thomas Frank Newhall*), restaurant, Main, cor. Depot
Smith & Walker, (*Leland A. Smith and Nathaniel B. Walker*), hardware and silver platers, Depot
Smyth Edward F. junk dealer, Wash. n. the Jail, house do.
Snell Oliver S. blacksmith, N. R. R. h. Thorndike, n. Main
Somers Tilsley, painter, 5 Chapel
Somerville Daniel, clerk, Elm House, house 25 Cross
Sommers Patrick, carcleaner, N. R. R. h. South, n. Fulton
Southmayd Henry H. stonecutter, boards Joseph Hook's
Souza A. J. hairdresser, boards 4 Call's block, State
Spain James, laborer, h. State, opp. the new cemetery
Spain Martin, laborer, house State, near the new cemetery
Spain Martin J. F. stone cutter, boards Michael Spain's
Spain Michael, stonecutter, house Cross, above State
Spain Michael, laborer, house State, n. Fosterville [Concord
Spaulding Addie Miss, weaver, bds. Baldwin Humphrey's, W.
Spaulding Eunice P. Mrs. widow of Roswell L. h. 4 Pearl
Spead George G. merchant, house South, near Iron Works
Spead Robert, stonecutter, house south end South
Speed John N. stonelayer, house West Concord [Concord
Speed Leonard, quarryman, bds. Baldwin Humphrey's, West
Spellman Henry T. baker, house 25 Cross
Spellman Martin, quarryman, b. D. Fish's, W. Concord road
Spellman Michael, laborer, house 13 1-2 Centre
Spellman Michael, blacksmith, house 198 Centre
Spiller John J. clerk, J. Brown & Co. house 6 Tahanto
Spiller Josiah G. salesman at Brown's, house 30 Washington
Springfield Fire and Marine Ins. Co. Springfield Mass. C. W. Moore, agent, Hill's block, Main
Stackpole James H. framemaker, 132 Main, bds. 24 School
Staniels Emery T. farmer, house School, cor. Merrimack
Staniels Rufus P. clerk, ins. office, Main, opp. P. O. house Vernon, cor. High [Hotel build'g, Main, h. 170 State
Stanley J. B. (*Stanley & Ayer*), watches and jewelry, Phenix
Stanley Solon W. bookbinder, boards E. L. Childs'
Stanley & Ayer, (*Joseph B. Stanley and Richard H. Ayer*), watches and jewelry, Phenix Hotel building
Stanyan David D. woodworker N. R. R. h. Wash. cor. Essex
Stark Betsey P. Mrs. widow of Samuel, house Centre, near Summer, Fisherville
Stark Philip, leather dresser, house 138 Spring
Stavens Frank, machinist, boards 33 Green
Stearns Charles O. boards 214 Main [head Jackson
Stearns Christopher H. car repairer N. R. R. house Church,
Stearns Frank A. stonecutter, boards James Blake's

Stearns Marcellus H. clerk, W. B. Stearns, b. 28 Merrimack
Stearns Onslow, Pres. Northern R. R. house 214 Main, above Free Bridge road [28 Merrimack
Stearns William B. carpetings &c. op. State House, Main, h.
Stetson Jabez S. bootmaker, house Wash. n. Walnut
Stevens Benjamin, restaurant, boards Sherman House
Stevens Benjamin F. machinist, Con. R. R. house 13 Monroe, near Free Will Church
Stevens Caleb, boards 14 Thompson
Stevens Chandler E. laborer at Abbot's, house 50 Spring
Stevens Edward R. laborer, house Turnpike, n. the brick yard
Stevens Edwin R. hostler, b. H. A. Stevens, Union, Fisherville
Stevens Henry A. livery stable, r. Washington House, house Union, Fisherville [h. 77 State, cor. Fayette
Stevens Josiah Jr. master of transportation C. M. & L. R. R.
Stevens Lyman D. (*Stevens & Lund*), lawyer, Main, house 14 Thompson
Stevens Prescott F. (*Stevens & Duncklee*), h. 8 Railroad Sq.
Stevens Samuel H. lawyer, house 162 State [house do.
Stevens Sylvester (*Tallant & Stevens*), merchants, E. Concord,
Stevenson Wm. blacksmith at Abbot's, house Allison, near Turnpike road
Stevens Zelotes, marble worker, house 3 Centre
Stevens & Duncklee (*Prescott F. Stevens and Charles H. Duncklee*), stoves and tinware, op. Phenix Hotel, Main
Stevens & Lund, (*Lyman D. Stevens and Charles C. Lund*), lawyers, Main, opp. School
Stewart Charles F. city clerk, house Main, cor. Franklin
Stewart Harris, carpenter, house Main, cor. Washington, Fisherville [Pearl, cor. State
Stewart John H. merchant tailor, (*T. W. & J. H. Stewart*), h.
Stewart Thomas W. (*T. W. & J. H. Stewart*), house 1 South
Stewart T. W. & J. H. merchant tailors, Rumford's block, Main
Stickney George H. laborer, bds. John B. Stickney's
Stickney John, teamster, house Prince, cor. Spring
Stickney John B. laborer, house Prince, near Spring
Stickney Joseph, farmer, house 212 Main
Stickney Sarah Miss, house 210 Main
Stiles Samuel, writing-master, house 169 State [Phenix Hotel
Stockbridge Edward A. book-binder, Morrill & Silsby's, bds.
Stockbridge Harrison, mason, house Tremont, near Union
Stockbridge Sewell, mason, house Tremont, near Union
Stokes Daniel H. blacksmith at Abbot's, house 13 Thompson
Stokes John K. blacksmith at Abbot's, house 19 Downing
Stone Benj. P., D.D. house 69 Main
Stone Benj. P. laborer, house Washington, near Centre
Stone Charles L. cutter, A. J. Edmunds, house 7 Hanover
Stone Michael, laborer, house 213 Main
Storin John, house Washington, near Liberty

Storin Michael, baker, house Main, near Winter
Storin Winnie, widow of Michael, house Washington, near Liberty
Storrs Wm. W. cashier, First National Bank, house Rumford, cor. Cambridge [Summer, Fisherville
Story Sarah P. Mrs. widow of Warren, house Cross, corner
Strauss Edward, clerk at Richard Mayers', bds. R. Mayers'
Strauss Herman, clothing-dealer, 1 Hill's block, bds. Phenix Hotel
Straw James B. carpenter, house School, cor. Spring
Straw Samuel E. sash and blind-maker, house Washington, near Union
Straw Trueman, engineer, bds. Columbian Hotel
Stuart Thomas, house 33 Warren
Studley Edward, foreman machine-shop, C. M. & L. Railroad, house 53 State, near Thorndike [bds. Phenix Hotel
Sturtevant George H. printer and publisher, Monitor Office,
Sturtevant Henry C. (*Sturtevant & Whittredge*), grocers, 6 Main, house 28 Main
Sturtevant Mary Mrs. bds. 28 Main
Sullivan Daniel, blacksmith, house West, near South
Sullivan Daniel, laborer, house Main, near the Gas Works
Sullivan David, teamster, house 227 State
Sullivan Dennis, laborer, house Main, opp. Abbots' factory
Sullivan James, laborer, house State, near West
Sullivan James, laborer, bds. H. Nason's, Monroe, n. Beaver
Sullivan James, wheelwright, Harvey, Morgan & Co.'s, bds. H. Nason's, Monroe, near Beaver
Sullivan John, stone-cutter, bds. Joseph E. Phelps'
Sullivan John, laborer, bds. Main, cor. Centre
Sullivan John N. clerk, house Hall, near Water
Sullivan Julia Mrs. widow of Edward, house Water, n. Main
Sullivan Michael, stone-cutter, bds. Sherman House
Sullivan Patrick, stone-cutter, bds. Columbian Hotel
Sullivan Philip H. stone-cutter, bds. Columbian Hotel
Sullivan Thomas, laborer, house Main, opp. Abbots' factory
Sullivan Timothy, stone-cutter, bds. Sherman House
Summers Mathew, carriage-painter, bds. 16 South
Summers Patrick, laborer, N. Railroad, house 16 South
Swain Levi, manufacturer of refrigerators, Warren, n. Main, house 9 Green, near Warren
Swain Wm. B. (*Pitman & Swain*), soda-water and pop-beer manufacturer, 17 Wall, house 14 Wall [7 Hanover
Swallow James R., Eagle book store, Stickney's new block, h.
Sweeney Dennis, tin-peddler, house Downing, near South
Sweeney Jeremiah, harness-maker, 151 Main, house rear Hill's block
Sweeney Timothy, moulder, house rear Hill's block
Sweetser Henry P. harness-maker, 151 Main, house Main, opposite Franklin

Swett Franklin B. blacksmith at Abbot's, house Turnpike, n. the brick-yard
Swett Stephen, laborer, house West Concord
Sylvester Silas G. trader, house Huntington, near Centre
Symonds David, harness-maker, house State, near Court

TAGGARD STEPHEN, stone-cutter, house 8 Chapel
Tallant Chas. H. clerk, C. M. & L. Railroad, house 48 State, cor. Thorndike [factory, bds. Phenix Hotel
Tallant James, painter, Abbot & Downing's carriage-manu-
Tallant John L. (*Tallant & Stevens*), merchants, East Concord, house do.
Tallant Mary A. widow of James, house 48 State
Tallant & Stevens, (*John L. Tallant and Sylvester Stevens*), merchants, East Concord
Tandy Calvin L. stone-cutter, house 10 Green
Tandy Charles H. stone-cutter, house Valley, cor. Forest
Tandy David, stone-mason, house High, near Franklin
Tandy David R. lather, house High, near Forest
Tandy Eben L. carpenter, house Chestnut, near High [lin
Tandy Elizabeth, widow of Franklin, house High, n. Frank-
Tandy Josiah, stone-cutter, bds. Mrs. E. Tandy's, High, near Franklin
Taylor Lucien C. farmer, house Fosterville
Taylor Wm. W. clerk Post Office, house 46 Warren
Tebaux Abigail C. widow of Lewis, house High, cor. Centre
Tebbetts Frank P. C. clerk, Phenix Hotel, bds. 33 Warren
Tebbetts Hiram B. physician, house 44 Main
Tebbetts Hiram W. physician, bds. 44 Main
Teel J. D. house 52 Main
Templeton Charles, machinist, house 41 Warren
Tenney Asa P. physician, house W. Concord [Spring
Tenney Franklin A. pattern-maker, N. Railroad, house 84
Tenney Gardner, carpenter, house East Concord
Thacher Henry S. house East Concord
Thayer Calvin, laborer, house 10 Tahanto
Thayer Eunice Mrs. widow of Charles G. house E. Concord
Thayer Wm. F. clerk P. O. boards 10 Tahanto
Therien Arsene, harness maker, 151 Main, bds. Amos Bean's
Thomas William W. stone cutter, boards Amos Bean's
Thompson Albert, machinist, house Merrimack, Fisherville
Thompson Albert H. mason, boards G. Thompson's, Hall
Thompson Ai B. captain U. S. Army, h. Union, n. Wash.
Thompson Charles B. hackman, Main, near Centre, boards 11 Montgomery
Thompson Charles E. mason, house 27 West
Thompson Cyrus A. express messenger, Depot, Railroad Sq.
Thompson Franklin W. stable keeper, Main, near Sherman House, house 11 Montgomery [n. Downing
Thompson George, moulder. at Ford & Kimball's, h. Spring,

Thompson George F. hoster, Main, opp. Free Bridge road, boards 11 Montgomery
Thompson George W. moulder, house Spring, near Clinton
Thompson Giles O. harness maker, bds. G. Thompson's, Hall
Thompson Goin, farmer, house Hall
Thompson Hannah J. Mrs. milliner, Main, b. Calvin Roberts'
Thompson Henry J. ten pin alley, Free Bridge road, boards Sherman House
Thompson Jas. laborer, b. J. C. Barnard's, High, n. Franklin
Thompson James, machinist, boards Sherman House
Thompson James, farmer, house Water, near Hall
Thompson John, laborer, house 211 Main
Thompson John E. (*J. L. Pickering & Co.*), grocers, 3 Masonic Temple, house 60 Pleasant, near Merrimack [South
Thompson John H. mason, house Downing, between State and
Thompson John S. insurance agent, boards Eagle Hotel
Thompson Philander, job wagon, house High, cor. Forest
Thorn Calvin, boot and shoe dealer, and city liquor agent, 240 Main, house 24 Centre
Thorn Charles H. boards 24 Centre
Thorn John C. clerk, 240 Main, boards 24 Centre
Thornton John, quarryman, house West Concord
Thurston Asa J. clerk, 1 Moore's block, boards C. C. Davis'
Tidd Pliny, blacksmith, house 48 Warren
Tilton Carey F. clerk, 132 Main, bds. A. J. Halls'
Tilton James M. teamster, house 20 Maple
Tilton Jesse J. stonecutter, boards Columbian Hotel
Tilton Jonathan L. farmer, house Main, cor. Penacook
Tilton Joseph E. carriage painter, house 128 State
Tilton Mary, widow of Andrew J. house South, near West
Tilton Samuel J. (*Dunklee & Tilton*), machinist, h. 165 State
Tinay Alice, wid. of Patrick, house rear Holden's Mill, West Concord
Titcomb John, wheelwright, house Washington, near State
Titus Charles D. cabinetmaker, h. Washington, Fisherville
Todd George E. supt. N. R. R. bds. H. Fessenden's, Spring, corner Pleasant
Topliff Charles C. physician, house Main, Fisherville
Towle Charles N. (*Murphy & Towle*), dentist, Masonic Temple, boards Eagle Hotel [Langley's, Perley
Towle Charles S. dentist, Masonic block, Main, boards A. J.
Towle Eben S. house State, cor. Franklin
Towle George S. lawyer, house Rumford, near Cambridge
Towle Lizzie S. Miss, tailoress, house 12 Chapel
Trainor Peter H. carpenter, house 11 Monroe
Tracy Luther, piano tuner, house Fulton
Trask Joseph O. wheelwright at Abbot's, house 12 Downing
Travellers Accidental Ins. Co., Hartford, Conn. C. W. Moore, agent, Hill's block, Main
Travers George, carpenter, house Rumford, near Centre

Treadwell Thomas P. house 46 Green
Trevor James A. house Wash. n. State [134 Main
Tripp David F. photograph artist, Merrimack block, house
Trussell Albert, clerk, boards Elm House
Trussell Samuel D. blacksmith, at Abbot's, h. 3 Downing
Tucker James J. house High, Fisherville [opp. Jackson
Tucker James, foreman at Wm. P. Ford & Co.'s, h. Franklin,
Tucker Fifield, cabinet maker, house High, Fisherville
Tucker Josiah P., Int. Rev. and Custom House Officer, house Main, opposite City Hall
Tucker Sarah M. widow of John T. house Green, n. Centre
Tucker William E. finisher, Prescott Bros'. house 1 Henry
Turner Charlès, stone cutter, boards Oliver Turner's
Turner Oliver, h. 34 Main [near Pleasant
Tuttle Hannah C. wid. of Hiram, carpet maker, house Spring,
Twombly Joseph C. teamster, house 227 State
Twomey John, baggage master, C. M. and L. R. R. house Main, near Franklin
Twomey Owen, laborer, house Forest, n. Valley
Tyner Richard, spinner, boards Joel D. Waller's

UNDERHILL CHARLES W. farmer, 8 Green
Underhill Fred. B. clerk R. Mayer's, house 17 Fayette
Underhill George F. (*Underhill & Kittredge*), druggist, State block, Main, house 5 Merrimack
Underhill Jonathan T. teller Union Bank, h. 50 Pleasant
Underhill & Kittredge, (*George F. Underhill and Perry Kittredge*), apothecaries, State block, Main
United States and Canada Express Co. Concord and Boston, &c. Depot, Railroad Square [junction of Railroads
Union Steam Mill Co.'s grist mill and planing mill, Main, n.
Upham Nathaniel G. house 6 Park
Upham Sidney S. blacksmith at Abbot's, boards 15 Downing
Upham Thomas, stone mason, house 15 Downing
Upton Grafton, carpenter C. R. R. h. 23 Thompson, c. Jefferson
Upton James H. tailor, 12 School, house Green, n. Centre
Urann George C. peddler, boards 68 Warren
Utley Samuel, clergyman, house Jackson, cor. Church

VANOS JOHN, harness maker, boards Philipye Pelkey's
Vatoon Charles T. fireman N. R. R. bds. Sherman House
Vaughn Marian Mrs. wid. of Almon, house West Concord
Verville Louis, laborer, house 3 Fosterville
Vesper Isaac N. machinist, house Summer, Fisherville
Vesper Joseph R. soapmaker, Washington, house do.
Vincent Francis, compositor, bds. O. Turner's, 84 Main
Vincent Morrison R. engineer Con. R. R. h. Hall, n. Water
Virgin Charles P. coachmaker at Abbot's, h. 12 State
Virgin John H. baker, house Clinton, opposite Spring
Virgin William W. pressman, boards Phenix Hotel

Virgin Wm. W. Mrs. clothes cleansing, 114 Main, h. do.
Vogler William, (*J. Brown & Co.*), furniture, Stickney's block, house 248 Main

WADKINS FREDERICK, cabinet maker, bds. J. B. Goldsmith's Main, corner Summer, Fisherville
Wadleigh Abbie T. Mrs. wid. Thomas, house 39 Main
Wadleigh Geo. W. milliner and millinery goods, Central buildings, bds. Phenix Hotel, h. Wash. cor. Union, Fisherville
Wadleigh Wm. R. saloon, Main, bds. G. W. Wadleigh's, Wash. corner Union, Fisherville
Wainwright Geo. A. tinsmith, house 14 Rumford
Waldron Dustin W. conductor N. R. R. house Fulton
Wales George W. house 10 Fayette
Walker Abigail B. Mrs. wid. of Timothy, Main, n. Penacook
Walker Elizabeth, wid. of Hazen, house 187 State
Walker Gust, hardware and agricultural tools, Phenix block, Main, house State, corner Centre
Walker Joseph B. pres. N. H. Savings Bank, 252 Main, house Main, near Penacook
Walker Judith Mrs. wid. of Flanders', boarding house 4 West
Walker Lyman A. farmer, house State, cor. Penacook
Walker Nathaniel B. (*Smith & Walker*), silversmith, Hutchins, house 29 South
Walker Priscilla C. Miss, tailoress, h. Rumford, cor. Short
Walker Stilman, brakeman, N. R. R. boards Wm. Walker's, Turnpike, near the brick yard
Walker Wm. 2d, h. Turnpike, near the brick yard
Walker Wm. R. cashier Merrimack County Bank, 252 Main, boards Porter Blanchard's, Main, near Montgomery
Walker & Co. (*Gust Walker and William D. Ladd*), iron and steel, Railroad square
Wallace Edwin P. clerk, bds. Hiram L. Wallace's, Summer, Fisherville
Wallace George H. stonecutter, b. David Silvers', E. Concord
Wallace Mary L. Miss, clerk, 8 Stickney's block, boards 36 Rumford [near Main, Fisherville
Wallace Nancy Mrs. wid. of John, bds. O. N. French's, Spring,
Wallace Samuel, stairbuilder, house Pearl, near State
Wallace William D. stairbuilder, bds. Samuel Wallace's
Waller Joel D. spinner woolen factory, house West Concord
Ward James F. carpenter, boards, 19 Union
Ward Lydia E. Mrs. widow of Thomas, house Summer, near Church, Fisherville
Warde David A. (*Warde, Humphrey & Co.*), hardware, &c. 1 and 2 Exchange block, house 66 Pleasant
Warde, Humphrey & Co. (*David A. Warde, Stillman Humphrey and George P. Cleaves*), hardware, 1 and 2 Exchange block
Warren Alpheus, machinist, Con. R. R. h. Perley, n. State

Warren Amos C., General Ticket Agt. N. R. R. office Depot, house 9 Green, corner Warren
Warren Benjamin S. physician, house Main, cor. Chapel
Warren John G. carpenter, house Church, Fisherville
Washburn James A. freight-conductor, bds. Columbian Hotel
Wason Charles T. carpenter, 53 Main
Watson Augustus, cigar-maker, 105 Main, boards 13 Wall
Watson Benjamin, cigars and tobacco, 105 Main, house Montgomery
Watson Jacob W. express-messenger, house 7 Union
Watson John B. carpenter, house 15 Washington
Wayland Christian, gardener at Morrill's, bds. E. Morrills' Spring, opp. Cross [Fisherville
Webber Daniel B. blacksmith, house Main, n. Washington,
Webster Albert, merchant, house Centre, near Union
Webster Andrew H. wheelwright, house 44 State
Webster Atkinson, carpenter, house 9 Tahanto
Webster Calvin C. wholesale and retail grocer, 2 & 3 Phenix block, house 40 Main
Webster Charles F. engineer, Con. Railroad, h. 18 Fayette
Webster Daniel S. teamster, house 4 Turnpike
Webster David, upholsterer, house 202 State [Thompson
Webster Freeman, conductor, Con. Railroad, house State, cor.
Webster George, laborer, bds. Joseph E. Phelps'
Webster Hannah C. Mrs. widow of Parker, house 18 Fayette
Webster J. Frank, cashier, C. M. & L. Railroad, house Cambridge, cor. Academy
Webster John C. (*Webster & Smith*), insurance agent, 12 State block, house Morse's block. 159 State
Webster John S. market-man, house 53 Warren
Webster Noah P. laborer, house West, near South [Wash.
Webster Oscar W. laborer, bds. Mrs. E. James, Walnut, near
Webster Peter W. carpenter, rear Low's block, house Washington, cor. Spring
Webster Robert S. house 62 Pleasant
Webster Stephen, foreman, Abbot's factory, house 68 Main
Webster Wm. E. machinist, house Spring, near Washington
Webster William L. market-man, opp. Phenix Hotel, boards 53 Warren [insurance agents, 12 State block
Webster & Smith, (*John C. Webster and George W. Smith*),
Weed Mary A. Mrs. widow of Monroe, bds. Ira E. Kenney's, Fisherville [South
Weeks George H. blacksmith at Abbot's, house Downing, n,
Weeks Hannah, widow of James, house Turnpike, near Allison [Rumford
Weeks Henry, machinist, N. Railroad, house 50 Warren, cor.
Weeks Henry M. blacksmith at Harvey, Morgan & Co.'s, bds. N. M. Weeks', Downing, near South
Weeks Jonathan B. farmer, house Turnpike, near Allison
Weeks Joseph S. painter, h. Turner's block, rear 26 Main

Weeks Nathaniel, carpenter, house West, near South [n. South
Weeks Nathaniel M. blacksmith at Abbot's, house Downing,
Welch Albion, farmer, house Walnut, near Tremont
Welch John, farmer, house East Concord
Welch Thomas, laborer, h. Main, opp. Church
Welcome Ambles, collar-maker, house Washington, n. Walnut
Welcome Field, carriage-maker, house Railroad Square
Welcome Joseph, carriage-builder, rear Low's block, house 48 Centre
Welcome Mark, collar-maker, house Centre, near Spring
Welcome Peter A. wheelwright, N. Railroad, house Prince, near Spring
Wellman Hannah K. Mrs. widow of Rev. J. h. 8 Pearl
Wells James M. wood-worker, Con. Railroad, bds. Mrs. J. N. Flanders', Perley
Wells Joseph, laborer, house East Concord
Wells Martin, fireman, house Hall, near Water
Wentworth Charlotte G. widow of Ephraim, dress-maker, Washington, near the jail, house do.
Wentworth Lydia Mrs. widow of Paul, house 24 Pleasant
Wentworth Philip, hair-dresser, Main, cor. Summer, house do. Fisherville [174 State
West Charles E. melodeon-maker at Parker & Secomb's, h.
West Christian, widow of Jacob W. house Rumford, corner Short
West John A. grocer, Main, cor. Ferry, house 3 Pearl
West Mary A. Mrs. widow of Joseph C. house 3 Pearl
West Nancy Mrs. widow of John, bds. 245 Main [Warren
West Ruel, plough-maker, Fords' foundry, house Spring, cor.
Weston Lon, agent, Charter Oak Life Ins. Co. Central block, bds. 25 Rumford [Co.'s, bds. J. P. Fay's, 15 Wall
Weymouth Worcester, book-keeper at N. S. Batchelder &
Whalan Lawrence, spinner, house W. Concord
Whalen Michael, laborer, house rear Robert Woodruff's
Wheeler Benj. farmer, house South, Wheeler's Corner
Wheeler Charles, reed-maker at Morgan's, bds. 4 West
Wheeler Giles, carpenter, house South, n. Wheeler's Corner
Wheeler Isaac F. b. Benj. Wheeler's, South, Wheeler's Corner
Wheeler John C. farmer, bds. Benj. Wheeler's, South Wheeler's Corner
Wheeler John, building-mover, house Green, cor. Centre
Wheeler Richard B. painter, 238 Main, bds. Centre, cor. Main
Whicher Simon B. teamster, house 52 Pleasant [erville
Whidden Henry R. farmer, house Cross, cor. Summer, Fish-
Whidden Jacob C. farmer, house Cross, cor. Summer, Fisherville [84 State
Whipple B. Plummer, ticket-seller, C. M. & L. Railroad, house
Whitaker Ruth Mrs. house West Concord
White Bessie Mrs. widow of Charles H. house Clinton
White Curtis, carpenter, house 64 Warren

White David, farmer, house Hall [ville
White Henry D. dentist, Mechanics block, house do. Fisher-
White John A. bds. 20 School
White John W. marble-worker, bds. Main, cor. Centre
White Nathaniel, express-man at U. S. and Canada Express Office, Depot, Railroad, house 20 School
White Simeon, carriage-smith at J. Welcome's, bds. J. Welcome's, Centre, opp. Hanover [Hotel
Whitford Edward L. clerk, N. Railroad Office, bds. Phenix
Whiting Charles, laborer, bds. Orin T. Clisby's
Whitmore John, wood-worker, C. Railroad, bds. 83 State
Whitney Edwin R. cooper, house Merrimack, Fisherville
Whitney George L. wood-worker, N. Railroad, house Union, cor. High [ney's
Whitney James K. painter, N. Railroad, bds. Joseph G. Whit-
Whitney Joseph G. blacksmith at Abbot's, b. Wm. Whitney's, West, near South
Whitney Wm. G. blacksmith at Abbot's, house West, n. South
Whittaker Gilman, stable-keeper, bds. Sherman House [erville
Whittaker John, lumber-dealer, bds. Washington House, Fish-
Whittemore George, hostler, bds. 350 Main
Whittemore Geo. P. carpenter, house Warren, near Liberty
Whittemore James C. mason, house 348 Main
Whittemore Wm. A. carpenter, bds. Warren, near Liberty
Whittle Wm. T. conductor, H. B. R. R., Depot, R. R. Square
Whittredge George B. (*Sturtevant & Whittredge*), grocers, 6 Main, house 10 Main
Whittredge Geo. F. dry goods, boots and shoes, &c. 10 Main, house 8 Main
Widmer Daniel, carriage-spring-maker at Abbot's, h. 7 Perley
Widmer Frederick W. miller, bds. Henry D. White's, Fisherville
Wiggin Albert W. house 164 State
Wiggin Augustus H. printer, house 5 Hanover
Wiggin Lucia A. Mrs. widow of Bradstreet, h. Chapel court
Wilder Robert H. carpenter, house 25 Union
Wilder Thomas, laborer, bds. 30 Warren
Wilder Thomas A. farmer, house Warren, near Washington
Wilkins George, carpenter, house 1 Main
Wilkins George H. machinist, house 36 West
Wilkinson Joseph H. clerk, h. Spring, n. Clinton
Willard Hattie E. Miss, boards 29 State
Willard Moses T., Postmaster, house 8 Centre
Willey Henry, stonecutter, boards Joseph E. Phelps'
Willey Zebulon, watchman C. M. & L. R. R. h. 32 Washington
Williams Andrew A. melodeon maker, h. Spring, n. Cross
Williams Danl. H. carriage trimmer at Abbot's, h. 73 South
Williams George H. A. trimmer at Abbot's, b. 10 Downing
Williams Isaac F. house 78 Main, corner Depot
Williams John, laborer, b. Mrs. Mary U. Scales', Clinton
Williams John, stonecutter, house 8 Union

Williams John, stonecutter, boards 4 Pearl
Williams John O. stonecutter, boards 4 Pearl
Williams Nathaniel, laborer at Abbot's, h. Turnpike, n. Main
Williams Otis A. house West Concord
Williams Willard, foreman at Abbot's, h. Main, n. Cross
Williamson Matilda Mrs. widow, house 24 Downing
Williamson William, blacksmith, house Downing, n. State
Wilson Edmund S. clerk Remick's, b. Thompson, c. South
Wilson George W. (*Wilson & Badger*), optical instruments, Exchange block, house Thompson, corner South
Wilson Nathaniel, hostler, boards Phenix Hotel
Wilson & Badger (*George W. Wilson and George A. Badger*), optical instruments, Exchange block, Main
Wilton George, painter, b. E. G. Cutting's, Summer, n. Court
Wing Albert T. stonecutter, house Pleasant, east Main
Winkley David, cutter at M. B. Critchett's, house 170 State
Winslow Dudley, laborer at Ford & Kimball's, house Hall, n. Water
Winslow John S. clerk Harris & Co's, boards Eagle Hotel
Withington James C. job compositor, boards 39 State
Wolcott Benj. F. woodworker N. R. R. house 34 Warren
Wolcott S. A. Mrs. fancy goods, 34 Warren, house do.
Wood Amos, house Spring, corner Pleasant
Wood Davis S. machinist N. R. R. house 19 Thompson
Wood Susan, widow of George, house Short, near Spring
Wood Tyler, stonecutter, boards Baldwin Humphrey's, West Concord
Woodbury Frank D. printer Monitor office, bds. 6 Pleasant
Woodbury Wm. W. carriage painter, Harvey, Morgan & Co's, house at West Concord [Allison, n. Turnpike
Woodman Addison L. machinist, boards Levi T. Woodman's,
Woodman Edgar H. bookkeeper, 2 Phenix block, b. Phenix Hotel [Allison
Woodman Edward S. machinist, boards Levi T. Woodman's,
Woodman Levi T. carpenter, house Allison, near Turnpike
Woodruff Robert, foreman Abbot's paint shop, house 22 Main
Woods Alba, brakeman N. R. R. house 6 Maple
Woods Dutton, bridge builder, house Merrimack, near School
Woods Levi C. engineer N. R. R. house 7 Summer
Woodward Alvin A. stonecutter, boards Amos Bean's
Woodward D. Rufus (*E. W. Woodward & Co.*), h. Elm, n. Thompson [tailor, Phenix Hotel building, h. 22 Pleasant
Woodward Ephraim W. (*E. W. Woodward & Co.*), merchant
Woodward E. W. & Co. (*Ephraim W. and D. Rufus Woodward*), merchant tailors, Phenix Hotel building
Woodward Jacob N. woodworker N. R. R. house Centre, cor. Rumford
Woodward Miss, tailoress, boards Main, corner Centre
Woolson Charlotte H. Mrs. widow of James, house Main, opp. Washington

Woolson Moses, principal High School, boards S. Quimby's, Tahanto, c. School
Worcester James, lumber dealer, house Spring, n. Pleasant
Worth Calvin, laborer, house Franklin, near Walnut
Worthen George W. soapmaker at M. Critchett & Son's, bds. M. Critchett's, Rumford, corner Washington
Worthington George, carriagesmith, house East Concord
Wright George (*J. W. & George E. Wright*), glove maker, Moore's block, Main, house at New York
Wright H. N. express messenger, boards Columbian Hotel
Wright J. W. & Geo. E. glovemakers, Moore's block, Main
Wright J. W. (*J. W. & George E. Wright*), Moore's block, house at New York
Wright Rensselaer O. cutter, Stickney's block, boards L. B. [Morrill's
Wright T. H. expressman, boards Columbian Hotel
Wyatt Hattie, widow Charles C. house Cross, corner State
Wyatt Joseph G. fish and provisions, 1 Warren, h. 36 Main
Wyman George A. fireman N. R. R. boards 141 State
Wyman Horace G. house 3 Winter
Wyman Jesse E. farmer, house 29 Warren
Wyman Jesse H. mechanic, b. Ezekiel S. Reed's, Fisherville
Wyman Jos. J. dealer in tripe, tallow, &c. Walnut, c. Church, house do.
Wyman Reuben G. butcher, house 141 State
Wyman Wm. H. jr. butcher, boards 141 State

YEATON ALBERT H. cutter, boards M. B. Critchett's
Young Alfred, butcher, boards Asa M. Bond's
Young Alva A. butcher at Bond's, boards Asa M. Bond's, Pleasant, near Main
Young Geo. A. (*Cummings & Young*), dentist, Phenix block, [Main, h. 1 Monroe
Young Geo. S. iron fence maker at Ford & Kimball's, house State, corner Winter
Young Levi T. carpenter, house 24 Thorndike
Young Thomas W. house Green, near Bowery avenue
Young William Henry, printer, boards T. W. Young's, Green, near Bowery avenue

# CONCORD BUSINESS

# DIRECTORY,

## FOR 1867-8.

### Agricultural Warehouses and Stores.

FORD WILLIAM P. & CO. 235 Main (see advt. opp. advt. index, p. 9)
MOORE & CILLEY, 212 Main (see adv. dept. page 4)
WALKER GUST., Phenix block (see adv. dept. p. 6)
WARDE, HUMPHREY & CO. 1 and 2 Exchange (see advt. on opposite page)

### Ale, Porter, &c.

ADAMS G. H. & C. G. opp. Phenix Hotel, Main (see adv. dept. p. 4)

### Apothecaries.

EASTMAN & CO., Hill's block, Main (see advt. inside front cover)
FOSTER H. B. 129 Main (see advt. first colored page)
Morgan James & Co. 103 Main
ROLLINS J. S. & Co., Main, Fisherville (see adv. dept. p. 17)
Rollins & Co. opp. State House, Main
UNDERHILL & KITTREDGE, State block, Main (see advt. opp. title-page)

### Architect.

DOW EDWARD, Masonic Temple, Main (see adv. dept. p. 22)

## Artificial Limbs.

JEWETT LEG CO., William Carr, manager, Central block, Main (see advt. opp. preface)

## Artists.

Clough D. Ansel, Exchange block, Main
Moore Henry P., Henry, corner Church

## Auctioneers.

Durgin Jeremiah S., Main, Fisherville
Shattuck S. W. 3 Moore's block (up stairs), Main

## Bakers.

Norris James S. & Co. 85 Main

## Bankers.

MINOT & CO. over Post Office, School (see adv. dept. p. 24)

## Banks.

(*See also Savings Banks.*)

First National Bank, Stickney's block, Main
National State Capital Bank, 11 State block, Main
Union Bank, Central block, Main

## Bedstead Manufacturers.

ELWELL ISAAC & SON, near Concord Railroad Freight Depot (see adv. dept. p. 24)

## Belting Manufacturers.

ROBINSON C. & SONS, Penacook (see advt. front colored page)

## Belting.

WALKER GUST., Phenix block (see adv. dept. page 6)
WARDE, HUMPHREY & Co. 1 and 2 Exchange (see advt. page 102)

## Billiard Halls.

Colston H. N. 99 Main
Pendergast John, Main, Fisherville
Rand Hamilton L., Hill's block

## Blacksmiths.

Chesley Samuel M., Union Steam Mill
Cochran J. C. old Downing Stand, opp. Phenix Hotel

Fuller Hilton, Turnpike, corner West
Gill Bradbury, rear Stickney's block
ROBINSON C. G., Warren (see index to adv'ts. page 7)
ROGERS BROOKS E., Main, opp. Spring, Fisherville (see adv. dept. p. 18)
Silver Wm. C., Warren, corner Pine
Welcome Joseph, rear Low's block

## Blank Book Manufacturer.

CRAWFORD FRED'K S., Statesman building (see adv. dept. p. 12)

## Boarding Houses.

Adams Benjamin O., Main, corner Centre
Baker Charles E. 9 West Canal
Blodgett Eliza Miss, 18 Centre
Brown John, 13 Wall
Choate Sarah G. Mrs. Summer, cor. Centre, Fisherville
Fish Daniel, West Concord road
Fitts Dexter, School, cor. Spring
Flanders Jane N. Mrs., Perley, near State
Flanders Mary J. Mrs., State, near Pleasant
French Richard J., West Canal, Fisherville
Hook Joseph B., Main, first door north of City Hall
Howe Isaac G. 33 Green
Johnson Warren, Washington, near Main, Fisherville
Mills Seba H. 1 State
Neal Mary N. Mrs., Ash, cor. Fayette
Pelkey Philipye, Short, near Spring
Sawin Harriet Mrs., 83 State
Smith Mahala D. Mrs. 11 Wall
Walker Judith Mrs., 1 West

## Booksellers and Stationers.

CHANDLER L. (periodicals), Main, c. School (see adv. dept. p. 3)
Eastman Edson C., 160 Main
Fisk William H., Eagle Book Store, Stickney's new block, Main
GUERNSEY D. L. & CO., State block, Main (see advt. opp. title page)
NOYES S. G., Main, Fisherville (see adv. dept. p. 13)
Sanborn B. W. & Co., Sanborn's block, Main

## Book Binders.

CRAWFORD FRED. S., Main, cor. Depot (see adv. dept. p. 12)
Giles Nicholas, Stickney's block, Main
Morrill & Silsby, Central block, Main

## Boots and Shoes, Retail.

Bean Moses H., 5 Mechanics block, Fisherville
Clifford Joseph E., Stickney's new block, Main
French Joseph, School, opp. Post Office
Gage & Andrews, Central block, Main
Gilman William, opp. Statesman building, Main
HARRIS & CO., State block, Main (see adv. dept. p. 17)
Moore George H., 5 Exchange block, Main
Moulton J. S., Main, opp. Free Bridge road
Munsey Frank P., City Block, Main
Sanders J. P., Main, Fisherville
Thorn Calvin, 240 Main
WHITTREDGE GEO. F., 10 Main, (see adv. dept. p. 20)

## Boots and Shoes, Wholesale and Retail.

BACHELDER G. H., 160 Main (up stairs), (see adv. dept. page 26)
Hazeltine Life A., 240 Main [dept. p. 15)
PIPER & CLOUGH, opp. State Capital Bank (see adv.
Smith J. M., 164 Main

## Boot and Shoe Findings.

Hill Chase, 147 Main

## Boot and Shoe Makers.

Bean Moses H., 5 Mechanics block, Fisherville
Clark Hiram, 71 South
Fairfield William B., Main, opp. Pearl
French Joseph, School, opp. Post Office
Gatley Richard, 7 Warren
Grover Loring, 5 Warren
Lacosse Joseph, 3 Warren
Pease John, South, cor. Cross
Rollins John, 143 Main
Saunders Daniel J. rear of the Depot, West Concord
Savary Thomas W., Main, Fisherville

## Boot and Shoe Manufacturers.

BACHELDER GEO. H., Main, opp. School (see adv. dept. page 26)
Gilman William, opp. Statesman building, Main
Munsey Frank P., City block, Main
PIPER & CLOUGH, opp. State Capital Bank, Main, (see adv. dept. p. 15)

## Brass Founders.

FORD & KIMBALL, Railroad Square (see adv. dept. p. 20)

## Brick Manufacturer.

Bowers Joseph R., Turnpike

## Broom Manufacturer.

Vogler William, 248 Main

## Builders.

Mead, Mason & Co., Union Steam Mill, Office School, opp. Post Office

## Business Colleges.

SHARPE WM. H., Main, cor. Depot

## Butchers.

*(See also Meat Markets.)*

Wyman Joseph J., Walnut, cor. Church
Wyman R. G., Main, opp. Free Bridge Road

## Cabinet Makers.

Hill Daniel A. rear of Stickney's block

## Candle Manufacturers.

Critchett M. & Son, Walnut, near Washington

## Carpenters and Joiners.

Brainerd Duane D., State, cor. Thompson
Clifford & Currier, rear Stickney's block
Dow Lorenzo, State, near Cross
HUTCHINSON E. B., Pleasant, near Main, (see adv. dept. p. 22)
Runals John B. Warren, near Prince
Shaw David, 25 Monroe
Webster Peter W. rear Low's block

## Carpets and Oil Cloths.

ALLEN W. H., Main, Fisherville, (see adv. dept. p. 19)
Stearns W. B. opp. State House, Main

## Carriage Hardware.

WARDE, HUMPHREY & CO. 1 and 2 Exchange (see advt. page 102)

## Carriage Manufacturers.

Abbot, Downing & Co., 17 Main
Griffin S. M., 253 Main
Harper Charles S., East Concord
HARVEY, MORGAN & CO. 58 Main
Welcome Joseph, rear of Low's block

## Carriage Painters.

Davis & Giles, rear Low's block

## Carriage Smiths.

Brockway George W. rear of the Depot, West Concord
Harper Charles S., East Concord [dept. p. 26)
ROBINSON CHESTER G., Warren, near Main (see adv.

## Car Wheel Manufacturers.

FORD & KIMBALL, Railroad square (see adv. dept. pp. 4 and 20)

## Churn Manufacturers.

BLANCHARD PORTER & SONS, 211 Main (see advertising department page 11)

## Cigars and Tobacco.

Watson Benjamin, 105 Main

## Civil Engineers.

DUNKLEE & TILTON, 60 Main, (see advt. dept. p. 16)

## Claim Agents.

Dewey H. K., Phenix block
STEVENS & LUND, Main, opp. School (see adv. dept. p. 7)

## Clairvoyant.

Hatch Robinson Mrs., Prince, near Spring

## Clergymen.

Adams Elisha, 205 State
Baker Osman C., 207 State
Barry John A., School, corner Huntingdon
Bouton Nathaniel, Main, opposite City Hall
Cooke Samuel, 56 State
Couch John, Rumford, near Cambridge

Cummings Eben E. 23 Green
Curtis Silas, Rumford, near Washington
Eames J. H., 33 Main
Faunce Daniel W., 29 Green
Fiske Albert W., Summer, opp. Church, Fisherville
Holman S., Chaplain at Prison
Kendall Henry A., East Concord
Kenney Ira E., Elm, Fisherville
Kittredge F. E., Eagle Hotel
Lovering Joseph F. 88 State
Merrill John W. 161 State
Moulton A. K., Fayette, near State
Patten David, 34 Washington
Stone Benjamin P. 69 Main
Utley Samuel, Jackson, corner Church

## Clocks and Watches.

DREW GEO. W. & CO., opposite State House, Main (see advertisement page following Business Directory)
Galloway J., 159 Main
Hall Ivory, 262 Main

## Clothing Dealers.

BROWN S. F., Main, Fisherville (see advt. dept. p. 12)
CRITCHETT M. B., Main, c. Warren (see advt. dept. p. 1)
EDMUNDS A. J., Eagle block (see advt. opp. preface, p. 6)
HILL JOHN H. 118 Main (see adv. dept. page 26)
LINCOLN & SHAW, Exchange bld., (see adv. dept. p. 7)
Peck F. S. & Co., 114 Main
STEWART T. W. & J. H., Rumford's block (see advertising department, page 15)
STRAUSS HERMAN, 1 Hill's block, Main (see advertising department, page 21)

## Clothes Cleansers.

VIRGIN WM. W. MRS., 114 Main (see adv. dept. p. 8)

## Coal and Wood.

Ranlet H. W. & Co., Hill's avenue, corner R. R. square

## Coffin Ware Rooms.

BROWN JOSEPH, Main, opp. Ford's Warehouse (see adv. dept. p. 2)
COBURN JOHN A., Main, Fisherville, (see adv. dept. p. 16)

## Collector.

CHASE DEXTER, Main, opposite State House

## Commissioners for Mass. and U. S. Courts.

FOWLER A. & F. A., 134 Main (see adv. dept. p. 4)

## Commission Merchants.

PRESCOTT E. P. & CO., 42 Railroad square (see advertising department page 22)
QUIMBY S. & CO., 6 Pleasant (see adv. dept. p. 19)

## Concord Axle Manufacturers.

BROWN D. ARTHUR & CO., Fisherville (see advt. front colored page)

## Confectionery, Fruits, &c.

BRADBURY F. C. & J. Y., Stickney's new block, Main (see adv. dept. p. 15)
CHANDLER L., Main, cor. School, (see adv. dept. p. 3)
Gillis Joseph, 14 School
Hoit Sewall, Main, near Columbian Hotel
MORRILL J. H. opp. State House, Main, (see advt. p. 5)
Niles S. W., Chase's building, Main
Norris Jas. S. & Co., 85 Main
PIPER & HASKINS, Central block, Main (see advt. front colored page)

## Cotton Goods Manufacturers.

BROWN H. H. & J. S., Fisherville

## Copper, Tin and Sheet Iron Workers.

CARROLL L. H., Moore's block, Main, (see adv. dept. p. 7)
CHASE J. H., Main, opp. Statesman building (see advt. last white page)
DANFORTH R. C. Fisherville, (see adv. dept. p. 18)
STEVENS & DUNCKLEE, Main, opp. Phenix Hotel (see advt. opp. Streets, Courts, &c. page 12)

## Crockery and Glass Ware.

Blood S., Central building, 132 Main
DANFORTH R. C., Main, Fisherville, (see adv. dept. p. 18)
Stearns W. B. opp. State House, Main

## Dentists.

Blaisdell J., Exchange block, Main
Cummings & Young, Phenix block
Fletcher William W., Stickney's block, Main
Little J. W. 176 Main
Murphy & Towle, Masonic Temple, Main
White H. D., Mechanics' block, Fisherville

## Deputy Sheriff.

Merrill J. B., Main, J. P. Johnson's, opp. State House

## Dining Room.

(*See also Eating Houses.*)

BRADBURY F. C. & J. Y. Stickney's block, Main, (see adv. dept. p. 15)
PIPER & HASKINS, Central block, Main, (see adv. front colored page)

## Dress Makers.

Abbott Esther N. Miss, Spring, cor. Pleasant
Brown S. K. Mrs. Main, bds. Washington House, Fisherville
Convers R. A. Miss, Central block, Main
Couch Mahala Mrs. 83 State
Crawford Jane L. Miss, City block, Main
Flanders Mary D. 157 State
Jones David B. Mrs. Central block, Main
Noyes Clary A. Miss, 4 State block, Main
Ordway H. S. Miss, Stickney's new block, Main
Piper Mary S. Mrs. 12 Tremont
Wentworth Charlotte G., Washington, near the jail

## Dry Goods Dealers.

ALLEN W. H., Main, Fisherville, (see adv. dept. p. 19)
Andrews William G., Central block, Main
Brown T. H. Mrs. 4 Statesman building, Main
BROWN & LINEHAN, Main, n. the bridge, Fisherville, (see adv. dept. p. 18)
Chadwick Hale, Main, Fisherville
Churchill, Kilburn & Co., Main, opp. Post Office
Clarke David E. 5 Exchange block, Main
Eastman & Currier, West Concord
Evans Franklin, Main, south of Pleasant
FARNAM & OSGOOD, Main, cor. Free Bridge road, (see advt. opp. preface)
FISK F. A. Main, opp. Church, (see adv. dept. p. 21)

FRENCH T. J. 153 Main, (see adv. dept. p. 11)
HARRIS & CO., State block, Main, (see adv. dept. p. 17)
HAZELTON JAMES, 158 Main, (see advt. p. 18)
Johnson John P. 8 Stickney's block, Main
Putnam & Hall, Main, Fisherville
Putney John, East Concord
Sanborn A. B. & Co. South end State block, Main
Tallant & Stevens, East Concord
WHITTREDGE GEO. F. 10 Main, (see adv. dept. p. 20)

## Dye House.

Holden B. F. & D., West Concord

## Engineers.

DUNKLEE & TILTON, 60 Main, (see adv. dept. p. 16)

## Expresses.

CHENEY & CO. UNITED STATES AND CANADA EXPRESS, Depot, Railroad Square, and I. C. Edgerly, agent, Washington House, Fisherville (see advt. front colored page)

## Fancy Goods.

BRADBURY F. C. & J. Y., Stickney's new block, Main, (see adv. dept. p. 15)
CARR NORMAN G., Statesman block (see advt. opp. preface, p. 2)
EASTMAN & CO. Hill's block, Main, (see advt. inside front cover)
FOSTER H. B. 129 Main (see advt. first colored page)
KNIGHT E. Stickney's block, Main, (see adv. dept. p. 16)
Moffatt Alexander, next door to Phenix block, Main
MORRILL SAM'L F. & CO. 119 Main (see adv. dept. page 1)
Morrill & Silsby, Central block, Main
NOYES S. G., Main, Fisherville, (see adv. dept. p. 13)
PIPER & HASKINS, Central block, Main (see advt. front colored page)
ROLLINS J. S. & CO., Fisherville (see adv. dept. p. 17)
Rollins & Co. opp. State House, Main
SHERMAN ALDEN P. 149 Main, (see adv. dept. p. 11)
STANLEY & AYER, Phenix Hotel building, (see adv. dept. p. 3)
UNDERHILL & KITTREDGE, State block, Main, (see advt. opp. title page)
Wolcott S. A. Mrs. 34 Warren
WHITTREDGE GEO. F. 10 Main, (see adv. dept. p. 20)

## Fish Markets.

Wyatt Joseph G. 1 Warren
MITCHELL & GALE, Main, opp. Depot, (see adv. dept. p. 8)
WEBSTER C. C. 2 and 3 Phenix block (see advt. front colored page)

## Flour and Grain, Wholesale and Retail.

Barron, Dodge & Co., Railroad Square
Barter Lewis & Co. 8 Pleasant
BATCHELDER N. S. & CO. 5 Statesman building, (see adv. dept. p. 6)
FISK F. A. 336 & 338 Main, (see adv. dept. p. 21)
FRENCH & COCHRAN, Main, cor. Pleasant, (see adv. dept. p. 13)
KILBURN E. G. & CO. 2 Moore's block, (see adv. dept. p. 4)
PEARSON J. H. & CO., Railroad Square (see advt. p. 4).
PRESCOTT E. P. & CO. 42 Railroad Square, (see adv. dept. p. 22)
QUIMBY S. & CO. 6 Pleasant, (see adv. dept. p. 19)
WEBSTER C. C. 2 and 3 Phenix block (see advt. front colored page)

## Fruit Dealers, Wholesale and Retail.

WEBSTER C. C. 2 & 3 Phenix block (see advt. front colored page)

## Furnaces and Ranges.

CARROLL L. H. Moore's block, (see adv. dept. p. 7)

## Furniture Dealers.

Bradford O. K., Washington Square, Fisherville
BROWN J. & CO., Stickney's block, opp. State House, Main, (see adv. dept. p. 15)
Hill D. A. 238 Main
Shattuck S. W., 3 Moore's block, (up stairs), Main

## Furniture Manufacturers.

CALDWELL & AMSDEN, Main, Fisherville, (see adv. dept. p. 18)
ELWELL ISAAC & SON, near Freight Depot, (see adv. dept. p. 24)

## Gas and Steam Fitters.

Badger William, office, Gas Light Co.
Morse & Putnam, School, near Post Office

## Gas Light Company.

Concord Gas Light Company, 4 White's block, Capital

## Gents' Furnishing Goods.

BROWN SAMUEL F., Main, Fisherville (see advertising department, page 12)
Chandler Frank, Main, Fisherville
CRITCHETT M. B., City block, Main, corner Warren, (see adv. dept. page 1)
EDMUNDS A. J., Eagle block (see advt. opp. index to advertisements, page 6)
HILL JOHN H. 118 Main (see adv. dept. page 26)
LINCOLN & SHAW, Exchange bldg. (see adv. dept. p. 7)
Sanders J. P., Main, Fisherville
SLEEPER J. T., Stickney's block, Main (see adv. dept. p. 16)
STEWART T. W. & J. H., Rumford block (see advertising department page 15)
STRAUSS HERMAN, 1 Hill's block, Main (see advertising department, page 21)

## Glove Manufacturers.

Wright J. W. & George, Moore's block, Main

## Grist Mill.

Union Steam Mill, Main

## Grocers.

Andrews Asa G., Washington, cor. Rumford
Batchelder J. & Co., Washington square, Fisherville
BROWN & LINEHAN, Main, Fisherville (see advertising department, page 17)
Eastman & Currier, W. Concord
Evans Franklin, Main, south of Pleasant
FARNAM & OSGOOD, Main, cor. Free Bridge road (see advt. opp. preface)
FISK F. A., Main, opp. Church (see adv. dept. p. 21)
HOIT J. F. & CO., Masonic Temple, Main (see advt. first colored page)
Marden Alfred L., West Concord
Pearson John M., State, cor. Downing
Pickering J. L. & Co. 3 Masonic Temple Pleasant
Pitman O. V. & W. H., Main, cor. Free Bridge road
Putnam & Hall, Main, Fisherville
Putney John, East Concord
Remick Granville L., Merrimack block, Main
Rowell & Clough, Washington, near Rumford
Sanborn A. B. & Co. south end State block, Main

STURTEVANT & WHITTREDGE, 6 Main (see adv. dept. p. 19)
Tallant & Stevens, E. Concord
Union Store, Main, Fisherville
West J. A., Main, cor. Ferry road

## Grocers, Wholesale and Retail.

BATCHELDER N. S. & CO., 5 Statesman building, Main (see adv. dept. p. 6)
Hutchins & Co., Depot square
KILBURN E. G. & CO., 2 Moore's block, opp. Masonic Temple (see adv. dept. p. 4)
PRESCOTT E. P. & CO., 42 Railroad square (see adv. dept. p. 22)
WEBSTER C. C. 2 and 3 Phenix block (see advt. front colored page)

## Guns, Rifles, and Fishing Tackle.

Eastman John J., 236 Main

## Hair Dressers.

Allen C. W. 145 Main
Anderson W. S. next door to Eagle Hotel, Main
Calif Joseph W. 2 Mechanics block, Fisherville
Cardenas M., City block, Main
CORNING W. H. under Phenix Hotel (see adv. dept. p. 9)
Proctor C. H., Masonic Temple, Main
Wentworth Philip, Main, cor. Summer

## Hair Worker.

GAWLER ROBERT A., Low's block, School (see adv. dept. p. 21)

## Hardware and Cutlery.

CARROLL L. H., Main, near Elm House (see adv. dept. page 7)
DANFORTH R. C., Main, Fisherville (see adv. dept. p. 18)
MOORE & CILLEY, 212 Main (see adv. dept. p. 4)
Rines Nathaniel P. 68 Warren
WALKER GUST., Phenix block, Main (see adv. dept. page 6)
WARDE, HUMPHREY & CO. 1 & 2 Exchange (see advt. p. 102)

## Harness Makers.

COBURN JOHN A., Main, Fisherville (see adv. dept. p. 16)
Comery Alex., 3 Warren
Cutler Israel P., Prescott's block, opp. Columbian Hotel, Main
Hill James R. & Co. 151 Main
Johnson J. D. 234 Main
Rogers William H., Main, opp. Free Bridge road
Shallies & Lawrence, 5 Warren

## Hats, Caps and Furs.

Coffin Oliver C., Stickney's new block, Main
CRITCHETT M. B., City block, Main, cor. Warren (see adv. dept. p. 1)
LINCOLN & SHAW, Exchange bldg. (see adv. dept. p. 7)
Sanger Austin T., Low's block, opp. Post Office
STRAUSS HERMAN, 1 Hill's block, Main (see adver. dept. page 21)

## Hoop Skirts and Corsets.

HALLETT G. W., Statesman block, Main (see adv. dept. p. 2)
QUIMBY NICHOLAS & CO. (manuf.) 232 Main (see advt. dept. p. 11)

## Horse Nail Manufacturer.

BROWN D. ARTHUR & CO., Fisherville (see advt. front colored page)

## Horse Shoers.

(*See also Blacksmiths.*)

Fitch George E., old Downing stand, opp. Phenix Hotel
ROGERS BROOKS E., Main, Fisherville (see adv. dept. page 17)

## Hotels.

Columbian Hotel, G. C. Fuller, Proprietor, 163 Main
Eagle Hotel, T. A. Ambrose, Proprietor, opp. State House, Main
Elm House, J. S. Dutton, Main, cor. Pleasant
PHENIX HOTEL, Langdon Littlehale, Proprietor, Main, n. Passenger Depot (see adv. dept. p. 5)
SHERMAN HOUSE, James Chesley, Proprietor, Main, opp. Free Bridge road (see adv. dept. p. 19)
WASHINGTON HOUSE, I. C. Edgerly, Proprietor, Washington square, Fisherville (see advt. p. 101)

## Ice Dealers.

Ranlet H. W. & Co., Hill's av. cor. R. R. square

## Ink Manufacturer.

FOSTER H. B. 129 Main (see advt. first colored page)

## Insurance Agents.

Campbell & Hall, 6 State block, Main
EASTMAN S. & S. C., Rumford block, Main (see adv. dept. p. 8)
HODGDON & MERRIAM, 9 State block, Main (see adv. dept. p. 20)
Jackman Lyman, 6 State block
Kayes H. G., Phenix Hotel building
MOORE CHARLES W., Hill's block, Main (see advt. opp. index to advertisements)
Osgood R. C., Stickney's new block, Main
Prescott Abraham J., Exchange block, Main
Robinson Wesley J., State block, Main
WEBSTER & SMITH, 12 State block, Main (see adv. dept. p. 10)
Weston Lon, Central block, Main

## Insurance Companies.

Ætna Fire Ins. Co., Hartford, Conn., C. W. Moore, agent, Hill's block, Main
ÆTNA LIFE INS. CO. of Hartford, Webster & Smith agents, 12 State block (see adv. dept. p. 10)
CITY FIRE INS. CO. of Hartford, Webster & Smith Agents, State block (see adv. dept. p. 10)
Commerce Fire Ins. Co., Albany, N. Y., Stickney's new block
EQUITABLE MUTUAL FIRE INS. CO., Mitchell Gilmore, Secy. and Treas., Sanborn's block, Main (see adv. dept. p. 14)
Hartford Accidental Ins. Co., Campbell & Hall Agents, 6 State block, Main
HARTFORD FIRE INS. CO., Webster & Smith, Agents, State block (see adv. dept. p. 10)
JOHN HANCOCK MUTUAL LIFE INS. CO. of Boston, Hodgdon & Merriam, Agents, 9 State block, Main, (see adv. dept. p. 20)
LORILLARD FIRE INS. CO. of New York, Hodgdon & Merriam, Agents, 9 State block, Main (see adv. dept. page 20)

Mutual Life Ins. Co. of New York, R. C. Osgood, agent, Stickney's new block, Main

NIAGARA FIRE INS. CO. of N. Y., Webster & Smith, Agents, State Block (see adv. dept. p. 10)

PHŒNIX MUTUAL LIFE INS. CO., Hartford, Conn., C. W. Moore, agent, Hill's block, Main (see advt. opp. index to advts. page 7)

Springfield Fire and Marine Ins. Co., Springfield, Mass., C. W. Moore, agent, Hill's block, Main

Union Mutual Life Ins. Co., Boston, Campbell & Hall, Agents, 6 State block, Main

## Iron Foundries.

FORD WM. P. & CO,, 235 Main (see adv. opp. adv. index to advertisements)

FORD & KIMBALL, near Freight Depot, Railroad square, (see advt. p. 4)

## Iron and Steel.

WALKER & CO., Railroad square (see adv. dept. p. 6)

WARDE, HUMPHREY & CO., 1 and 2 Exchange (see advt. page 102)

## Job Wagons.

Foster Ira, State, cor. Thorndike

Morrill Willis H. 12 State

Nye George S., Cross, near Jefferson

Thompson Philander, High, cor. Forest

## Kitchen Furnishing Goods.

CARROLL L. H., 4 Moore's block, Main, near Elm House (see adv. dept. p. 7)

## Lace Leather.

ROBINSON C. & SONS, Penacook (see advt. front colored page)

## Last Manufacturers.

HAYNES JOHN, Union Steam Mill (see adv. dept. p. 26)

## Lawyers.

Albin J. Henry, Central block, Main

BADGER BENJ. E., Stickney's block, Main

BADGER STEPHEN C., Stickney's block, Main

Blanchard George S., Exchange building, Main

Butterfield J. Ware, Stickney's block, Main

DANA S., office Rumford block, Main
Eastman Ira A., Central block, Main
EASTMAN S. C., Rumford block, Main (see adv. dept. p. 8)
Fletcher Arthur, Main, opp. School
FOGG GEORGE G., Main, opp. Court House
Foster & Sanborn, Sanborn's block, Main
Fowler George R. 312 Main
FOWLER A. & F. A., Merrimack block, 134 Main (see adv. dept. p. 4)
GEORGE JOHN, Sanborn's block, Main (see adv. dept. p. 3)
George John H., White's block, Capital
Goodwin William F. 45 School
HADLEY AMOS, Monitor office, School
Lane S. G., Hill's block
MARSHALL & CHASE, 2 and 3 State block, Main (see adv. dept. p. 6)
Minot & Mugridge, Hill's block, Main
Perkins Hamilton E., Stickney's block, Main
Potter Alvah K., Stickney's block, Main
Rolfe Henry P., Stickney's block, Main
Stevens Samuel H. 162 State
STEVENS & LUND, Main, opp. School, (see adv. dept. p. 7)
Towle George S., Rumford, near Cambridge

## Leather Belting.

(*See Belting.*)

## Liquor Agent.

Thorn Calvin, 240 Main

## Machinists.

BROWN D. ARTHUR & CO., Fisherville (see advt. front col. page)
DUNKLEE & TILTON, 60 Main (see adv. dept. p. 16)

## Mackerel Kit Manufacturer.

Humphrey Moses, West Concord

## Maps and Pictures.

GUERNSEY D. L. & CO., State block (see advt. opp. title page)

## Marble Workers.

Cummings G. A., 89 Main
FARLEY H. N. & CO., Main, cor. Depot
Farley Nathan, Main, cor. Depot

## Meat Markets.

Bond A. M., Pleasant, near Main
Hart William & Co., 16 School
MITCHELL & GALE, opp. Depot, Main (see adv. dept. page 8)
Moores Nathan W., Main, opposite Free Bridge road
Peaslee Cyrus, Main, near Free Bridge road
Webster John S., opp. Phenix House, Main
Wyman R. G., Main, opp. Free Bridge road

## Masonic Regalias.

DREW GEO. W. & CO, opp. State House, Main (see advt. page 130)
MORRILL S. F. & CO., Central block Main (see adv. dept. page 1)

## Masons.

Bean J. W. & Bros., Pleasant, near Main
Dow, Kenney & Clifford, Main, opp. Columbian Hotel
Ordway & Robinson, 7 Warren

## Melodeon and Organ Manufacturers.

AUSTIN CHARLES E., Railroad sq. (see adv. dept. p. 11)
PARKER & SECOMB, warerooms, Phenix block, manuf'y opp. Court House (see adv. dept. p. 17)
PRESCOTT JOSEPH W., Exchange block, Main (see adv. dept. p. 8)

## Melodeon and Organ Reed Manufacturers.

Austin Charles, Railroad square
Davis & Morgan, Union Steam Mill

## Melodeon, Organ, and Piano Stool Manuf.

PARKER & SECOMB, Phenix block (see adv. dept. p. 17)
Prescott Brothers, Exchange block, Main

## Milliners and Millinery Goods.

Batchelder Addie M. Mrs., 4 Mechanics block, Fisherville
Brown T. H. Mrs., 4 Statesman building, Main
Butters S. F. Miss, Sanborn's block, Capital
Crawford Jane L. Miss, City block, Main
HAZELTON JAMES, 158 Main (see adv. dept. opp. first page general directory)
Jones David B. Mrs., Central block, Main

MARSHALL E. H. MRS. & CO., Stickney's new block, Main (see adv. dept. p. 14)
SMITH M. M. MRS. 164 Main (see adv. dept. p. 8)
Thompson H. J. Mrs., Main, Fisherville
Wadleigh Geo. W. 130 Main, Central building

## Newspaper Publishers.

CONCORD DAILY MONITOR, Durgin's block, School, Independent Press Association, Publishers, (see adv. dept. p. 25)
INDEPENDENT DEMOCRAT, Durgin's block, School, Independent Press Association, Publishers (see adv. dept. p. 25)
NEW HAMPSHIRE PATRIOT & STATE GAZETTE, Sanborn's block, Main, Wm. Butterfield, Publisher
NEW HAMPSHIRE STATESMAN, Main, cor. Depot, McFarland & Jenks, Publishers

## Notaries Public.

(*See also City and County Register.*)

Dewey H. K., Phenix block
GEORGE JOHN, Sanborn's block, (see adv. dept. p. 3)
Lane S. G., Hill's block

## Nurserymen.

Main & Nutter, 3 Merrimack

## Nurses.

Ashton Elizabeth Mrs. 39 State
Coburn Elizabeth, Liberty, cor. Warren

## Optical Instruments.

Wilson & Badger, Exchange building, Main

## Painters, House and Sign.

Abbott Geo. jr., 9 Warren
Bradford O. K., Washington Square, Fisherville
Carpenter Preston J., West Concord
Cutting Amos D., Academy, near Washington
Cutting Eben E., Summer, near Court
Estabrooks A. G., opp. Phenix Hotel
Moulton Edward A. 30 Union
Rounsefell James, (sign), Pleasant, near Main

## Paints, Oil and Glass.

EASTMAN & CO., Hill's block, Main, (see adv. inside front cover)
Morgan James & Co. 103 Main

## Paper Hangings.

ALLEN W. H., Main, Fisherville, (see adv. dept. p. 19)
Blood S., Central building, 132 Main
Fisk William H., Stickney's new block, Main
Stearns W. B. opp. State House, Main

## Patent Solicitors.

STEVENS & LUND, Main, opp. School, (see adv. dept. p. 7)

## Patent Spring Bed Manufacturers.

CHASE DEXTER, Main, opp. State House

## Periodicals and Newspapers.

CHANDLER L. 161 Main, (see adv. dept. p. 3)

## Photographic Artists.

CARR BENJ., 108 Main
Currier Herman J., Washington Square, Fisherville
Hoit William P., Exchange block, Main
KIMBALL BROS. State block, Main (see adv. opp. list of streets)
Morgan J., Moore's block, opp. Masonic Temple
NOYES E. R., City block, Main, (see advt. opp. first page general directory)
TRIPP DAVID F. Merrimack block, 134 Main, (see adv. dept. p. 10)

## Physicians.

Abbott Ezra W. 9 Warren
Bancroft Jesse P., Insane Asylum
Blodgett John H. 18 Centre
Carter Ezra, 249 Main
Conn G. P., 220 Main
Crosby A. H. Stickney's block, Main
Gage Charles P. 2 Montgomery
Gage & Conn, Stickney's block, Main
Gallinger Jacob H. 153 State
Goodwin B. S. 4 Centre
Haynes Timothy, 8 Park

Hildreth Charles F. P., 9 State block, Main
Hosmer Wm. H., Merrimack, cor. Centre, Fisherville
Lockerby Charles A., Merrimack building
McIntire H. G. (specialist), Tahanto, cor. School
Moore Ebenezer G., Main, corner Pleasant
Moore James M., Main, corner Pleasant
Morrill Shadrach C. (hom.), 82 Main
Morrill Alpheus, (hom.), 82 Main
Moulton Albert A. 1 Call's block, State
Prescott William, Elm, near Pleasant
Robinson A. H. 1 Park
Russell Moses W. 28 School and Central block, Main
Simpson S. L. F., Main, near Pleasant
Smart William H. 73 Main
Tenney Asa P., West Concord
Topliff Charles C., Main, Fisherville
Warren B. S. (bot.), Main, cor. Chapel

## Piano Stool Manufacturers.

PARKER & SECOMB, Phenix block, Main, (see adv. dept. p. 17)

## Piano Forte and Melodeon Key Manufs.

Crockett & Pillsbury, 16 Warren

## Picture Frame Manufacturers.

Blood Samuel, Central building, 132 Main

## Planing Mills.

ELWELL ISAAC & SON, near Freight Depot, (see adv. dept. p. 24)
Union Steam Mill, North end of Main

## Plaster Mill.

Clough J. T., East Concord

## Plough Manufacturer.

Robinson E. B. rear of Stickney's block

## Plumber.

Eves John, 5 Tremont

## Printers, Book and Job.

Butterfield William, Sanborn's block, Main
INDEPENDENT PRESS ASSOCIATION, Durgin's block, School (see adv. dept. page 25)
Jones A. G., Exchange building, Main
McFARLAND & JENKS, Main, corner Depot
Morrill & Silsby, Central block, Main
NOYES SAMUEL G., Main, Fisherville (see adv. dept. page 13)

## Provision Dealers.

(*See also Meat Markets.*)

Baker Charles P. 1 Walnut
DAVIS C. C. 1 Moore's block, opp. Masonic Temple (see adv. dept. page 22)
Foss John H. under Washington House, Main, Fisherville
KILBURN E. G. & CO. 2 Moore's block (see adv. dept. page 4)
WEBSTER C. C. 2 and 3 Phenix block (see advt. front colored page)
Wyatt Joseph G. 1 Warren

## Pump Maker.

Button Reuben, Warren, near Main

## Real Estate Agents.

Lane S. G., Hill's block

## Refrigerators.

Swain Levi, Warren, near Main

## Restaurants.

(*See also Dining Saloons.*)

Colston H. N. 99 Main
Dow Frank, Main, two doors south Sherman House
Gale Albert W., Depot R. R. square
Smith & Newhall, Main, cor. Hutchins

## Roofer, (Slate and Gravel.)

Tamblyn T. B., near Sherman House

## Root Beer Manufacturer.

Grover Loring, 5 Warren

## Saddlery Goods.

Hill James R. & Co., 151 Main

## Saddlery Hardware.

Smith & Walker, Depot

## Saloons.

Dow Frank, 3 doors north of American House, Main
Hart Christopher, Depot, near Railroad square
Hart Thomas, Depot, near Railroad square
Wadleigh William R., Main, Fisherville

## Sashes, Doors and Blinds.

Bunker Andrew, Union Steam Mill

## Savings Banks.

(*See also Banks.*)

NEW HAMPSHIRE SAVINGS' BANK, Pres. Joseph B. Walker. Treas. Chas. W. Sargent, 252 Main, (see adv. dept. last white page)

## Sewing Machines.

DREW GEORGE W. & CO., opp. State House, Main (see adv. dept. p. 130)
Cooke Howard M., Agent, (Howe Sewing Machine), Exchange block, Main
KIMBALL BROTHERS, State block (see adv. opp. list of streets)
MORRILL S. F. & CO., Central block, Main (see adv. dept. page 1)
NOYES S. G., Main, Fisherville (see adv. dept. p. 13)
STANLEY & AYER, (Weed Sewing Machine) Phenix Hotel bldg. (see adv. dept. p. 3)

## Silk Dyer.

Farrar Cyrus, East Concord

## Silversmith.

Durgin Wm. B., School, near Main

## Silver Platers.

Smith & Walker, Depot Street

## Skirt Supporters.

QUIMBY N. & Co. 232 Main (see adv. dept. p. 13)

## Soap Manufacturers.

Critchett M. & Son, Walnut, near Washington
Gardner & Blood, Free Bridge road
Vesper Joseph R., Washington, Fisherville

## Soda Water and Beer Manufacturers.

Pitman & Swain, 17 Wall
UNDERHILL & KITTREDGE, State block, (see advt. opp. title page)

## Spring Bed Manufacturers.

Robinson Wesley J., Central block, Main

## Spring Manufacturers.

Palmer, Warde & Co., Railroad Square

## Stables, Livery, Boarding, and Sale.

Brown David A., West Canal, Fisherville
Eagle Hotel Stable, T. A. Ambrose, Proprietor
Foster A. & G. A., 6 Warren
Norton Charles H. rear Eagle Hotel
PHENIX HOTEL STABLE, P. Dudley & Co., proprietors, rear Phenix Hotel, (see adv. dept. p. 13)
Stevens Henry A. Merrimack, Fisherville
Thompson F. W., Main, opp. Free Bridge road

## Stairbuilders.

WALLACE SAMUEL & SON, Pearl, near Main, (see adv. dept. p. 21)

## Stationery, Blank Books, &c.

Morrill & Silsby, Central block, Main

## Stone Cutters.

Concord Granite Co., E. C. Sargent, agent, Ferry, North Railroad Crossing
Donagan & Davis, State, near Fosterville
Emerton Geo. W., Walker, cor. Union
Granite Railway Co., Office, near Union Steam Mill

## Stoves and Tinware.

CARROLL L. H., Main, near Elm House, (see adv. dept. p. 7)
CHASE J. H. opp. Statesman building, (see adv. dept. last white page)
DANFORTH R. C., Main, Fisherville, (see adv. dept. p. 18)
FORD WM. P. & CO. 235 Main, (see adv. dept. opp. index to advts.
STEVENS & DUNCKLEE, Main, opp. Phenix Hotel, (see advt. opp. streets, courts, &c. p. 10)

## Straw Bleachery.

MARSHALL E. H. MRS. & CO. Stickney's new block, Main, (see adv. dept. p. 14)

## Sulpher Baths.

COBURN JOHN A. 1 Mechanics' block, Fisherville, (see (adv. dept. p. 16)

## Tailors, Merchant.

BROWN S. F., Main, Fisherville, (see adv. dept. p. 12)
CRITCHETT M. B., City block, Main, (see adv. dept. p. 1)
DAVIS JAMES, Main, opp. School
EDMUNDS A. J., Eagle block (see advt. opp. index to advts.)
HILL JOHN H. 118 Main, (see adv. dept. p. 26)
SLEEPER J. T., Stickney's block, Main, (see adv. dept. p. 16)
STEWART T. W. & J. H., Rumford block, opp. Post Office, (see adv. dept. p. 15)
Upton J. H. 12 School
Woodward E. W. & Co., Phenix Hotel building

## Tanners and Curriers.

Blake J. Mellen, rear 105 State
ROBINSON C. & SONS, Penacook, (see advt. front colored page

## Teacher, Private School.

Merrill Dora P., Green, near Centre

## Teachers, Music.

Davis & Morey, Masonic Temple, Main

## Teacher, Painting.

Gates A. M. Miss, Central block

## Telegraph Co.'s.

Northern Telegraph Co., State block, Main
Western Union Tel. Co. Depot, Railroad Square

## Tin and Wooden Ware.

(*See also Kitchen Furnishing.*)

CARROLL L. H., Moore's block, (see adv. dept. p. 7)
CHASE J. H., Main, opp. Statesman block (see adv. dept. last white page)
Crummett J. B. opp. Statesman building, Main

## Tobacco and Cigars.

(*See also Cigars and Tobacco.*)

Graham H. E., Stickney's block, Main
Parker H. M. 101 Main
Watson Benjamin, 105 Main

## Toys and Fancy Articles.

MORRILL J. H. opp. State House, Main, (see advt. p. 3)

## Trunks and Valises.

Hill James R. & Co. 151 Main
COBURN JOHN A. Main, Fisherville, (see adv. dept. p. 16)

## Trusses, Supporters, and Shoulder Braces.

ESATMAN & CO., Hill's block (see advt. innside front cover)

## Turner.

DUNLAP MORRILL, Union Steam Mill

## Undertakers.

BROWN JOSEPH, Main, opp. Ford's Warehouse, (see adv. dept. p. 2)
COBURN JOHN A. 1 Mechanics' block, Fisherville, (see adv. dept. p. 16)

## Upholsterers.

Aldrich H. H., School, near Main
Annable J. 116 Main

## Watches, Clocks and Jewelry.

Bell William H., Main, Fisherville
CARR NORMAN G., Statesman block, (see adv. opp. preface)
DREW GEO. W. & CO. opp. State House, Main, (see advt. p. 130)
Hall Ivory, 262 Main
KNIGHT E., Stickney's block, Main, (see adv. dept. p. 16)
MORRILL S. F. & CO., Central block, Main, (see advt dept. p. 1)
SHERBURNE A. P. 149 Main, (see adv. dept. p. 11)
STANLEY & AYER, Phenix Hotel building, (see adv. dept. p. 3)

## Watchmaker and Engraver.

Nelson N. C., School, near Post Offiee

## Wagon Axles.

BROWN D. ARTHUR & CO., Fisherville, (see advt. front colored page)

## Wheelwrights.

*(See also Carriage Manufacturers.)*

Eastman Chandler, West Concord
Sanborn Carroll, State, near West

## Windmills.

BROWN D. ARTHUR & CO., Fisherville, (see advt. front colored page)

## Wood and Coal Dealers.

Ranlet H. W. & CO., Hill's Avenue, cor. Railroad Square
Saltmarsh A. G. rear of Stickney's block

## Woolen Mill.

Holden B. F. & D., West Concord

# GOVERNMENT

OF  THE


# CITY OF CONCORD,

INAUGURATED TUESDAY, MARCH 19, 1867.

---

HON. JOHN ABBOTT, *Mayor*.

BOARD OF ALDERMEN.

Ward 1. Jeremiah S. Durgin, Fisherville.
" 2. John P. Locke, East Concord.
" 3. George W. Flanders, West Concord.
" 4. Charles H. Herbert, 185 State Street.
" 5. Abraham G. Jones.
" 6. Henry T. Chickering.
" 7. Isaac Clement.

Charles F. Stewart, *Clerk*.

COMMON COUNCIL.

William S. Curtis, *President*.

Ward 1. Edward Runnells, Hiram Simpson.
" 2. Thompson Tenney, David A. Morrill.
" 3. Harrison Partridge, Jacob N. Flanders.
" 4. George W. Emerton, Daniel Farnum.
" 5. Philip Flanders, Daniel F. Secomb.
" 6. Lewis L. Mower, N. H. Haskell.
" 7. William S. Curtis, N. W. Gove.

Amos Hadley, *Clerk*.

ASSESSORS.

| | | | |
|---|---|---|---|
| Ward 1. | Timothy C. Rolfe. | Ward 4. | Horace A. Brown. |
| " 2. | James Frye. | " 5. | Nicholas Quimby. |
| " 3. | Hiram Farnum. | " 6. | George S. Dennett. |

Ward 7. William H. Proctor.

---

*City Clerk.* — C. F. Stewart. Office in City Hall building, south entrance, house 267 Main Street.

*City Treasurer.* — Samuel C. Eastman. Office, Rumford block, Main street, up stairs.

*City Solicitor.* — John Y. Mugridge.

*Collector of Taxes.* — William H. Buntin.

*City Marshal.* — William H. Buntin.

*Assistant Marshals.* — John Connell, John A. Coburn.

*Night Watch.* — James E. Rand, William T. Locke.

*City Physician.* — Benjamin S. Warren.

*Overseer of the Poor.* — John Abbott.

*Health Officers.* — William H. Buntin, Dr. Benjamin S. Warren, Dr. G. P. Conn.

*Police Justice.* — Sylvester Dana.

*Special Police Justice.* — S. C. Badger.

*Superintending School Committee of Wards* 1, 2, *and* 7. — Edward T. Rowell, L. T. Flint, A. K. Potter.

*Board of Education for Union District.* — Asa Fowler, J. B. Walker, S. C. Eastman, D. Patten, Hazen Pickering, J. P. Bancroft, A. J. Prescott, P. B. Cogswell, J. V. Barron.

*Trustees of the Public Library.* — John A. Holmes, Benj. L. Larkin, Geo. W. Flanders, Amos Hadley, Henry P. Rolfe, L. D. Stevens, Jonathan B. Weeks.

*"Old" and Blossom Hill Cemetery Committee.* — Edward Dow, Joseph B. Walker, Cyrus W. Paige.

*Superintendent of Repairs of Highways and Bridges.* — John Abbott.

*City Messenger and Lamplighter.* — Josiah S. Ingalls.

## POLICE DEPARTMENT.

*Police Officers.* — John Connell, James E. Rand, William T. Locke, John A. Coburn, Charles C. Bean, Chas. W. Davis, and John Foss.

*Special Police Officers.* — Baruch Biddle, Josiah C. Shaw, George G. Virgin, E. S. Gilman, E. A. Miller, Jacob E. Hutchins, Samuel R. Mann, Charles T. Lane, True Osgood, J. S. Ingalls, Luther P. Fuller, Nathaniel H. Johnson, A. G. Saltmarsh, George W. Chesley, Westley J. Robinson, A. W. Gale, Benjamin F. Holden, Josiah Cooper, Heman Sanborn, George Partridge, E. H. Houston, George W. West, Samuel S. Pickard, J. C. Eaton, Curtis White, R. M. Ordway, Noah P. Webster, John Corlis, Horace S. Abbott, Isaac P. Baker, H. B. Rand, I. W. Hatch, Robert Crouther.

# FIRE DEPARTMENT.

TRUE OSGOOD, *Chief Engineer.*

Abel B. Holt, John D. Teel, John M. Hill, Alonzo Downing, Joseph S. Merrill, Chandler Eastman, James Frye, David A. Brown, *Assistant Engineers.*

## ENGINE COMPANIES.

"*Concord*" *Engine Company, No.* 2, *Ward* 4. J. N. Ryder, *Foreman*; J. F. Scott, *Clerk.*

"*Merrimack*" *Engine Company, No.* 3, *Ward* 6. John J. Mills, *Foreman*; James M. Otis, *Clerk.*

*No.* 1. *Steamer* "*Gov. Hill,*" Daniel W. Long, *Foreman*; W. D. Ladd, *Clerk*; ——— ———, *Teamster.*

*No.* 2. *Steamer* "*Kearsarge,*" David L. Neal, *Foreman*; George Burns, *Clerk*; Frank Smart, *Teamster.*

"*Cataract*" *Engine Company, No.* 6, *Ward* 3, I. H. Farnum, *Foreman*; Moses F. Clough, *Clerk.*

"*Old Fort*" *Engine Company, No.* 7, *Ward* 2, George H. Curtis, *Foreman*; John E. Frye, *Clerk.*

"*Pioneer*" *Engine Company, No.* 8, *Ward* 1, John Whittaker, *Foreman*; Calvin Roberts, *Clerk.*

*Concord R. R. Hydrant and Hose Company No.* 1, J. M. Foss, *Foreman*; Philip Flanders, Jr., *Clerk.*

*Northern R. R. Hydrant and Hose Company, No.* 2, James M. Lauder, *Foreman*; Luther W. Nichols, *Clerk.*

*Hook and Ladder Company, No.* 1, Eben B. Hutchinson, *Foreman*; J. B. Smart, *Clerk.*

*Eagle Hose Company, No.* 1, J. L. Green, *Foreman*; M. T. Palmer, *Clerk.*

## FIRE POLICE.

William H. Buntin, *Captain*; J. L. Pickering, Charles W. Davis, John Connell, D. S. Webster, James E. Larkin, Joseph S. Prescott, Samuel M. Griffin, Thompson Rowell, William T. Locke, James E. Rand, Josiah Cooper, James H. Rowell, Charles H. Critchett, Thomas F. Newhall, Curtis White, George A. Foster, Josiah S. Ingalls.

---

## FENCE VIEWERS.

John Abbott, Daniel Knowlton, Moses H. Farnum.

## SURVEYORS OF WOOD AND LUMBER.

Nicholas Quimby, John S. Mason, Joseph T. Clough, Eben F. Elliott, John G. Warren, T. W. Emery, John P. Locke,

Andrew Moody, Jeremiah S. Noyes, George S. Dennett, Abel B. Holt, Curtis White, John T. Batchelder, Rodney G. Cutting, Samuel Eastman, John Abbott, Henry M. Moore, Sewell Hoit, Shadrach Seavey, Albert C. Holt, William Ballard, Daniel Farnum, Erastus C. Currier, Daniel A. Hill, Joel Ingalls, George Frye, Jeremiah F. Runnells, George Wilkins, Saml. Shute, Joseph S. Lund, Leonard Holt, Jehiel D. Knight, Cyrus Runnells, J. B. Weeks, Elbridge Dimond, Henry Martin, Timothy Carter, Alfred L. Marden, T. J. Carpenter, Harrison Partridge, Joshua Chapman, Edward Dow, Ira C. Edgerly, Henry T. Chickering, A. B. Cook, William H. Buntin, George A. Pillsbury, Richard M. Ordway, Henry L. Elliott, Philip Flanders, Jr., Ebenezer B. Hutchinson, Asa H. Morrill, Jeremiah S. Abbott, William Carr, Orrin T. Clisby, Isaac Clement.

## SURVEYORS OF STONE.

Henry H. Brown, Nathaniel Smith, Josiah Cooper, Daniel S. Clark, Richard M. Ordway, Edward Dow, George W. Emerton.

## SURVEYORS OF MASONRY.

Richard M. Ordway, Jefferson Noyes, Charles E. Thompson, Albert H. Drown.

## WEIGHERS OF HAY.

John Batchelder, James F. Hoit, T. J. Carpenter, Francis A. Fiske, George F. Whittredge, Noah Ranlett, Henry W. Ranlett, Henry T. Chickering, Albert A. Currier, George H. Whittredge, Sylvester Stevens, George S. Morrill.

## SEALERS OF LEATHER.

Cyrus Robinson, Enos Blake, Chase Hill, Jacob P. Saunders, William Gilman, Calvin Thorn, Charles E. Robinson, James Mallon Blake.

## SEALERS OF WEIGHTS AND MEASURES.

James H. Chase, William Carr.

## CULLERS OF STAVES.

Isaiah Robinson, Leonard Bell, William Haywood, Joseph B. Abbott, Stephen Quimby, John Hoyt.

### POUND KEEPER.

Ephraim S. Gilman.

### HIGHWAY SURVEYORS.

District No. 1, Samuel Hutchins; No. 2, Enoch Jackman; No. 3, George Graham; No. 4, Thompson Tenney; No. 5, D. A. Morrill; No. 6, William B. Fletcher; No. 7, Josiah S. Locke; No. 8, George W. West; No. 10, Hiram Farnum; No. 11, Alfred C. Abbott; No. 12, John A. Holmes; No. 13, Joseph B. Knowlton; No. 14, E. C. Ellicott; No. 15, Cyrus Runnells; No. 16, Robert B. Hoyt; No. 17, Augustus C. Carter; No. 18, Andrew S. Farnum; No. 19, Daniel C. Tenney; No. 20, Jacob N. Flanders; No. 21, Daniel Farnum; No. 22, Charles Hall; No. 23, Jeremiah S. Abbott; No. 24, Moses E. Brown; No. 25, Moses B. Abbott; No. 26, George Frye; No. 29, Alexander Thompson; No. 30, Elbridge Dimond; No. 31, Samuel Clifford.

## PUBLIC SCHOOLS IN CONCORD.

### HIGH SCHOOL.

Moses Woolson, *Principal*; Mrs. Abby G. Woolson, Misses Sarah E. Blair, E. J. Sherman, Julia C. Hunt, Helen E. Gilbert, and Mary H. Brooks, *Assistants.*

### GRAMMAR SCHOOLS.

MERRIMACK—Misses Lucy R. Hill and Kate A. Shumway, *Principals;* Mrs. R. Akerman, *Assistant.* CENTRE — Miss Mary A. Eaton, *Principal;* Miss Mary O. Carter, *Assistant.* RUMFORD — Miss Julia Jones, *Principal;* Miss Metta C. Davis, *Assistant.*

### INTERMEDIATE SCHOOLS.

STATE STREET, NORTH END—Miss D. E. E. Hill; MERRIMACK—Miss S. F. Emery; CENTRE—Miss E. F. Ordway; MYRTLE STREET—Miss Julia M. Johnson; RUMFORD—Miss H. M. Putney; WEST STREET, SOUTH END—Mrs. P. S. Bowen.

### PRIMARY SCHOOLS.

STATE STREET, NORTH END—Miss Helen McG. Ayers; MERRIMACK—Miss Eliza J. Day; FRANLIN STREET—Miss M. E. Hoag; UNION STREET—First, Miss Susan R. Moulton; Second, Mrs. S. R. Crockett; CENTRE—Miss A. M. Nutter; SPRING STREET—First, Miss Isabella Nutter; Second,

Misses Clara E. Batchelder and Sarah A. Day; MYRTLE STREET—Miss Z. H. Morgan; SIXTH WARD HOUSE—Misses Hanah Bell and H. Addie Monroe; RUMFORD—Misses Mary E. F. Andrews and E. J. Wallace; WEST STREET, SOUTH END—First, Misses M. E. and Lucy A. Greene; Second, Misses Ellen A. Reed and Anna E. Shute.

### MIXED SCHOOLS.

BOW BROOK—Misses H. Addie Monroe and Ellen A. Reed; ELEVEN LOTS—Misses H. Josephine Sleeper, Abby A. Flint and Eva E. Piper.

## St. Paul's School.

Endowed by Dr. George S. Shattuck of Boston. Incorporated 1855. Rev. Henry A. Coit, D. D., *Rector;* Joseph H. Coit, M. A., *Vice-Rector;* Rev. Thomas G. Valpey, M. A., Rev. Hall Harrison, M. A., Rev. Wm. Schouler, Jr., and Rev. John Hargate, *Masters.*

## CHURCHES.

### FIRST BAPTIST CHURCH.

The First Baptist Church and Society was organized in the year 1818. Their house of worship, situated on State Street, was built in 1825, and was enlarged in the year 1846, and remodeled in the year 1860. Their Sunday School was commenced in the year 1828. Their officers are as follows:—*Pastor,* Rev. D. W. Faunce; *Deacons,* Benj. Damon, David Winkley, Isaac Elwell, and J. B. Flanders; *Clerk,* A. J. Prescott; *Treasurer,* Isaac Elwell. Committee of the Society are Isaac Elwell, L. D. Brown, and George A. Pillsbury; Treasurer of Society, Henry Foster; Clerk, A. J. Prescott.

### PLEASANT STREET BAPTIST CHURCH.

Church edifice dedicated Jan. 11th, 1854. Rev. E. E. Cummings, D. D., *Pastor;* Wm. H. Howe, *Clerk;* James S. Crockett, and James Morgan, *Deacons;* James S. Crockett, *Church Clerk;* Nahum Robinson, Daniel Y. Bickford, Daniel C. Peasley, James S. Crockett, John C. Hancock, Wentworth G. Shaw, *Trustees.*

SABBATH SCHOOL—George P. Harvey, *Superintendent.* Number of scholars, 175. Number of volumes in the Library 600.

PLEASANT STREET FEMALE CHARITABLE SOCIETY—Mrs. J. Sanborn, *President;* Mrs. W. H. Howe, *Secretary.*

## FIRST BAPTIST CHURCH OF FISHERVILLE.

Organized Aug. 6, 1845. Present Church built 1858.

Rev. Ira E. Kenney, *Pastor;* H. H. Brown, Frank Abbott, and William H. Allen, *Deacons;* William H. Allen, *Treasurer;* J. S. Brown, *Clerk.*

SABBATH SCHOOL—Henry H. Brown, *Superintendent;* Edward H. Gilmore, Quincy Bean, *Librarians.* Number of Scholars, about 275. Number of Volumes in Library, about 1,000.

## FREEWILL BAPTIST CHURCH.

State Street. Incorporated 1857.

Rev. A. K. Moulton, *Pastor;* Joshua Heath, Joseph B. Fellows, and David Batchelder, *Wardens;* D. L. Guernsey, *Clerk;* Joshua Heath, *Sexton;* Josiah S. Ingalls, and D. S. Webster, *Deacons.*

SABBATH SCHOOL—Josiah S. Ingalls, *Superintendent;* Augustus Chesley, *Librarian.* Number of Scholars, 150. Number of Volumes in Library, 700.

## FIRST CONGREGATIONAL CHURCH.

Main Street. Incorporated Nov. 18th, 1730.

Rev. Nathaniel Bouton, *Pastor;* Benj. Farnum, Charles F. Stewart, and John Ballard, *Deacons.*

SABBATH SCHOOL, Established 1818 — Edward A. Moulton, *Superintendent.* Number of Scholors, 180. Number of volumes in Library, 300.

## SOUTH CONGREGATIONAL CHURCH.

Pleasant Street, near State. Incorporated Feb. 1st, 1837.

—— ——, *Pastor;* Caleb Parker, Greenough McQuesten, Hazen Pickering, and George G. Sanborn, *Deacons.*

SABBATH SCHOOL—Lon Weston, *Superintendent.* Number of Scholars, 466.

## WEST CONCORD CHURCH.—TRINITARIAN.

Organized April 22, 1833.

Rev. Asa P. Tenney, *Pastor*, installed April 23, 1833; Ira P. Rowell, *Deacon* and *Clerk.*

SABBATH SCHOOL—Asa P. Tenney, *Supt.;* Timothy Carter, *Vice Supt.;* J. D. Knight, *Librarian.*

Number of Scholars, about 150. Number of Volumes in Library, 350.

Connected with the Society is a Ladies' Charitable Society, Mrs. Mary Tenney, *Pres.*

## EAST CONGREGATIONAL CHURCH.

East Concord. Organized March, 1842.

—— ——— *Pastor;* James M. Carlton, Henry A. Kendall, *Deacons.*

SABBATH SCHOOL — George H. Curtis, *Supt.;* Samuel Merriam, *Librarian.*

Number of Scholars, about 75. Number of Volumes in Library, 250.

## ST. PAUL'S CHURCH.—EPISCOPAL.

Park Street.

This Church was organized under the name of St. Thomas Chapel, January 5th, 1817; the name was afterwards changed to St. Paul's Church, July 13th, 1835. Rev. Dr. J. H. Eames, *Rector;* Charles Minot, James N. Blake, Edward A. Abbott, Charles J. Conner, Henry P. Rolfe, *Vestrymen;* Abel Hutchins, *Clerk;* J. H. Albin, *Treasurer.*

Horace A. Brown, Charles S. Eastman, *Wardens.*

SUNDAY SCHOOL—Horace A. Brown, *Supt.*

Number of Scholars in School, 125. Number of Volumes in Library, 400.

## FIRST METHODIST EPISCOPAL CHURCH.

State Street.

Rev. E. Adams, *Pastor;* Albert Langmaid, Benj. F. Holden, Henry C. Sanborn. Joshua B. Merrill, I. C. Weeks, David F. Brown, Jacob B. Rand, Nath. P. Rines, John S. Mason, *Trustees;* John P. Johnson, Geo. W. Richardson, Timothy R. Elwell, Amos H. Curtice, Wm. P. Hoit, Daniel Widmer, Thos. J. Sanborn, Geo. W. Drake, Geo. A. Young, *Stewards;* Luther P. Durgin, Israel C. Bailey, John Saunders, Edwin Gary, Wm. H. Currier, *Class Leaders.*

SABBATH SCHOOL—Luther P. Durgin, *Supt.;* John S. Mason, *First Ass't;* John Gordon, *Second Ass't.*

Number of Officers and Teachers, 36; number of Scholars, 250; number of Volumes in Library, 700; membership of the Church, 330.

There are several Benevolent Societies connected with the Church.

## METHODIST EPISCOPAL CHURCH OF FISHERVILLE.

Main Street.

Rev. Page Philbrook, *Pastor;* J. C. Elsworth, *Sec.;* L. K. Hall, *Treas.;*

SABBATH SCHOOL—Fifield Tucker, *Supt.;* Walter Sweet, *Librarian.*

Number of Scholars, about 105. Number of Volumes in Library, 600.

### ST. JOHN'S CHAPEL.—Roman Catholic.

Merrimack St., Fisherville. Organized 1854.
Present Church dedicated 1867. Rev. J. E. Barry, *Priest.*

### ADVENT CHURCH.

Washington Street.

### FIRST UNIVERSALIST CHURCH.

School, corner State Street. Incorporated 1850.

Rev. F. E. Kittredge, *Pastor;* J. F. Whittredge, Robert Hall, *Deacons;* Joel C. Danforth, *Clerk and Treas.*

Sabbath School—James E. Larkin, *Supt.;* George F. Underhill, *Librarian.*

Number of Scholars, 200. Number of Volumes in Library, 1000.

### SECOND CONGREGATIONAL CHURCH.

Unitarian.

State Street, north of School. Organized August, 1827.

First Church built in 1829, and burnt November, 1854; present Church built 1855.

Rev. Joseph F. Lovering, *Pastor;* William Kent, Daniel F. Secomb, Benjamin Grover, *Deacons;* Daniel F. Secomb, *Clerk.*

Sabbath School—Asa Fowler, *Supt.*

Number of Scholars, about 100. Number of Volumes in Library, 970.

## MASONIC.

### GRAND ROYAL ARCH CHAPTER OF NEW HAMPSHIRE.

Annual convocation at Concord on Tuesday preceding the 2nd Wednesday in June.

Officers—N. W. Cumner, Manchester, *M. E. Gr. High Priest;* Daniel R. Marshall, Nashua, *E. Dep. Gr. High Priest;* John A. Harris, Concord, *E. Gr. King;* Edward Gustine, Keene, *E. Gr. Scribe;* John Knowlton, Portsmouth, *E. Gr. Treasurer;* Horace Chace, Hopkinton, *E. Gr. Secretary;* James Adams, Candia, *E. Gr. Chaplain;* Asahel A. Balch, Manchester, *E. Gr. Capt. of Host;* Thomas Spurlin, Dover, *E. Gr. Pr. Sojourner;* William Barrett, Nashua, *E. Gr. Royal Arch Captain;* Edward Bond, Claremont, *Gr. Master Third Veil;* Hiram Clark, Plymouth, *Gr. Master Second Veil;* L. J. Graves, Langdon, *Gr. Master Third Veil;* George H. True, Manchester, M. L. Morrison, Peterboro', *Gr. Stewards;* George L. Reed, Concord, *Gr. Tyler.*

## TRINITY CHAPTER, NO. 2, ROYAL ARCH MASONS.

Stated convocations fourth Tuesday in each month in Masonic Temple.

OFFICERS.—Thos. J. Sanborn, M. E. High Priest; John A. Harris, E. King; Elijah Knight. E. Scribe; Geo. P. Cleaves, Treasurer; Luther W. Nichols, Secretary; Samuel Utley, Chaplain; Isaac N. Elwell, Capt. of Host; Chas. W. Harvey, Principal Sojourner; Augustus G. Harris, Royal Arch Capt.; John E. Rollins, Wm. W. Storrs, Norman G. Carr, Grand Masters of Veils; Frank W. Hayes, Wm. Carr, Stewards; Geo. L. Reed, Tyler.

## MOUNT HOREB COMMANDERY, NO. 5, OF KNIGHTS TEMPLAR.

Regular meetings at their Asylum, in Masonic Temple, the fourth Monday of each month.

OFFICERS.—Josiah Stevens, Jr., E. Commander; Wm. W. Taylor, Generalissimo; George P. Cleaves, Capt. General; Charles W. Harvey, Prelate; Wm. W. Storrs, Treasurer; Luther W. Nichols, Recorder; Joseph W. Robinson, Senior Warden; Abel Hutchins, Junior Warden; Norman G. Carr, Sword Bearer; John A. Harris, Standard Bearer; Samuel D. Baker, Warder; George L. Reed, Sentinel.

## GRAND COUNCIL ROYAL AND SELECT MASTERS OF THE STATE OF NEW HAMPSHIRE.

OFFICERS.—John R. Holbrook, Portsmouth, M. I. Gr. Master; Thomas J. Sanborn, Concord, R. I. Gr. Master; George H. True, Manchester, I. Gr. Master; Daniel R. Marshall, Nashua, Gr. Treasurer; Luther W. Nichols, Concord, Gr. Recorder; Thomas Snow, Somersworth, Gr. Capt. of Guard; Leland J. Graves, Langdon, Gr. Conductor; Charles G. Pickering, Portsmouth, Gr. Marshal; John A. Harris, Concord, Gr. Steward; John D. Patterson, Manchester, Gr. Chaplain; George L. Reed, Concord, Gr. Sentinel.

## HORACE CHACE COUNCIL, NO. 4, ROYAL AND SELECT MASTERS.

Regular meetings at Masonic Temple, the third Monday in each month.

OFFICERS.—John A. Harris, T. I. Gr. Master; Thomas J. Sanborn, R. I. Gr. Master; George P. Cleaves, I. Gr. Master; Wm. W. Storrs, Gr. Treasurer; Edward Dow, Gr. Recorder; Luther W. Nichols, Gr. Capt. of Guard; Isaac N. Elwell, Gr. Conductor; Norman G. Carr, Gr. Master; Geo. L. Reed, Gr. Steward.

## GRAND LODGE OF NEW HAMPSHIRE.

Annual Communication at Concord, 2d Wednesday in June.

OFFICERS.—John H. Rowell, Franklin, M. W. Gr. Master; Alex. M. Winn, Farmington, R. W. Dep. Gr. Master; John R. Holbrook, Portsmouth, R. W. Sr. Gr. Warden; N. W. Cumner, Manchester, R. W. Jr. Gr. Warden; John Knowlton, Portsmouth, R. W. Gr. Treasurer; Horace Chase, Hopkinton, R. W. Gr. Secretary.

### DISTRICT DEP. GRAND MASTERS.

District No. 1 John Dame, Portsmouth.
" " 2 Franklin McDuffee, Rochester.
" " 3 Ezra Huntington, Manchester.
" " 4 Charles H. Burns, Wilton.
" " 5 Eli Dodge, Newbury.
" " 6 John Blackmer, Sandwich.
" " 7 Don H. Woodward, Keene.
" " 8 A. M. Gove, Lebanon.
" " 9 T. J. Smith, Wentworth.
" " 10 Hazen Bedel, Colebrook.

### GRAND LECTURERS.

Washington Freeman, Portsmouth; Thomas Snow, Somersworth; Edward Parker, Nashua; Warren Pratt, New Ipswich; John A. Harris, Concord; J. W. Dearborn, Effingham; Jesseniah Kittredge, Walpole; Albert S. Waite, Newport; Hiram Clark, Plymouth; Benj. F. Hunking, Lancaster.

### GRAND CHAPLAINS.

Elisha Adams, William Morse, Roger M. Sargent, Solomon Laws, G. W. H. Clark, E. A. Smith, Anthony C. Hardy, William Barrett, Nashua, Sr. Gr. Deacon; Francis A. Perry, Keene, Jr. Gr. Deacon.

### GRAND STEWARDS.

Aaron King, E. F. Lane, D. W. Edgerly, Hiram Clark, Lewis W. Clark, J. D. March, Henry B. Atherton, Nashua, Gr. Marshal; Luther W. Nichols, Concord, Gr. Sword Bearer; O. A. Woodbury, Nashua, Gr. Pursuivant; George L. Reed, Concord, Gr. Tyler.

## BLAZING STAR LODGE, NO 11.

Instituted May 6, 1799.

Meeting on the Wednesday, on or before the full of the Moon in each month.

OFFICERS.—J. W. Robinson, W. M.; A. B. Sanborn, S. W.; S. F. Morrill, J. W.; J. H. Chase, Treasurer; J. F. Cotton, Secretary; J. E. Rollins, S. D.; C. H. Herbert, J. D.; John Quimby, L. Merrill, Stewards; T. J. Sanborn, Chaplain; G. L. Reed, Tyler.

## EUREKA LODGE, NO. 70.

Chartered June 13, 1860.

Regular meetings first Thursday of each month.

OFFICERS.—George P. Cleaves, W. M.; James E. Larkin, S. W.; M. T. Palmer, J. W.; Darius Morrill, Treasurer; C. A. Colbath, Secretary; F. D. Woodbury, S. D.; W. E. Tucker, J. D.; George W. Estabrook, Chaplain; J. T. Gordon, Marshal; W. H. Kenny, N. C. Nelson, Stewards; Geo. L. Reed, Tyler.

## HORACE CHACE LODGE, NO. 72.

Fisherville.

Meetings Tuesday on or before the full of the Moon.

OFFICERS.—Albert H. Drown, W. M.; Samuel N. Brown, S. W.; Gilman H. Dimond, J. W.; Charles C. Bean, Treasurer; D. Arthur Brown, Secretary; D. A. Macurdy, Chaplain; Levi N. Barnes, S. D.; Isaac N. Vesper, J. D.; Rufus D. Scales, Marshal; John Chadwick, Henry L. Clough, Stewards; Elkanah P. Everett, Tyler.

# Independent Order of Odd Fellows.

## PENACOOK ENCAMPMENT, No. 3.

Instituted Nov. 26th, 1844.

OFFICERS—Curtis White, *C. P.;* George W. Crockett, *H. P.;* Charles F. P. Hildreth, *S. W.;* Edward N. Doyen, *J. W.;* Joseph B. Smart, *Scribe;* William Hart, *Treas.;* Herman Strauss, *Sent.;* Joseph S. Merrill, *G.;* Jesse C. Cochran, *First W.;* Frank D. Woodbury, *Second W.;* Robert A. Gawler, *Third W.;* Orrin T. Carter, *Fourth W.;* George A. Cummings, *First G. of T.;* James H. Goodrich, *Second G. of T.*

Meets at Odd Fellows' Hall, in Central Block, on the second and fourth Tuesday evenings in each month.

Amount of Funds, about One Thousand Dollars, well invested. Numbers One Hundred Members.

## WHITE MOUNTAIN LODGE, No. 5.

OFFICERS—William P. Hoit, *N. G.;* James N. Green, *V. G.;* Frank D. Woodbury, *Sec.;* Geo. Crockett, *Treas.;* Seth R. Dole, *Chap.;* Edwin N. Doyne, *Warden;* Harlan F. Brown, *Conductor;* John F. Scott, *I. G.;* Geo. L. Reed, *O. G.;* John D. Teel, *R. S.N. G.;* James S. Norris, *L. S. N. G.;* Moses Ladd, *R. S. V. G.;* Grafton Upton, *L. S. V. G.;* James H. Goodrich, *R. S. S.;* A. C. Ferrin, *L. S. S.*

This Lodge nambers 234 members. They hold their meetings at Odd Fellows' Hall, on Friday evenings. They have a Fund of Four Thousand Six Hundred Dollars, well invested.

## Independent Order of Good Templars.

DUSTIN ISLAND LODGE, No. 20.

Fisherville. Instituted Jan. 8, 1866.

Officers—Chas. H. Amsden, *W. C. T.;* Lizzie M. Morse, *W. V. T.;* William W. Cilley, *W. C.;* Millard F. Johnson, *W. S.;* Abbie M. Everett, *W. A. S.;* Timothy E. Rolfe, *W. F. S.;* Edwin P. Wallace, *W. T.;* David E. Jones, *W. M.;* Nellie A. Eastman, *W. D. M.;* Nellie M. Brown, *W. I. G.;* Chas. V. Fisher, *W. O. G.:* Mary J. Crowther, *W. R. S.;* Helen A. Brown, *W. L. S.*

Meets every Monday evening, at Catholic Vestry.

STATE CAPITAL LODGE, No. 19.

Instituted January 8, 1866.

Meets on Wednesday evenings, at Tahanto Hall.

## Sons of Temperance.

GRAND DIVISION SONS OF TEMPERANCE, OF NEW HAMPSHIRE.

Annual Meeting at Concord, third Wednesday in October.

CONCORD DIVISION, No. 2.

Meets Monday evenings.

CRYSTAL FOUNT DIVISION, No. 16.

Meets Tuesday evenings, at Tahanto Hall.

NEW HAMPSHIRE STATE TEMPERANCE LEAGUE.

Officers—Hon. Samuel Upham, Manchester, *Pres.;* Fred. S. Crawford, Concord, *Sec.;* Caleb Parker, Concord, *Treas.*

## SOCIETIES, LIBRARIES, ETC.

NEW HAMPSHIRE HISTORICAL SOCIETY.

No 250 Main Street. Incorporated 1823. Number of volumes in Library, 5,000.

Joseph B. Walker, Esq., *President;* Asa McFarland, Esq., 1*st Vice President;* Hon. Franklin Pierce, 2*nd Vice President;* Rev. Dr. N. Bouton, *Cor. Sect.;* Samuel C. Eastman, Esq., *Rec. Sect.;* William R. Walker, Esq., *Treas.;* Charles W. Sargent, Esq., *Librarian;* Amos Hadley, Esq., *Assist. Librarian.*

Hon. Samuel D. Bell, Rev. Dr. E. E. Cummings, William S. Foster, Esq., *Publishing Committee.*

Rev. Dr. B. B. Stone, Dr. William Prescott, S. C. Eastman, Esq., *Standing Committee.*

Abel Hutchins, Esq., P. B. Cogswell, Esq., *Auditing Committee.*

## NEW HAMPSHIRE MISSIONARY SOCIETY.

Room 5, State block, Main Street. Instituted 1801. Incorporated 1807.

Rev. Asa Smith, President; Lyman D. Stevens, Esq., Vice President; Rev. William Clark, Secretary; Rev. B. P. Stone, Treasurer.

The object of this Society, is to assist churches that are unable to support the gospel ministry.

Persons contributing $2. yearly, to its funds, become members.

Thirty dollars constitutes Life Membership.

## NEW HAMPSHIRE BIBLE SOCIETY.

Room 5, State block, Main Street. Instituted 1810.

Edward Spaulding, President; Rev. Benj. P. Stone, Treasurer.

## FISHERVILLE LIBRARY ASSOCIATION.

Main street, Fisherville. Organized August, 1865.

Nehemiah Butler, *President*; Isaac K. Gage, *Secretary;* William H. Allen, *Treasurer.*

Henry H. Brown, Ira E. Kenney, Nehemiah Butler, *Trustees.*

Stewart I. Brown, *Librarian.*

Number of volumes, about 1,000.

## LADIES' BENEVOLENT ASSOCIATION.

Fisherville.

Mrs. Pratt, *President.*

## LADIES' BENEVOLENT ASSOCIATION,

East Concord.

Mrs. Sarah A. O. Fifield, *President.*

## PUBLIC LIBRARY.

Frederick S. Crawford, Librarian.

The Public Library is in the upper story of the City Hall building. It is open every Monday, Thursday, and Saturday; in the afternoon from two to four o'clock, in the evening from seven to nine.

Whole number of books in Library, 5,000.

# RAILROADS.

## CONCORD, MANCHESTER AND LAWRENCE RAILROAD.

From Manchester to Lawrence, 26 miles. Office at Concord. Asa Fowler, President; James R. Kendrick, Superintendent; E. W. Harrington, Treasurer; Wm. C. Clarke, Clerk; Asa Fowler, E. A. Straw, W. W. Stickney, Geo. B. Chandler, E. A. Abbot, I. T. Goss, B. A. Martin, Directors.

## MANCHESTER AND NORTH WEARE RAILROAD.

From Manchester to North Weare, 19 miles. Office at Concord. Operated by the Concord Railroad,

JAMES R. KENDRICK, Supt.

## BOSTON, CONCORD AND MONTREAL R. R.

From Concord, N. H., to Wells River, Vt., 93 miles.

John E. Lyon, Boston, Mass., President; Edward D. Harlow, Boston, Mass., Treasurer; Charles Lane, Laconia, N. H., Secretary; Joseph A. Dodge, Plymouth, N. H., Superintendent.

John E. Lyon, Boston, Mass.; Peter Butler, Boston, Mass.; J. A. Parks, Boston, Mass.; A. H. Tilton, Sanbornton, N. H.; J. P. Pitman, Laconia, N. H.; Jos. W. Lang, Meredith, N. H.; John L. Rix, Haverhill, N. H., Directors.

## NORTHERN RAILROAD.

Concord to White River Junction, 69 miles, with branch Franklin to Bristol, 13 miles, single track.

President, Onslow Stearns; Superintendent, Geo. E. Todd; Treasurer, Geo. A. Kettell; Directors, Onslow Stearns, Geo. A. Kettell, Josiah Minot, Geo. W. Nesmith, Uriel Crocker, John A. Burnham and J. W. Clark.

## CONCORD AND CLAREMONT RAILROAD.

Concord to Bradford, 27 miles, single track, operated by Trustees of 1st Mortgage.

Trustees, Onslow Stearns, Geo. W. Nesmith, Geo. A. Kettell; Superintendent, Geo. E. Todd; Treasurer, Geo. A. Kettell.

## CONCORD RAILROAD.

From Concord to Nashua, 35 miles, (double track.)

Josiah Minot, President; James R. Kendrick, Superintendent; Nathan Parker, Treasurer; Samuel N. Bell, Clerk;

Josiah Minot, F. M. Weld, Thomas Chase, Nathan Parker Phineas Adams, J. S. Abbot, R. H. Messer, Directors.

### CONCORD AND PORTSMOUTH RAILROAD.

From Concord to Portsmouth, via., Manchester. Distance 59 miles.

Stephen Kendrick, President; Wm. H. Hackett, Portsmouth, Clerk; Moody Currier, Manchester, Treasurer; James R. Kendrick, Concord, Superintendent.

Stephen Kenrick, Franklin; S. Plumer Dow, Newmarket; Benj. F. Martin, Manchester; Joseph B. Walker, Concord; Samuel N. Bell, Manchester, Directors.

### CONTOOCOOK RIVER RAILROAD.

Contoocook to Hillsborough Bridge, 14 miles, single track.

President, Theo. French; Superintendent, Geo. E. Todd; Treasurer, Geo. A. Kettell; Directors, Onslow Stearns, Theo. French, Stephen Kenrick, Geo. A. Kettell, Charles Minot.

## NEWSPAPERS.

NEW HAMPSHIRE PATRIOT AND STATE GAZETTE, Sanborn's block, Main Street, William Butterfield, Publisher, (Weekly), $2 per year.

NEW HAMPSHIRE STATESMAN, Main, corner of Depot, McFarland & Jenks, Publishers, (Weekly), $2 per year.

CONCORD DAILY MONITOR, Durgin's block, School, Published by the Independent Press Association, (Daily), $6 per year.

INDEPENDENT DEMOCRAT, Durgin's block, School, Published by the Independent Press Association, (Weekly), $2 per year.

## Incorporated Companies, etc.

### CONCORD GAS-LIGHT COMPANY.

Office, No. 4 White's Block, Capital St. Incorporated 1854.
Capital, $60,000.

OFFICERS—Nathaniel White, *Pres.;* Sylvester Dana, *Clerk;* John M. Hill, *Treas. and Agent;* N. White, S. Eastman, B. Grover, J. H. George, A. C. Peirce, E. H. Rollins, S. Dana, *Directors.*

The Concord Gas-Light Company have laid about sixty thousand feet of main pipe. There are about seven hundred consumers, and eighty street lights.

## BANKS.

### NATIONAL STATE CAPITAL BANK.

11 State Block, Main Street.

Incorporated 1853. Re-organized 1865. Capital, $150,000.

OFFICERS—J. V. Barron, *Pres.;* P. S. Smith, *Cash.*
Discount Day, Tuesday.

### FIRST NATIONAL BANK.

Stickney's Block, Main Street. Incorporated March 15, 1864.

Capital, $500,000.

OFFICERS—George W. Pillsbury, *Pres.;* Wm. H. Storrs, *Cash.;* Geo. A. Pillsbury, Enos Blake, William Walker, Benning W. Sanborn, Timothy Haynes, James W. Johnson, Peter Dudley, *Directors.*

Banking Hours from 9 1-2 to 12, and 2 to 4. Closed Saturday afternoons. Discount Day, Tuesday.

### UNION BANK.

Central Block, Main Street. Incorporated 1856.

Capital, $100,000.

OFFICERS—Nathaniel White, *Pres.* A. C. Peirce, *Cash.*
Discount Day, Tuesday.

## INSURANCE COMPANY.

### EQUITABLE MUTUAL FIRE INSURANCE CO.

Office, Sanborn's Block, Main Street. Incorporated 1846.

OFFICERS—Caleb Parker, *Pres.;* Mitchell Gilmore, *Sec. and Treas.*

## PUBLIC INSTITUTIONS.

### STATE'S PRISON.

Located on State Street. Whole No. of inmates during 1866,—156.

OFFICERS.—Joseph Mayo, *Warden;* Augustus Bean, *Deputy Warden;* A. A. Moulton, *Physician;* Rev. Sullivan Holman, *Chaplain.*

OVERSEERS.—Alvah H. Bickford, *Overseer of Prison Hall and Cook Room;* Augustine L. Gale, *Overseer of the Shoe Shop;* Charles Elwell, *Overseer of First Cabinet Shop;* Charles H. Ordway, *Overseer of Second Cabinet Shop;* Francis W. Kilbourn, *Instructor in the Cabinet Shop.*

GUARDS.—Orrison Dudley, Z. T. Cutler, Levi R. Laney, George Snow. G. H. Chadwick, *Night Watchman.*

## N. H. ASYLUM FOR THE INSANE.

Pleasant Street.

This Institution was opened in 1842. Whole No. of inmates during the year,—353.

OFFICERS OF THE INSTITUTION.

---

BOARD OF VISITORS, (ex-officio.)—His Excellency, Frederick Smyth, *Governor*; Hon. Horton D. Walker, Hon. Benjamin J. Cole, Hon. Isaac Spalding, Hon. John H. Elliott, Hon. Luther B. Hoskins, *Councillors*; Hon. Daniel Barnard, *President of the Senate*; Hon. Austin F. Pike, *Speaker of the House.*

BOARD OF TRUSTEES.—Charles Burroughs, D.D., Portsmouth, *President*; Joseph B. Walker, Esq., Concord, *Secretary*; Isaac Adams, Esq., Sandwich; Waterman Smith, Esq., Manchester; George B. Twitchell, M.D., Keene; Woodbury Melcher, Esq., Gilford; Hon. Isaac Spalding, Nashua; John Conant, Esq., Jaffrey; Ebenezer S. Towle, Esq., Concord; Charles A. Tufts, Esq., Dover; William G. Perry, M.D., Exeter; Hon. Denison R. Burnham, Plymouth.

J. P. Bancroft, M. D., *Superintendent and Physician*; J. P. Brown, M. D., *Assistant Physician*; A. A. Porter, M. D., *Second Assistant*; J. C. Shaw, *Steward*; Miss H. W. Moore, *Matron.*

# COUNTY OFFICERS.

## MERRIMACK COUNTY

Was incorporated July 23, 1823, and contains twenty-five towns. Shire town, Concord; population by last census, 41,409.

*County Solicitor*—Daniel Barnard, Franklin.

*County Commissioners*—Nehemiah Butler, Boscawen; Dan'l E. Hill, Northfield; Enoch G. Wood, Boscawen.

*County Treasurer*—Joseph T. Goss, Hooksett.

*Register of Deeds*—William O. Folsom, Henniker.

*Sheriff*—Henry L. Burnham, Dunbarton.

*Clerk S. J. Court*—Jonas D. Sleeper, Concord.

*Jailer*—Charles C. Davis, Concord.

*Coroner*—Seth Eastman, Concord.

## NOTARIES PUBLIC IN CONCORD.

Nathaniel G. Upham, Ebenezer S. Towle, Arthur Fletcher, Elisha Morrill, Lyman D. Stevens, Elbridge G. Carter, Chas. Minot, Preston S. Smith, Samuel C. Eastman, William M. Chase, Wm. W. Storrs, Hiram K. Dewey, Robert C. Osgood, Isaac A. Hill, William R. Walker, Darius Merrill, Sullivan Holman.

## JUSTICES OF THE PEACE IN CONCORD.

Benjamin F. Prescott, Asa Fowler, Sylvester Dana, Josiah Minot, Edward H. Rollins, William Prescott, Lyman D. Stevens, Joseph B. Walker, Henry P. Rolfe, Isaac A. Hill, Wm. H. Bartlett, Anson S. Marshall, Amos Hadley, William L. Foster, John Y. Mugridge, Peter Sanborn, Samuel G. Lane, Benning W. Sanborn, Luther Roby, Ira A. Eastman, William E. Chandler, Onslow Stearns, William M. Chase, Joshua B. Merrill, Charles P. Sanborn, Jonas D. Sleeper, Hazen Pickering, John Kimball, Elisha Adams, Hiram K. Dewey, Hamilton E. Perkins, Joseph Robinson, Josiah Stevens, Richard Bradley, John H. George, James W. Carr, Nicholas Quimby, William A. Clough, William R. Walker, Richard Harcourt, Sam'l D. Baker, John A. Holmes, Aldrich B. Cook, Joshua Chapman, Wm. F. Goodwin, Stephen C. Badger, Arthur Fletcher, Moses Humphrey, Nathan W. Gove, Geo. G. Fogg, Chas. A. Colbath, Jona. E. Pecker, *State;* George Abbott, Jeremiah S. Noyes, Henry D. White, William W. Taylor, John Abbott, Mitchel Gilmore, William H. Buntin, Isaac N. Elwell, Seth K. Jones, Perkins Gale, Shadrach Seavey, Eliphalet S. Nutter, *Quorum;* Heman Sanborn, Thomas D. Potter, True Osgood, Atkinson Webster, George W. Wadleigh, John F. Brown, Jonathan L. Cilley, Benjamin Grover, John P. Johnson, Benj. F. Gale, George A. Pillsbury, Benj. E. Badger, David Abbott, George G. Virgin, Charles Minot, William H. Smart, John Ballard, George F. Whittredge, Calvin Howe, Hazen G. Kayes, Henry B. Foster, Andrew S. Smith, Charles C. Davis, George H. Chandler, George E. Holden, Stillman Humphrey, Joseph Eastman, Amos C. Warren, John George, William Ballard, Abraham G. Jones, Joseph S. Abbott, 2d, Isaac N. Abbott, Woodbridge Odlin, David J. Abbott, Alvah K. Potter, David M. Carpenter, Moody S. Farnum, John Foss, Samuel C. Eastman, Seth Eastman, Caleb Jackman, Charles W. Sargent, Frank A. Fowler, Barnard D. Eastman, Jacob B. Rand, William W. Storrs, Sylvester Stevens, Charles C. Lund, Charles F. Stewart, George S. Blanchard, J. Frank Webster, P. Brainard Cogswell, George E. Jenks, Darius Merrill, John H. Albin, Enoch Gerrish, George W. Ela, Lyman B. Hamilton, George Noyes, Wm. W. Hunt, G. R. Fowler, A. J. Prescott, J. P. Bancroft, G. E. Holden.

## POST OFFICE.

School Street.

Moses T. Willard, *P. M.*; W. W. Taylor, W. H. Thayer, G. W. Hook, and D. V. Everett, *Assistants.*

OFFICE HOURS.—Winter months from 7 1-2 A.M., to 9 P.M. Summer months from 7 A.M. to 9 P.M.

### DAILY MAILS.

MANCHESTER AND NASHUA, Close 9 1-2 A.M., 2 1-2 and 8 1-2 P.M.; Due 10 1-2 A.M., 3 and 8 1-2 P.M.

LOWELL AND BOSTON, MASS., Close 9 1-2 A.M., 2 1-2 and 8 1-2 P.M.; Due 10 1-2 A.M., 3 and 8 1-2 P.M.

PORTLAND, *via* NEWMARKET JUNCTION, Close 8 1-2 P. M.; Due 8 1-2 P.M.

PORTSMOUTH RAILROAD, Close 2 1-2 and 8 1-2 P.M.; Due 10 1-2 A.M., and 8 1-2 P.M.

NORTHERN RAILROAD, Close 9 1-2 A.M., and 7 P.M.; Due 7 A.M., and 3 1-2 P.M.

BOSTON, CONCORD AND MONTREAL R. R., Close 9 1-2 A. M., and 2 1-2 P.M.; Due 10 1-4 A.M., and 3 1-2 P.M.

MERRIMACK AND CONN. RIVER R. R., Close 9 1-2 A.M.; Due 3 P.M.

CONTOOCOOK VALLEY R. R., close 9 1-2 A.M.; Due 3 P.M.

LAWRENCE, MASS., Close 2 1-2 and 8 1-2 P.M.; Due 10 1-2 A.M.

HOPKINTON, N. H., Close 2 1-2 P.M.; Due 9 1-2 A. M.

PITTSFIELD, Close 2 1-2 P. M.; Due 9 1-2 A. M.

NORTHWOOD AND NEWMARKET, Close Tuesdays, Thursdays and Saturdays, 9 1-2 A. M. Mondays, Wednesdays and Fridays, 8 1-2 P. M.; Due Tuesdays, Thursdays and Saturdays, 5 P. M. Mondays, Wednesdays and Fridays, 7 1-2 P. M.

LOUDON, GILMANTON IRON WORKS, AND ALTON, N. H,, Close Tuesdays, Thursdays and Saturdays, 9 1-2 A. M.; Due Mondays, Wednesdays and Fridays, 3 P. M.

DUNBARTON, Close Tuesdays, Thursdays and Saturdays, 11 A. M.; Due Tuesdays, Thursdays and Saturdays, 5 P. M.

BOW, Close Wednesdays and Saturdays, 11 A. M.; Due Wednesdays and Saturdays, 5 P. M.

---

☞ Letters, Transient Newspapers, aud all other printed matter, to any part of the United States, must be prepaid by stamps. Postage to the Canadas, 10 cents—paid or unpaid. Drop letters must be prepaid by stamps.

MAILS CLOSE SUNDAY EVENING AT 8 O'CLOCK.

N. B. Strict adherence to the above hours for closing the Mails will be regarded, except in case of sickness.

www.ingramcontent.com/pod-product-compliance
Lightning Source LLC
LaVergne TN
LVHW012330100826
845148LV00017B/2104

*9780788428517*